Catholic Shrines in Chennai, India

T0383751

Though proportionally small, India's Christians are a populous and significant minority. Focusing on various Roman Catholic churches and shrines located in Chennai, a large city in South India where activities concerning the revival of saint cults and shrinal development have taken place in the recent past, this book investigates the phenomenon of Catholic renewal in India. The author tracks the changing local significance of St. Thomas the Apostle who, according to local legend, was martyred and buried in Chennai and details the efforts of the Church hierarchy in Chennai to bring about a revival of devotion to St. Thomas. In so doing, the book considers Indian Catholic identity, Indian Christian indigeneity, and Hindu nationalism, as well as the marketing of St. Thomas and Catholicism within South India.

Thomas Charles Nagy is currently a research associate in the religious studies program at Victoria University of Wellington, New Zealand. He received a BA in religion from Whitman College in Walla Walla, WA, his MA in comparative religion from Miami University of Ohio, and his PhD in religious studies from Victoria University of Wellington. His research interests include Indian Christianity with a focus on Catholicism, global Christian studies, the veneration of relics, religious marketing and tourism, and wayang puppetry.

Catholic Shrines in Chennai, India

The politics of renewal and apostolic legacy

Thomas Charles Nagy

Routledge
Taylor & Francis Group

LONDON AND NEW YORK

First published 2017 by Routledge

2 Park Square, Milton Park, Abingdon, Oxfordshire OX14 4RN
52 Vanderbilt Avenue, New York, NY 10017

Routledge is an imprint of the Taylor & Francis Group, an informa business

First issued in paperback 2019

Library of Congress Cataloging in Publication Data
Names: Nagy, Thomas Charles, author.
Title: Catholic shrines in Chennai, India : the politics of renewal and
apostolic legacy / Thomas Charles Nagy.
Description: 1 [edition]. | New York : Routledge, 2016. | Includes
bibliographical references and index.
Identifiers: LCCN 2016010491 | ISBN 9781472485175 (hardback :
alk. paper)
Subjects: LCSH: Christian shrines–India–Chennai. | Catholic
Church–India–Chennai.
Classification: LCC BX2320.5.I4 N34 2016 | DDC 282/.5482–dc23
LC record available at https://lccn.loc.gov/2016010491

ISBN: 978-1-4724-8516-8 (hbk)
ISBN: 978-0-367-88211-2 (pbk)

Typeset in Sabon
by Cenveo Publisher Services

Contents

Figures

Acknowledgements

This book is dedicated to the memory of my father Richard M. Nagy who passed away on December 7, 2012. From an early age, my father instilled in me the importance of education and inspired me to pursue my graduate studies. He served as my reader through several of the preliminary drafts of this work when it was still in the early stages of a PhD dissertation, and I believe he would have been proud of its final outcome. Thank you Dad!

Of course, my book would not have been as robust a work if it were not for the guidance of my thesis supervisor Dr. Rick Weiss. I met Dr. Weiss back in 2002 when he was a sabbatical replacement at Whitman College, my undergraduate alma mater. In 2008 I initiated a correspondence with Dr. Weiss inquiring about graduate schools outside the US. He promptly recruited me for the PhD program at Victoria University of Wellington and the rest is history. I am certain that without Dr. Weiss's involvement, comments, and candour this book would not have been anywhere near as competent as it is today. I would also like to thank my secondary-supervisor, Dr. Geoff Troughton, whose expertise and suggestions on my final drafts went a long way in improving the coherency of my work. A special thanks to my examination committee, which consisted of Dr. Joseph Bulbulia, Dr. Will Sweetman, and Dr. Joanne Waghorne, whose collected input helped to improve the quality of my project in its final form.

I would like to extend my thanks to all my informants and acquaintances in India whose words and commentary helped to make this book a reality. A warm thank you to Mr. Dorairaj Prabakar, who took the time out of his busy schedule in order to help me secure long-term lodgings for my initial trip to Chennai. I would especially like to thank Fr. Lawrence Raj who also, despite a very busy schedule, made time to converse with me about the state of Catholicism in India today. I am indebted to his insight, openness, and generosity.

A final thanks to my friends and family who encouraged me all the way to the end, especially my mother, Linda Nagy, and my brothers Jeff and Will, I thank you for your patience. Additional thanks to Atsushi Iseki my eternal officemate for nearly five years, and to my special angel Patricia Yee, who served as my reader for the final drafts of my work and who greatly helped in eliminating redundancies and streamlining it into a more cohesive whole. Her presence and assistance was undeniably the most significant factor towards the completion of my thesis and book!

1 A brief history of Indian Christianity and the politics of modern-day Catholic renewal in Chennai, Tamil Nadu

Research objectives and methodology

Introduction to themes and objectives

Though proportionally small, India's Christians are a populous and significant minority. According to the 2011 Census of India, 27,819,588 people (or 2.3 percent) of India's one billion plus population are Christian, making Christianity the third most popular religion in India after Hinduism and Islam.[1] Roman Catholics make up the majority of India's Christian population at somewhere between 17–20 million people.[2] Most of these Christians are situated in the southern-most Indian states of Kerala and Tamil Nadu. This study focuses on the Catholic shrines of Chennai, Tamil Nadu (Figure 1.1). Drawing on extensive ethnographic field work, it examines renewal and revivalist strategies associated with selected Catholic shrines and sacred sites. In so doing, it adds to the small but growing body of research into Indian Christianity.

In the most general sense, this book is about the politics of religious renewal – a theme that encompasses issues ranging from contests over indigeneity to concerns about social justice. I use the term renewal to mean a Church's basic desire for revitalization in the face of perceived spiritual and community decline, and not in any theological sense or as an umbrella term for modern-day Pentecostal and charismatic movements. That being said, Catholic renewal in India is inevitably political partly due to the minority status of Indian Christians, and also because there are those within the Indian government and its political landscape who desire to obstruct Christian growth and evangelization. As such, this book covers a variety of significant themes pertaining to Catholic renewal in Chennai and elsewhere in India.

St. Thomas the Apostle's missionizing legacy is a significant theme throughout this book. His first-century CE voyage to India reputedly led to the founding of the first Christian communities there, and his supposed martyrdom in the ancient Tamil city of Mylapore is still preserved by way of several significant Catholic shrines in modern-day Chennai. Thus, especially for the Catholics of Chennai, St. Thomas's death and martyrdom play an important role in the fight for recognition of their indigeneity in the face

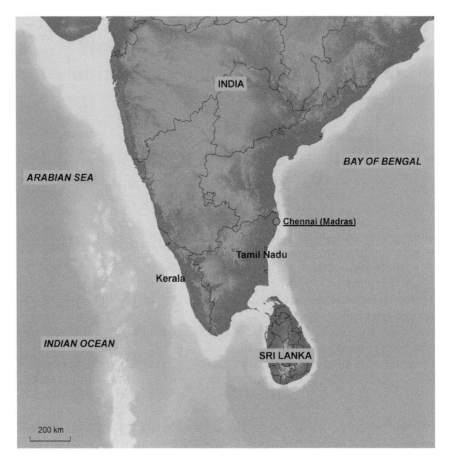

Figure 1.1 Map of South India showing the states of Kerala and Tamil Nadu, as well as the location of Chennai.
Map: T. C. Nagy using StepMap: Design Your Map, http://www.stepmap.com/.

of the political ideology of Hindutva (Hindu-ness). For the Church in Chennai, the imagery of St. Thomas's shed blood upon Indian soil is a significant symbol of Indian Christianity's first-century origins in Tamil Nadu that also serves to validate its claim for religious indigeneity in India. Accordingly, St. Thomas's apostolic legacy in India also becomes a point of political contention, and St. Thomas himself, a figure of political controversy.

In order to highlight the general political dimension inherent to contemporary Indian Christian identity and Christian evangelization efforts in India today we only have to look as far as the official Indian census figure listed in the opening paragraph of this chapter. For many scholars of Indian Christianity the Census of India is actually seen as a highly problematic political tool, whose dubious history goes back to its inception during the era of British colonialism.[3] More specifically, the Census of India represents the Indian Government's purposefully conservative enumeration of Indian Christians living in India today. According to Kumar Singh, who was the Director General of the Anthropological Survey of India from 1984–1993, Indian Christians (c. 1992) actually make up 7.3 percent of India's population.[4] Furthermore, in a more recent tabulation, the World Christian Database (2015) places the number of Indian Christians at 63,396,832 people, which totals a more conservative 4.8 percent.[5] If we take these figures at face value, the Census of India's set estimate of nearly 28 million Christians is a far cry from reality.

Robert Frykenberg, a historian of South Asia whose work has contributed greatly to the study of Christian missions and Indian Christianity, cites both of the above statistical sources in his criticism of the Census of India. According to Frykenberg, the huge disparity between population figures is due to the influence and policies of various Hindu nationalist political organizations that have had some level of control within India's government, and that have seemingly created an atmosphere within India's political landscape in which, "historical understanding has become more of a hostage to ideological and political warfare, so that findings are themselves used as weapons for destroying what are deemed to be unpalatable verities and putting something more palatable in their place."[6] Many Indian Christians, especially those of a lower caste, are not afforded equal rights within their own country, and to some degree, not considered fully "Indian" by a substantive portion of their Hindu countrymen. There have been many instances in recent Indian history of militant Hindu nationalists perpetrating religiously motivated violence against Indian Christian and Muslim communities, which will be examined in Chapter 3. Thus, as highlighted by Frykenberg, many Indian Christians, "as tactics for their own self-defence," choose not to identify themselves as Christians on any official government records or forms.[7]

Michael Bergunder, a specialist on Indian Christian Pentecostalism, also criticizes the Census of India for being an inaccurate representation of the Indian Christian population. Bergunder explains that this discrepancy is more a result of many Christian Dalits (low caste) not identifying themselves as such in order to maintain the "privileges" afforded them as Hindus.[8] Combined with Frykenberg's observations, it is easy to see how Christian identity has become a political issue in India today, especially for new and prospective converts.

On the other hand, India's government was technically established as a secular democracy via its national constitution, which was officially adopted in 1950. Why then does the government, through the Census of India, wish to maintain that the country's Christian population remains consistently, over several decades, at 2.3 percent of the nation's population? Frykenberg and Bergunder seem to imply that the Indian government has its reasons for not wanting to fully acknowledge the rapid and real growth of Christianity in India. It seems obvious that the rising influence of certain forms of Hindu nationalist ideologies within the Indian government's power structure has much to do with this attitude, and while the most mainstream forms of Hindu nationalism have become politically moderate in most respects, they still maintain a wariness of Christian population growth. By extension then, it is easy to see why Christian evangelization efforts within modern-day India have become an intrinsically political issue. As this book is about Indian Catholic renewal, which encompasses both evangelization and missionization, it is clear that such a political dimension extends even to a Church as globally influential as the Roman Catholic Church, if not especially so due to the nature of Catholic origins in India, as I will discuss further in this chapter.

Another important theme of this book is religious marketing, which provides a precise way of understanding and writing about modern-day Catholic processes for evangelization and missionization in today's technological world. This marketing highlights Catholicism's foreign and global character: when one joins the Catholic community, one becomes a part of an international community that shares a common faith and ritual system. For instance, the San Thome Cathedral Basilica in Chennai has the prestigious distinction of being one of only three apostolic tomb sites in the world. As a site of international significance, it spiritually connects Christian India to the rest of the Christian world. In this book I utilize some marketing terminology in order to better highlight many of the marketing strategies used by the Chennai Church towards the development of some of its shrines. Above all else, my examination of Catholic shrines in Chennai is about identifying religious innovation, in so far as to determine where and how history and tradition play as much a part in the development of modern-day Catholic evangelization as nation-wide economic growth and technological advancement

A third connecting theme in this book concerns the tensions and seeming contradictions of modern Catholic evangelization practices. On the one hand, these emphasize claims for Indian indigeneity, while on the other hand they highlight the importance of participation in a universal and international Church community. This tension is apparent in the religious marketing of Chennai's recent Catholic renewal and St. Thomas revival, as well as in the Church's current shrine-based evangelization strategy.

I would also like to note a second seemingly related contradiction with regard to Catholic evangelization practices in Chennai. Throughout this book I discuss two respective Church goals that at first sight appear to be separate issues. The first, as already mentioned, is Catholic evangelization, which pertains to the avid seeking out of new converts to the Catholic faith in order to grow and strengthen the local Catholic community. The second goal is communal preservation, which entails those preventive measures taken by the Church in order to curb the number of already baptized

Catholics from leaving the Church. As this book will demonstrate in later chapters, such measures include greater emphasis on certain Catholic beliefs, as well as the fostering of a better communal awareness about local history and tradition, especially concerning the Indian legacy of St. Thomas. For the purposes of my project, I understand both of these agendas as parts of the same Catholic enterprise of missionization, which looks to strengthen the community of faithful through both the bringing in of new converts via evangelization, and the maintenance of the already established congregation via community support and education programs, as well as continued spiritual guidance. Both goals are equally significant parts and simultaneous steps within the Church in Chennai's over-arching strategy of evangelization through the development of its many shrines. The basic premise is that before a parish can convince a potential convert to join the Church, it should be able to present to the individual the happy, knowledgeable, and welcoming community that he or she would hopefully join.

There is no statistical data that I have access to that validates the Church's fear that significant numbers of Indian Catholics are leaving the Church in India. However, there are several socio-religious and political factors at play within the context of modern-day India that have given the Church cause for concern. This book discusses two significant factors. The first is the steady growth of right-wing Hindu nationalism within India's political arena, whose most extreme factions have become hostile to the nation's Christian minorities. This development has led many within the Church to speculate that some congregants would leave due to social pressures or even out of fear for their lives, as also noted by Frykenberg and Bergunder.

Second, and equally important, is the rising tide of Evangelical and Pentecostal Christian sects that have recently gained a surprising foot-hold in South India, especially in Chennai. This phenomenon has prompted the Church to take considerable notice of allegations of "sheep-stealing" supposedly occurring in relation to Catholic youths who are being enticed away from the religion of their birth by more ecstatic and emotional forms of worship typical of Pentecostalism. This topic is discussed in more detail towards the end of this book.

Finally, I wish to make clear a specific theoretical agenda that I have maintained throughout the writing of this book. This is simply the purposeful avoidance of a post-colonial perspective with regards to Christianity in India. In other words, for the purposes of my project, I do not see post-colonial theory as being a necessary requirement for the study of contemporary Indian Christianity. In fact, it is my opinion that post-colonial theory only serves to muddy the waters within this context, especially since many of my informants are not interested in deconstructing their colonial pasts, but in progressing forward with their present-day identities as Indian Roman Catholics. In maintaining a focus primarily free of post-colonial discourses, I believe that I am better able to a present an original and empathetic discussion on contemporary Indian Catholicism and Christianity at work within Indian today. Indeed, I believe that the originality and creativity of my project owes much to the fact that I have chosen to distance it from the commonality of post-colonial theory.

It should be clear by now that the majority of this book is based on data collected in the city of Chennai (formerly Madras), which is Tamil Nadu's capital and India's fourth largest city (see Figure 1.1). Over a period of nearly six months in 2009, with a follow-up trip of three weeks in December of 2010, I conducted interviews with several Indian Catholics from within and outside the local Church hierarchy and collected documents and photographs. By analyzing the Roman Catholic shrinal renewal that has occurred throughout Chennai, especially at San Thome Cathedral Basilica the tomb site of St. Thomas the Apostle, this project will endeavor to answer the following sets of questions regarding the last decade or so of Catholic renewal and the revival of saint cults in Chennai: What strategies has the Roman Catholic Church in Chennai, India employed for religious renewal and maintenance in the face of current political and social issues? Furthermore, how has the Church utilized these strategies, how have they been informed by local culture and customs, and why were certain specific strategies adopted over others?

Using these questions as guidelines, I argue that in the context of Chennai's growing economy and urbanization, contemporary Catholic renewal can be viewed in terms of the development of shrines. In this book, the term "shrine" is used to denote any sacred site or edifice that serves as a focal point for prayer and worship by any number of visitors, most commonly pilgrims and practitioners of popular devotion. The designation of shrine often implies a more intimate setting or locale than one would find at a church or temple, but churches and temples can also be sites for shrinal worship due to innovative structures within their grounds, and/or due to a historical or spiritual connection with a god or saint. Since this book is about Roman Catholic shrines in Chennai, it mainly recognizes the Church's official designation for sites that have been bestowed with the title of shrine as sanctioned by the Vatican. But at the same time, it also takes into consideration the existence of unofficial shrines, edifices that are akin to the Hindu road-side shrines found throughout India. In fact, it is not uncommon to find Christian road-side shrines in Chennai, which demonstrates a cultural sensibility shared between South Indian Christians and Hindus. As such, the unofficial shrines discussed in this book are purposefully constructed structures built at the behest of the parish priest in order to specifically foster shrine-based devotion and development.

Shrinal development entails the construction of new church edifices and the refurbishment of existing ones, several of which are of historical and spiritual significance to Chennai's past. In this way, Catholic renewal and the active revival of saint cults can be seen as hierarchal movements, as opposed to grass-roots movements in that it is predominantly initiated by the Church's administrative hierarchy and not through the spontaneous efforts of its congregants. More specifically, it is at the parochial or parish level of the hierarchal institution that such movements primarily take place. This is because, within the Church, it is the parish priest who acts a bridge of sorts between the community and the upper-echelons of the Catholic hierarchy as it is the parish priest, and not the bishops or higher administrative clergy, who is among the people on a day-to-day basis. Thus, such parochial hierarchal movements are apparent due to the various ways in which local parish Church administrators have recently adopted various marketing strategies in order to facilitate evangelization, communal preservation, and touristic promotion at Catholic shrines in Chennai.

The remainder of this chapter is divided into three primary sections. The first section will provide background information and establish some context regarding the history and setting for the recent revival of St. Thomas at his shrines in Chennai. The second section will provide some historical background relating to the origins and spread of Roman Catholicism in India, with a focus on those Catholic shrines that claim association with the Apostle. This topic will then lead into a discussion that will analyze the significant roles played by local parish priests in the execution of religious renewal and the fostering of certain saint cults in Chennai. I will then examine the current economic context from which this recent Catholic renewal has taken place, as well as highlight some prior scholarship that has also touched upon India's economic growth since the early 1990s and its effects on Indian religious institutions. The final section of this chapter will be devoted to discussing various academic theories concerning indigeneity, marketing, and politics, and why I favor some theoretical notions over others. This section is capped with both an outline of all subsequent chapters and a brief explanation of the methodology used in researching this project.

A brief introduction to the legend of St. Thomas the Apostle and the Thomas Christian community in India

The mytho-historical origins of Christianity in India include St. Thomas's first-century CE mission to India, and later, the early Syrian migrations from the West. It was not until the advent of European colonialism that Christianity's presence in India would become historically prominent. The historian Leslie Brown at the beginning of his book *The Indian Christians of St. Thomas* states:

> Most of the considerable number of books written about the St. Thomas Christians of Malabar attempt to trace their history from its beginning, starting with an examination of the tradition of St. Thomas's mission to south India. But such a method is unsatisfactory because the sources for our knowledge of the first fifteen centuries are of very different

degrees of historical worth, and the reader cannot easily get an uncon-
fused picture of the events which certainly happened because of the
entanglement of legendary, or only doubtfully probable, incident.[9]

In other words, the St. Thomas tradition is not historically substantiated.
There are pieces of the story that are rooted in historically validated truths
but, for the most part, it falls within the realm of myth or legend, hence my
understanding of this tradition as being mytho-historical. On the other
hand, for the many Indian Christians who see St. Thomas as the progenitor
of their Christian faith and identity, the St. Thomas tradition is historical
fact.

The bulk of scholarship that is written about the St. Thomas tradition
tends to thoroughly analyze all the possible historical threads attached to
the Saint's mythos and then extrapolates the most probable explanation as
to the reality of St. Thomas's journey. Scholarly authors who are themselves
Indian Christians are obviously invested in the legitimacy of the apostolic
foundation. Historians of a more objective ilk tend to claim that there is
insufficient historical evidence to either prove or disprove the St. Thomas
story. According to the historian Leslie Brown, "The only certain conclu-
sion which can be drawn from an examination of the St Thomas tradition
is that at any rate such a visit was physically possible."[10] Indeed, for many
pious historians this is reason enough to continually return to the historical
validity of the St. Thomas story.

The St. Thomas tradition begins with the New Testament, in which Judas
Thomas or Didymus is named as one of Jesus' Twelve Apostles within all
four of the gospels. Extracanonically, the St. Thomas tradition has its foundation in both Western Christian sources and South Indian oral tradition.
The earliest and most complete written source detailing the missionary
work of St. Thomas is the *Acts of Thomas* (from now on *Acts Thom.*), a
popular Christian romance believed to have been written in Edessa (modern
day Urfa, Turkey) c. 230–250 CE in the Syriac language.[11] The *Acts Thom.*
is a lengthy work that has survived more or less intact into the modern day.
Divided into nine parts the *Acts Thom.* reads as a polemic against marriage
and espouses the spiritual superiority of celibacy as St. Thomas (aka Judas
Thomas or Didymus) travels from Jerusalem to the court of the Indian king
Gondophares and onto other nearby kingdoms, with miraculous occur-
rences along the way. St. Thomas finally meets his death by order of
another local king in some unspecified place.[12] The Edessene or Chaldean
Church of that day stated that they held in their possession the relics of St.
Thomas, said to have been removed from India. As such, the *Acts Thom.*
was most likely written in order to magnify the prestige of the Edessene
Church and highlight their claim to St. Thomas's relics.[13]

Alongside the *Acts Thom.* are the oral traditions of the South Indian
Christians themselves. Many of these stories surrounding St. Thomas's
work in South India were collected and written down by either Portuguese

adventurers or other Western Christian missionaries. To this day, these same stories and others are repeated, echoed, and maintained by the living communities of South Indian Christians, especially those communities who believe themselves to be the direct decedents of Hindus converted by the Apostle himself, hence the moniker "Thomas Christians." Two prominent South Indian song traditions that tell the St. Thomas story are the *Thomma Parvom* (Thomas's Song) or *Rabban Song* and the *Margam Kali* (first performed c. 1732 CE). They were both composed in Kerala and were written and performed in Malayalam.[14] It is difficult to date oral traditions, and one could assume that such sources are more dubious than the *Acts Thom.* in terms of historical validity, but I agree with historian Stephen Neill when he states, "Oral traditions linger long in the East. In all the Syriac sources relating to the early history of the Thomas Christians and to the coming of Thomas to India, certain features constantly recur, and through all the differences a common pattern appears."[15] It is this common pattern that inspires scholars and historians to continually revisit the validity of the St. Thomas tradition, and because this project focuses on some of the communities that maintain these stories, it is worth investigating.

As stated previously, the only fact that can be derived from the legend of St. Thomas is that it was physically possible for a first-century Jew, living in Roman ruled Jerusalem, to make a voyage to lands east of the Indus River (modern-day India and Pakistan respectively).[16] The historian John Keay states, "This was the age of Rome's commercial expansion. The new empire's demand for exotica was insatiable, and the acquisition of Egypt in 30 BC had opened the maritime route to the East to Roman investors."[17] The first-century CE text the *Periplus of the Erythraean* maps out the various ports of call for Roman/Indian trade, as does Pliny the Elder (23–79 CE) in his writings. Archaeological finds in Kerala, Tamil Nadu, and other areas of India have unearthed hordes of Roman coins and other artefacts dating from the time of Emperor Augustus (r. 31 BCE–14 CE), who is known to have received embassies from India.[18] Again, this historical reality does not prove St. Thomas visited India, only that the trip was historically viable. Regardless, it is the existence of these Roman trade routes that form the foundation for the plausibility of St. Thomas's initial sea voyage to India and other places.[19]

As implied by the *Acts Thom.* if we assume that St. Thomas followed the Roman spice route, he would likely have made his way north to the ancient city of Taxila, the historic capital of Gondophares's Indo-Parthian Kingdom.[20] King Gondophares's existence as an actual living person within Indian history has been verified by at least two significant archaeological discoveries, which date him as a contemporary of St. Thomas.[21] Proving the existence of Gondophares does not prove the reality of St. Thomas's missionary journey. However, due to tradition and perhaps embellishment on the part of the *Acts Thom.* the characters of Judas Thomas and Gondophares have become inexorably linked within the St. Thomas tradition of India. If the *Acts Thom.* are to be believed, St. Thomas found missionary success in the court of Gondophares, and by extension Taxila and the greater Indo-Parthian Kingdom.

The *Acts Thom.* does not give a definitive reason for St. Thomas's departure from the kingdom of Gondophares. However, the impending Kushan invasion (c. 50 CE) may have provided him with the historical impetus to leave and move his missionary activities to the south.[22] Thus, as South Indian oral tradition holds, after setting sail from Socotra (an island off the coast of modern-day Yemen) St. Thomas arrived in Muziris (modern-day Kodungallur/ Cranganore in Kerala, India) in c. 52 CE continuing his missionary enterprise along the Malabar Coast (India's south-western coast).[23] Muziris was another important port city utilized by the Roman trading routes and would have been the logical place to land when coming to the Malabar Coast for the first time. As South Indian tradition states, St. Thomas would go on to found seven and a half churches in what is now modern-day Kerala. These are as follows: Kodungallur (Muziris or Malankara), Palayur, Kottakkavu (Parur), Kokkamangalam, Niranam, Chayal, Kollam (Quilon), and the "half" church at Thiruvancodu. All of these sites were either near important trade centers of their day or were themselves important trade centers; some were even known to be home to established Jewish communities.[24] It is said that the first churches erected in these cities were built by the Apostle himself. While none of these "original" churches still stand, each of these cities, save for Chayal, is still home to Indian Christian communities that maintain the historical validity of an apostolic foundation.[25]

As South Indian tradition states, after many years of working along the Malabar Coast and elsewhere, St. Thomas eventually headed for the lands of the Tamils where he came to the coastal city of Mylapore (located on the Coromandel Coast or the south-east coast of India, just south of modern day Chennai, Tamil Nadu), meaning the "City of Peacocks". Here, he founded a church and took up hermitage in a nearby cave located in what is now called the Little Mount or Chinnamalai. Sometime later, circumstances brought St. Thomas to the adjoining hill, a place called Periamalai also known as the Big Mount, Adampamala, or St. Thomas Mount, where he was finally martyred with a spear or lance c. 72 CE. His body was then taken to and buried in the church he originally founded, which is now the modern-day site of the San Thome Cathedral Basilica.[26] To this day, Western Christian (Syrian and Roman Catholic) tradition, the Malabar Christian tradition, and the Coromandel Christian tradition agree that Mylapore is the site of St. Thomas's tomb, supported by the fact that no other city in India claims or contends to be the actual tomb site of the Apostle.[27]

The long span of time between St. Thomas's death in 72 CE and the arrival of the Portuguese (and Roman Catholicism) in 1498 CE does not provide the historian with many concrete details about the development and survival of Christianity in India. At present, Christianity in India is most prevalent in the state of Kerala, on the Malabar Coast, a prevalence that seems to have arisen very early in the history of Indian Christianity. Christianity in North and West India, and along the Coromandel Coast did not experience the same growth and maintenance that consistently invigorated the Thomas Christian communities on the Malabar Coast. Catholic priest and Indian Church historian James Kurikilamkatt argues that Christianity in North and West India died out due to both external and internal problems faced by the local Christians, the most devastating of those being the onset of consecutive foreign invasions.[28] Additionally, Christians living along the Coromandel Coast were also fraught with constant turmoil and violence due to natural disasters and persecution from local Cola rulers.[29]

South India seems to have avoided the onslaught wrought by foreign invasion and other such issues, with people living in relative peace and prospering due to friendly trade with foreign merchants. Kurikilamkatt proposes that any and all surviving Christian communities in North and western India would have logically migrated to South India in order to avoid the turmoil of war and religious intolerance.[30] Kurikilamkatt states, "In South India, Christianity was always favored by the kings and rulers, which is clear from the various privileges accorded to them by the kings … It was followed by many more privileges which were accorded to the Christians with an eminent status in the society and the Christians of Kerala ever remained in this particular status and it accounted for the growth and survival of the Christians in Kerala."[31] This is also coupled with the tradition that East Syrian missionaries came into India as early as 250 CE and 300 CE, initiating South India's long-standing communion with the East Syrian Chaldean Church.[32] This official communion, as well as reinvigoration from East Syrian, Mesopotamian, and Persian immigrants did much to preserve the traditions and maintain the longevity of the Thomas Christian communities along the Malabar Coast. The most important of these immigrations was led by a Babylonian or Armenian called Thomas of Cana who brought several families from Jerusalem, Baghdad, and Nineveh and settled them in Cranganore c. 345 CE.[33] Thus, when the Portuguese finally arrived in India they found many thriving communities of Thomas Christians along the Malabar Coast who were very willing, at first, to ally themselves with a powerful Christian empire from the West.

As we can see, the story of St. Thomas's journey to and throughout first-century India, as well as the subsequent preservation of the Christian communities he founded, is an intriguing blend of historical fact and pious tradition. The two main issues that weaken the historicity of the St. Thomas story and thus make St. Thomas a controversial figure in the modern day, is the reliance on the *Acts Thom.* as a pseudo-historical document, as well as the flimsiness of oral tradition as an accurate recording of history. Additionally, while the various arguments regarding the preservation of

early Christian communities along the Malabar Coast are far more historically viable, they also cast some doubt over the validity of the St. Thomas
tradition. It seems far more logical that Christianity was introduced to India
by way of the Eastern Syrian Church, maybe as early as the fourth century
CE, and maintained by subsequent migrations from those regions of the
Middle East that fell under the jurisdiction of the Eastern Syrian Church.

While the idea of a historical St. Thomas may prove problematic for a
reliable historical investigation, in terms of Christianity in India the validity
of such traditions are given clout by the living communities of Thomas
Christians who live and die by these traditions and do not look kindly upon
the scepticism of academics and other outsiders. The historian Stephen
Neill states it best when he writes, "Millions of Christians in South India
are certain that the founder of their church was none other than the apostle
Thomas himself. The historian cannot prove to them that they are mistaken
in their belief. He may feel it right to warn them that historical research
cannot pronounce on the matter with a confidence equal to that which they
entertain by faith."[34] For instance, as recently as 2006 Pope Benedict XVI
made certain public remarks that placed doubt on St. Thomas's evangelization of South India. Of course, these remarks were met with anger and
dismay by many Indian Christians, clearly demonstrating St. Thomas's
importance to Indian Christian identity, especially in South India.[35]

The Thomas Christians today are still primarily located in the Indian
state of Kerala, although communities can be found elsewhere in India such
as in Tamil Nadu. This moniker is not indicative of a sole Christian denomination, but is more akin to an ethnic identity. As such, Thomas Christians
are found across a wide range of Christian denominations with the majority
being from one of two Eastern Catholic Churches currently in communion
with Rome: the Syro-Malabar Church and the Syro-Malankara Church.
Those Thomas Christians who are not in communion with Rome tend to
belong to either the Jacobite Church or the Orthodox Syrian Church, as
well as a smattering of various Protestant Churches, the most unique being
the Mar Thomite Church. For the most part, Thomas Christians do not
typically belong to or inter-marry into the Roman Catholic (Latin-rite)
Church, as they tend to see the Syrian liturgy of their ancestors as being
superior, which is bolstered by the fact that they retain a unique and
entrenched high-caste cultural identity that is not typical to most Indian
Catholics.[36] The holy sites associated with the missionary journey of
St. Thomas the Apostle are popular pilgrimage destinations for the many
Thomas Christians who hold the Saint in reverence. Chief among these is
the tomb of St. Thomas located at the Roman Catholic San Thome
Cathedral in Chennai. The fact that all three sacred sites in Chennai associated with St. Thomas are under the jurisdiction of the Roman Catholic
Church is an interesting point of contention for the Thomas Christians. For
the purposes of my research, however, this provides an interesting lens
for examining the ways in which the Catholic Church attempts to make

St. Thomas its own without the shared ethnic identity enjoyed by the Thomas Christians.

A brief introduction to the history of Catholicism in India

On May 21, 1498 CE, the Portuguese explorer Vasco da Gama landed his ship in the Indian port city of Calicut (Kozhikode) located on the Malabar Coast. This expedition would be the first of three voyages he would make for the Portuguese crown; ultimately initiating Portugal's centuries-spanning presence in India. In 1503 CE the Portuguese established the first Catholic Church in India in the city of Cochin (Kochi), which is also on the Malabar Coast.[37] Over the course of several decades, the Portuguese gained several significant footholds in India (Calicut, Cochin, Cannanore, Pulicat, Nagapattinam, Goa, and Mylapore (which was renamed São Thomé), just to name a few), which helped to establish many new trade routes between Portugal and India, as well as providing them with the means to economically compete with their Muslim adversaries.

Obviously, the Portuguese were devout Roman Catholics, and as such, maintained close ties to Rome. In turn, the Pope invested the Portuguese crown with the authority to exercise ecclesiastical power, as they saw fit, to any region that fell under their royal jurisdiction, such as India. This authority, known as the *Padroado* or patronage, was developed over an extended period of time via several papal letters and bulls, beginning as early as 1442, and was finally solidified in 1481 by Pope Sixtus IV.[38] This most recent bull gave the Portuguese unrestricted access to those lands they discovered, as well as to any future lands they would eventually discover. It allowed them to establish and build all manner of religious edifices, and assign clergy with full spiritual authority. The *Padroado* also provided the Portuguese with the administrative rights for the establishment and financial maintenance of any new diocese created therein.[39] The *Padroado* would have far-reaching effects on Indian Christianity, and in the way Roman Catholicism would be administered throughout colonial India. It would last well into the twentieth century and be the cause of several inter-Catholic disagreements along the way.

By the authority of the *Padroado*, in 1534, the Portuguese established the first Roman Catholic diocese in India: the Diocese of Goa, which roughly covered all lands colonized and yet to be colonized by the Portuguese. As such, all of India fell under the jurisdiction of the Bishop of Goa.[40] As the Portuguese presence grew, it became unrealistic to maintain only a single diocese in India. Thus, in 1558, it was decided that a second diocese in India would be established: the Diocese of Cochin, which was comprised of the southern and eastern parts of India, of which the Tamil lands belonged. This too was deemed too large an area to efficiently govern. Consequently, in 1606, the Diocese of São Thomé in Mylapore was established out of the Diocese of Cochin, and the church of St. Thomas became the seat for the newly appointed Bishop of Mylapore.[41]

The relationship between the Thomas Christians and the Portuguese started out well enough since the Portuguese were happy to find Christians in India, while the Thomas Christians were happy to have powerful benefactors in the Portuguese. However, within fifty years, the Thomas Christians were deemed borderline heretical due to Hindu and "Nestorian" influences within their religious practice. According to historian M. N. Pearson, the number of Thomas Christians at this time (mid-to-late sixteenth century CE) was somewhere between 80,000–200,000 people. This time period also saw the beginning of the Catholic Counter-Reformation in Europe, which fueled the Church's zeal for maintaining doctrinal purity across the globe.[42] By 1560, a Holy Office of the Inquisition was established in India in order to oversee the Latinization of the Thomas Christians, as well as to contend with a host of other perceived impurities within the Church in India.[43] However, the Thomas Christians did not technically fall within the authority of the *Padroado*, but were by that time under the authority of the Syriac Patriarch of Chaldea, whom the Pope officially recognized. This technicality was finally overcome in 1599 when the Synod of Dampier officially placed the Thomas Christians under the authority of the *Padroado*, and allowed the Portuguese to take it into their own hands to purify the Thomas Christians of their doctrinal and ritual deviations.[44] With both the rulings of the Inquisition and the Synod put into effect, the Thomas Christians were forced to fall in line or else suffer persecution. Some communities chose to stay under the Catholic Church, others broke away and embraced Orthodoxy, and others would forge their own path. Ultimately, for the Thomas Christians, the Synod of Dampier would set into motion a path strewn with persecution, schism, and other such denominational divisions.[45]

Initially, the Portuguese experienced some missionary successes under the *Padroado*, however, as their empire declined so too did their desire and ability to administer to the many congregations they had founded. Eventually, the Portuguese and their missionaries grew to have a negative reputation among the Indians, which all but killed their original missionary agenda, while the Synod of Dampier earned them disdain from the Thomas Christians.[46] Rome was not impressed and started taking steps to relinquish its initial allowance of support. By the end of the sixteenth century the influence of the *Padroado* was well established, and not easy to do away with, but in 1622 Pope Gregory XV instated the Congregation of *Propaganda Fide* in order to reform and minimize the authority that colonial powers had over missionary activities. [47] While the *Propaganda* did not abolish the *Padroado*, it did provide Rome with the justification to send in its own missionaries and establish its direct authority above the *Padroado*. Of course, the *Propaganda* was viewed by the Portuguese as an unwelcome intrusion into their already established jurisdiction, leading to various conflicts between official representatives of Rome and those loyal to the *Padroado*. Regardless, such instances of rebellion against Rome did very little in the way of improving the situation for Portugal. In India, at this time, the tide of power was turning over to the British, who were more inclined towards Rome than Portugal.[48]

The British had gained their first foothold in India in 1611, and by 1639–1640 had negotiated with the local Nayak ruler to establish a southern base of operations in the small coastal fishing village of Madraspatnam or Chennapatnam, which was only a few miles north of São Thomé. In 1641, Fort St. George was erected and became the local headquarters for the British East India Company, recognized as a presidency in 1652. Eventually, as the commercial success of the Company in Madraspatnam grew, so did its indigenous population, enticed by the possible security that British rule provided. Thus, in 1688 the municipality of Madras was established.[49] Madras's growing prosperity, coupled with a succession of unfortunate events in São Thomé, provided the impetus for many Indian Christians living around São Thomé to migrate to Madras. With the Portuguese presence at São Thomé diminished, Madras officially annexed it in 1749, which allowed the former Portuguese holding to return to its indigenous name of Mylapore. By 1801, after a century or so of consecutive wars in and outside of India, the British Empire was left practically unopposed in South India, and by 1820 had conquered most of the Indian subcontinent, initiating the so-called "Pax Britannica."[50]

By the early eighteenth century, Rome and the British Empire began negotiations to further limit the *Padroado's* influence in India.[51] By the early nineteenth century there was an estimated quarter of a million Catholics living in India, spread over four *Padroado* bishoprics: Goa, Cochin, Cranganore, and Mylapore; and three vicariates apostolic: Pondicherry, Bombay, and Varappoli. Rome found this situation logistically chaotic and politically less than satisfactory. Thus, four more vicariates apostolic were established by Pope Gregory XVI and later by Pope Pius IX. The first of these, established in 1832, was the Vicariate Apostolic of Madras.[52] In 1838 the pope issued the brief *Multa praeclare* that declared, once and for all, Rome's authority over every Catholic in India, and which, more or less, signaled the proverbial death blow to the *Padroado's* long-standing influence. This, in turn, opened the way for a Catholic resurgence in India.[53]

In 1885 Pope Leo XIII set into motion the foundation for establishing a fully Indian Catholic Church with the bull *Humanae salutis*.[54] In 1886–87, three significant events took place. First, Pope Leo XIII pushed for the transfer of ecclesiastical authority over to a completely Indian church hierarchy.[55] Second, the Vicariate Apostolic of Madras was elevated to the Archdiocese of Madras. And third, the first of a new crop of Jesuit (Society of Jesus) missionaries were allowed to return to India after having been repressed by the Vatican for the previous 64 years. During this era of Catholic expansion, the Jesuits became important players in the rejuvenation and organization of Church assets in India. Frykenberg asserts, "Jesuits would become the instrument by which many Roman Catholic institutions would be forged into a sharp-edged instrument of Vatican power that was second to none in the world."[56] As a result of this, they have since become the most prominent Catholic organization in India today, producing more Jesuit priests than in any other country in the world.[57]

With a Catholic hierarchy that now fully answered directly to Rome, the Church began to develop a comprehensive educational system within India in order to better train and educate an indigenous clergy. By 1950 this system was fully in place. As Frykenberg states, "This system for producing an indigenous priesthood for the Indian hierarchy was so successful that it was eventually to accomplish what almost no other Catholic hierarchy accomplished so well – namely, the production of a surplus of Catholic priests, missionaries, and scholars."[58] The high percentage of Roman Catholic Christians in India today is a testament to the success of this late nineteenth-century resurgence of Catholic missionization and enterprise.[59] Today, Indian Roman Catholics remain proud of their education system and all indigenous hierarchy, as more than one of my informants reported. I would argue that the modern-day character of Indian Roman Catholicism has more to do with the Catholic renewals of the late nineteenth century than with the era of Portuguese colonialism.

Studying Catholicism in modern-day Chennai and the three St. Thomas shrines as they stand today

One of the main difficulties facing the present project is the complexity of Indian Christian identity due to its broad makeup of denominations, ethnicities, and historical or mytho-historical origins. While it is obvious that Indian Christianity cannot be simply explained away as a foreign or colonial element that has forced its way into India, neither can it be touted as a purely Indian indigenous movement. I agree with Robert Frykenberg's progressive stance that, "Christianity within India is 'Indian,'" but that ultimately, "Writing about Christians *in* India or about Christianity *in* India is not the same as writing about Christians *of* [emphasis in original] India, 'Indian Christians', or 'Indian Christianity'. So many and varied are the different Christian communities that the historian is faced with seemingly limitless sets of difficulties and dilemmas in defining the contours of particular phenomena that can be fitted within the broader concept."[60] With this in mind, the present project focuses mainly on a small, yet significant, demographic within the Tamil Roman Catholic communities situated around the three major St. Thomas sites and elsewhere within the city of Chennai. Since many of this project's informants are either members of the Catholic clergy or middle-class laity, this book will be heavily influenced by their top-down perspective on religious marketing and revival as high-status members within the diversely stratified Catholic community of Chennai. I believe it is important to remember that the Catholic hierarchy in India consists of individuals indigenous to India, and their decisions and interpretations of Vatican decree are of their own agency, influenced by their indigenous culture and personal inclinations.

So, why make Chennai, Tamil Nadu the focus of this book when the ancient cities of Kerala contain such rich examples of Indian Christianity? Simply, this book focuses on modern-day Indian Christian/ Catholic religious innovation, and not so much on history and ritual. I agree with prominent South Asian historian Roger Hedlund that, "More than any other city, Chennai is the home of indigenous Christian action, organizations and churches."[61] In other words, Chennai, as the largest urban metropolis in South India, is a prime hub for Christian religious innovation in general, across multiple Christian traditions. Although the Indian state of Kerala boasts a larger number of Indian Catholics, and Christians in general, Tamil Nadu is also a significant region from which to inquire into Indian Christian sacred sites and how they are perceived and maintained in the modern day. Tamil Nadu is home to a number of significant Roman Catholic churches, but only in the single metropolitan area of Chennai do you find three acclaimed shrines associated with the life and death of St. Thomas the Apostle. Chennai also boasts a population of over four million people within the municipal area alone.[62] This extraordinary context, one which has often been overlooked by scholars, provides an intriguing viewpoint with regard to the study of religious ritual processes within a highly urbanized setting.

The three sacred sites in Chennai that are associated with St. Thomas are San Thome Cathedral Basilica, St. Thomas Mount, and Little Mount (Figure 1.2). All three sites serve as sacred centers for the Tamil Roman Catholic and Malayalee Syro-Malabar/ Malankara Orthodox communities that visit and worship there. In the last ten years there has been a large-scale revival of the cult of St. Thomas in Tamil Nadu, with the sacred sites of Chennai acting as its focus. I argue that renovation work and the employment of a marketing strategy by local leaders presiding over these sites owe much to India's rising economy, growing foreign interest, and the rise of an Indian middle class who have become the pillars for local heritage preservation in Chennai.[63]

As already established, many modern-day Indian Christians identify themselves as Thomas Christians because they believe that their religious origins stem from the Apostle's missionary activities during the latter half of the first century CE.[64] How then do the Tamil Roman Catholics in and around Chennai express their devotion and identification with St. Thomas within a modern religious and social context? In many ways, the Church in Chennai's emphasis on St. Thomas is on the notion of elaborating and clarifying Tamil and/or Indian Christian identity in association with the Saint. For instance, one local epitaph regarding San Thome is that, "the tomb [of St. Thomas] is the womb of Christianity in India."[65] However, Tamil Catholics have neither a long-running ethnic identity associated with St. Thomas nor any deeply-rooted sense of loyalty or lineage to the Apostle's legacy. Thus, for many Tamil Catholics, in Chennai and elsewhere,

Figure 1.2 Map of modern-day Chennai showing the locations of San Thome, St. Thomas Mount, and Little Mount.

Map: T. C. Nagy using StepMap: Design Your Map, http://www.stepmap.com/.

San Thome and St. Thomas Mount are seen as sites of local interest for their historic architecture or scenic viewpoint, but their significance as the tomb and martyrdom sites of St. Thomas is largely forgotten. Consequently, the Church in Chennai's immediate goal is to foster a better Tamil Indian Christian awareness of St. Thomas's Indian legacy, starting with those sites most closely tied to St. Thomas's physical presence on Indian soil. It may then be possible for the Church to further inspire a unique Tamil Catholic identity that conveys a deeper spiritual and physical connection to the Apostle by way of his auspiciously located sacred sites in Chennai.

As we already know, the ancient Indian port city of Mylapore was the urban hub from which St. Thomas undertook his missionary activities along the Coromandel Coast, and would also later become a Portuguese holding during the early half of the sixteenth century. It was here that the Portuguese were shown the tomb of the Apostle Thomas, and where they would eventually erect a church and subsequent cathedral in his name. The area surrounding the tomb of St. Thomas became the Portuguese fort city, named São Thomé in the Saint's honor. The original Portuguese fort and church complex are now gone, but in their place stands a tall white-washed neo-Gothic cathedral that guards the supposed site of St. Thomas's tomb. Under the direct jurisdiction of Rome, this structure was completed in 1896 and since then has gone through several renovations, the most recent being in 2004 (Figure 1.3). This particular area of Mylapore is still referred to as San Thome, emphasizing its Latin-rite jurisdiction. Within the vicinity of the Cathedral are three other historically significant Portuguese churches: Luz Church, Descanco Church, and Rosary Church, as well as the region's most spectacular Hindu Shaiva temple Kapaleeswara.[66] Many locals consider Mylapore to be the main spiritual center of the Chennai metropolis.[67]

Separated from each other by only a few kilometers, St. Thomas Mount and Little Mount are both located on the congested GST Road that runs through most of Chennai's southwestern sector. Little Mount is considered to be the least significant of the three St. Thomas sites, and as such, does not figure as prominently within this book as the other two sites. Just as its name implies, this site sits on a small hillock that is difficult to recognize due to the storefronts and residential buildings that surround the parish grounds. According to common legend, this is the site of St. Thomas's hermitage, in the form of a cave accessible through the historic Shrine of Our Lady of Good Health, which was built by the Portuguese in 1551 CE. The most significant structural work done on this site took place in 1972 with the demolition of the main parish church in order to build a larger one to accommodate the growing community (Figure 1.4).[68] Due to its limited size and space, expansion and renovation of the level found at San Thome and St. Thomas Mount is not likely to occur at Little Mount.

St. Thomas Mount, also known as Big Mount or *Parangi Malai* (hill of the foreigners), is far more successful in drawing large crowds of visitors to its grounds due, in part, to its location, which is situated on top of a noticeably larger hillock.[69] Most Indians visit St. Thomas Mount not so much for its associations with the Christian saint, but for its impressive panoramic view of Chennai. According to local and Syrian Christian tradition, this is the site of St. Thomas's martyrdom, where it is said he was speared to death by an enemy assailant while kneeling in prayer. As with San Thome and Little Mount, this site was claimed by the Portuguese in the early sixteenth century, when they erected a church complex that is still standing (Figure 1.5). It was also during this time that the Portuguese unearthed the site's most famous possession, the miraculous Bleeding Cross, which is said to have been carved by St. Thomas himself. As the design of this cross is

Figure 1.3 San Thome Cathedral Basilica as it stands today after the 2004 renovations.
Photo: T. C. Nagy.

stylistically a Persian cross, it was most likely placed there by Syrian
Christian visitors prior to the arrival of the Portuguese, which still attests
to the cross's antiquity.[70]

During my initial visit to Chennai in 2009, St. Thomas Mount was
undergoing considerable renovations. By the end of my time in India,
St. Thomas Mount had undergone a complete physical transformation.
When I visited again a year later in 2010, St. Thomas Mount was still in the

Figure 1.4 The main entrance to Little Mount. Notice the modern "saucer" shaped parish church, which was built adjacent to the historical Portuguese chapel.

Photo: T. C. Nagy.

process of expansion because it has an entire hillock at its disposal. Given this recent context of expansion and renovation at St. Thomas Mount and San Thome, I have been able to obtain a great deal of data pertaining to the marketing of Catholicism in India, especially with regard to these specific Christian sacred sites. Also, the general timing of these renovations clearly demonstrates that the administrations of these particular sacred sites in Chennai are taking it upon themselves to generate a better and more informed Tamil Catholic understanding of St. Thomas's importance to Indian Christianity and Indian Christian identity.

Brief history of Catholic revival at St. Thomas's tomb

As stated previously, it is important to qualify my use of the term "revival," because this term is often utilized within the context of Protestant Evangelical history and theology. Even within Protestant Evangelical circles the meaning and understanding of this religious concept is debatable.[71] In the most basic sense, revival or revivalism implies an initial state of decline or falling into sin by a community of believers, who, after being overcome

Figure 1.5 The historic grounds of St. Thomas Mount's hilltop shrine.
Photo: T. C. Nagy.

with the Spirit, proceed to recommit themselves to their Christian faith. It is essentially a spontaneous movement that comes about as a response to the community's loss of grace, and is not typically associated with evangelization or missionization.[72] Clearly, this is not my intended understanding of the term revival, especially since my book is not situated within the context of Evangelical Protestantism, but of Indian Roman Catholicism.

For the purposes of this book, the idea of revival and the Church's use of revivalist strategies are meant to describe the Church's efforts towards the revitalization of interest and worship of the cult of St. Thomas in Chennai. In a similar sense, my use of revival does imply an initial, often repeated state of decline or disinterest on the part of the local Catholic community for St. Thomas, hence the need for revival. The renewal and revivalist strategies I focus on were neither spontaneous nor at a grass-roots level, but were instead planned and initiated by the Church hierarchy for purposes closely related to evangelization and missionization. As such, my project's main focus revolves around local Catholic strategies for the revival of a cult of St. Thomas at San Thome and St. Thomas Mount that takes place within the greater context of Catholic renewal and evangelization in the city of Chennai.

The current revivals in Chennai are not the first time the Catholic Church and local Christian communities have attempted to popularize St. Thomas in India via the sacrality of the Apostle's tomb site in Mylapore. The early attempts at religious revival and marketing lacked many of the advantages that the Chennai Church currently possesses, such as the presence of modern mass-media technologies, as well as the existence of a greater national infrastructure and global tourism industry. It can be assumed that the ancient East Syrian Church attempted to locate and mark the tomb site of St. Thomas, but to what extent it succeeded in establishing pilgrimage routes between the Malabar and Coromandel Coasts is unknown. However, beginning with the colonization of Mylapore by the Portuguese, and followed by their excavation of St. Thomas's tomb in 1523, these early Portuguese settlers purposefully set out to actively revive and propagate the cult of St. Thomas within the region.[73]

By the early eighteenth century, Madras was home to a thriving Armenian community. One notable member of this community was Petrus Uscan, a wealthy merchant who generously donated much of his wealth toward various city projects such as the first bridge across the Adyar River at Saidapet, which is near St. Thomas Mount, in 1726. As a devout Christian, he donated regularly to the local churches, including San Thome, and was the benefactor in 1728 for the construction and upkeep of the original stone walkway up St. Thomas Mount. In 1729, the tomb of St. Thomas was opened for public worship for the second recorded time since the initial Portuguese excavations a couple of centuries before. Petrus Uscan himself was present at the tomb's solemn opening, an honor afforded him by his outstanding patronage to the community and his role in maintaining the St. Thomas tradition in Madras.[74]

The next great building project to arise in relation to local veneration of St. Thomas was the construction of the current neo-gothic cathedral in 1893. The new cathedral was consecrated in 1896, with additional renovation work on St. Thomas's tomb completed in 1903. Prior to this project, the tomb site was located in a side chapel adjacent to the old Portuguese cathedral. The new and current cathedral was purposely built on top of the site of St. Thomas's tomb in order to better highlight its significance to locals and visiting pilgrims.[75] Finally, in 2003–2004, St. Thomas's tomb was once again opened as part of the Cathedral's extensive renovation, in which the actual tomb site was transformed into an underground crypt chapel. This location demarcates the tomb from the Cathedral grounds above in order to further emphasize its sacrality.[76] However, there are various factors that make this most recent revival different from its predecessors. For example, the Cathedral is now attempting to capitalize on the tourist industry by utilizing mass media (print, television, film, and internet) through the overall use of a more sophisticated marketing strategy. As the following subsections will demonstrate, the execution of this revival required the coming together of several key factors working in conjunction with each other. The most significant factors involve the insight of individuals within the Church hierarchy, as well as the context of Chennai's growing economy and the subsequent bourgeoning of its middle class, heritage preservation programs, and tourism industry.

It takes a special kind of priest

One interesting fact about the current St. Thomas revival and Catholic renewal in Chennai is that a great deal of the inspiration, organization, and groundwork for this endeavor can be traced back to a single individual within the Church's administration. Fortunately, I developed a good rapport with this individual early on in my field work in Chennai. This project's scope owes a great deal to my access to the opinions and experiences of Fr. P. J. Lawrence Raj, the current parish priest of St. Teresa's in Nungambakkam district of Chennai. Fr. Lawrence, in over 25 years of active service as a priest in the Roman Catholic Church, has carried and maintained several significant positions and assignments within the Archdiocese of Madras-Mylapore, which have included but are not limited to "pastor, consulter, member of the finance committee, property committee, and administrator of properties."[77]

In these various roles, Fr. Lawrence has overseen the location and construction of several new churches and parish buildings all over Chennai, as well as the renovation of several older and established sites within the Archdiocese. Quite clearly, his most ambitious project to date involved the full-scale renovation of San Thome Cathedral in 2004, which took place during his six-year tenure as parish priest of the Cathedral from January 2001–May 2007.[78] Also during this time, Fr. Lawrence accomplished the equally daring project of simultaneously constructing a new underground tomb chapel directly beneath the Cathedral's floors. Since the 2004 renovation of San Thome features heavily in this book, it was fortuitous that I was able to interview Fr. Lawrence several times during my two trips to Chennai, in addition to numerous less formal conversations. Fr. Lawrence's many contributions to shrinal and Church development in Chennai demonstrates how a single person's drive and ambition can shape modern-day urban renewal and religious revival. Fr. Lawrence was involved with many, if not most, of the Church-building projects undertaken in Chennai since the mid 1980s. Based on my research, I would go so far as to assert that such Catholic revivals hinge on the far-sightedness and managerial abilities of individuals like Fr. Lawrence, more than on the abilities and desires of the congregation. In other words, it takes a special kind of priest to lead his flock towards revival and renewal.

However, as my Catholic informants often noted to me, such priests within the Church administration are rare. This may help to explain, alongside other factors, why the renovation and revival of such significant sites as the tomb of St. Thomas and St. Thomas Mount have only occurred within the last decade. Sr. Merrill, one of the senior nuns stationed at San Thome shared this assertion, calling Fr. Lawrence a "true man of action" because most priests could not be described as such.[79] Additionally, what has undoubtedly helped Fr. Lawrence in his long-term bid to develop Church lands and shrines throughout the region is that he himself is a local, and, as such, he is very familiar with the concerns of Chennai's Catholic community, as well as with the city in general. Fr. Lawrence was born and raised in a large Catholic household (the second of six children) in the small village of Ottanthangal, which is located on the western fringes of Chennai, but is still a part of the same diocese as St. Thomas Mount. His childhood was spent tilling the fields and taking care of the cattle on his father's farm, as well as attending a nearby Catholic school for his early education. During this time, he decided that he wanted to eventually attend seminary and become a Catholic priest, which he accomplished by 1982 when he was ordained.[80]

In my first interview with Fr. Lawrence, he told me how, as a young priest, he would walk from village to village in the surrounding area in order to celebrate mass and preach sermons wherever he was needed. His first introduction to the St. Thomas tradition took place early in his career when he was briefly assigned as an assistant priest at St. Thomas Mount. It was there that Fr. Lawrence began to consider the marketing potential of such shrines and the local significance of St. Thomas's Indian legacy. What motivated him most towards his revivalist goals was the fact that at that time the Church did very little to promote the St. Thomas tradition and neglected the Apostle's holy shrines.[81] Over the years, he would gain the skills and experience necessary to take on high-scale renovation projects like at San Thome. As one long-time parishioner at San Thome stated, "what he [Fr. Lawrence] has achieved nobody has achieved so far."[82]

In my opinion, what is most extraordinary about Fr. Lawrence is that at the core of his revivalist agenda is a general guiding ethos that has served to inspire him and other local Catholic priests, and which, it seems, has been more or less adopted by the Church in Chennai as a whole. To paraphrase Fr. Lawrence, this ethos is the basic idea that through the construction and renovation of local Catholic churches and shrines, the Church in India can better evangelize and missionize to non-Christian Indians. In essence, the idea is to build the kingdom of God through the literal and physical building of Catholic shrines. Throughout this book I refer to this basic tenet and guiding principle of Fr. Lawrence's work, as undertaken by him and others within the administration of the Catholic Church in Chennai, as a "shrine-based strategy" for the marketing and evangelization of Catholicism in India.

Self-reflexively, however, I do realize that there are limitations to my research approach and my insistence on maintaining a focused top-down perspective within my project. The primary perspective that I am presenting in this book belongs to Fr. Lawrence and other informants who are either

clergy or well-to-do and educated members of the local Catholic community, and who, more or less, agree with the spirit of Fr. Lawrence's endeavors. This book remains mostly silent regarding the perspectives of low-class
members of the various congregations I discuss, as well as practitioners of
popular Christianity. As such, my project shies away from any deep engage-
ment with ritual, hybridity, and local caste demographics. Additionally, I
do not attempt to gauge or estimate the popularity or success, or lack
thereof, of Fr. Lawrence's work in terms of the general community, but in
how he executed and perceived his own challenges and "accomplishments."
Nor do I attempt to investigate too deeply the perspectives that challenge
or criticize Fr. Lawrence's character and undertakings. Although such data
does exist, I do not wish to turn this book into an exposé on the Archdiocese.
Thus, I do not overtly challenge or scrutinize Fr. Lawrence's words, or the
words of his supporters, but instead trust in their candor.

This is not to say that I blindly trust my data or the words of my informants, but that I am simply trying to present my findings free of any subjec-
tive pretext. In other words, I utilize this top-down perspective in order to
analyze the perception of Church leaders regarding their role in Catholic
renewal and shrinal development in Chennai. I do realize that Fr. Lawrence
and my other informants are not above reproach, and that, in addition to
my own research, the perspectives of the bottom and middle looking up
would provide a more complete insight into the nature of contemporary
Catholic renewal in Chennai. However, I firmly believe that the top-down
perspective that I have chosen to focus on is, nonetheless, a significant
perspective to analyze, and in terms of scholarly efforts, the road less
traveled, as I will explicate later in this chapter. I must also admit that
although I have empathy for my informants and for what Fr. Lawrence is
trying to accomplish within the context of India's unpredictable socio-
religious and political landscape, I doubt they would appreciate or accept
my book's heavy-handed application of marketing theory to the recent
revivals at San Thome and St. Thomas Mount.

Economic context of recent revivals and heritage preservation in Chennai

The recent Catholic renewal that was focused around reviving the
St. Thomas shrines in Chennai has been able to emerge, in part, due to the
larger context of India's growing economy and burgeoning middle class.
Chennai has followed this national economic trend and has enjoyed the rise
of its own middle class. With this new-found prosperity, Chennai's middle
class has become more invested in the preservation of their local heritage
and in the patronization and development of local religious institutions.
Scholars C. J. Fuller and Joanne Waghorne have shown in their respective
research that India's growing middle class has indeed reshaped and transformed religious institutions and practices within modern-day India.

Fuller's book, *The Renewal of the Priesthood*, explores ways in which the Minakshi Temple in Madurai and its administration have prospered and profited from recent political and socio-economic trends that produced a larger, more generous and entrepreneurial Indian middle class.[83] Joanne Waghorne convincingly demonstrates in her book *Diaspora of the Gods* how Chennai's new middle class have physically transformed the city's urban context through the building of new and innovative Hindu temples, creating in the process a uniquely middle-class Hindu temple aesthetic. I believe the same can be said about Chennai's Catholic middle class. Unsurprisingly, newly constructed and/ or renovated Catholic shrines have also enjoyed the patronage of the Church's middle-class congregants, something that will be further analyzed in Chapter 5.

Another related dimension of India's economic growth has been the emergence of a community-minded heritage preservation movement. Sites like San Thome and St. Thomas Mount, as well as several other notable Catholic shrines in the city, are living examples of Chennai's "heritage-conscious cityscape," and something Fr. Lawrence and other Church administrators hope to highlight within the greater scheme of Chennai's tourism industry and heritage preservation. Historian and anthropologist Mary Hancock, in her book *The Politics of Heritage from Madras to Chennai*, explores the intricate web of history and politics that has recently transformed Chennai from a post-colonial metropolis into a modern city invested in its own memorialization through both the preservation of its political and cultural heritage and the development of a tourism industry.[84] In short, Hancock asserts that Chennai has created its own distinct "brand" in order to better market itself internationally.[85] I agree with Hancock's assertion of the existence of a Chennai brand. From what I have seen at San Thome and other such shrines, the spirit of the times has certainly inspired priests like Fr. Lawrence to take their religious marketing in a far more modern direction. For Fr. Lawrence specifically, who is keenly aware of Chennai's economic growth and potential, the concept of "branding" has also taken on a life of its own, especially during his tenure at San Thome Cathedral.

Theories of contemporary religious and Hindu marketing models

Perhaps the most significant theoretical material utilized in this project deals with the issue of religious marketing, which captures much of the character of Catholic renewal and revival in Chennai today. This book focuses on the many ways in which the Church in Chennai utilizes structural renovation and shrinal development as a means to market St. Thomas to local, national, and international audiences. It utilizes insights from tourism marketing and religious marketing research, since high-profile sites such as San Thome and St. Thomas Mount purposefully attempt to attract both pilgrims and tourists to their respective shrines.

My project engages extensively with Mara Einstein's book entitled *Brands of Faith: Marketing Religion in a Commercial Age*.[86] Einstein's research focuses primarily on the "branding" of religious merchandise, or what she calls "faith brands." This encompasses a diverse range of religious oriented goods and merchandise that can include, but are not limited to: movies, books, self-help courses, institutions, and even individual religious personalities and their affiliated churches or denominations.[87] India's religious landscape is no stranger to religious marketing, especially in the context of the nation's growing middle class and the way this has improved the patronage of Hindu temples throughout the country, as both Fuller and Waghorne have noted.[88] Lise McKean's book, *Divine Enterprise*, offers a deep anthropological look at the diverse world of the burgeoning realm of Hindu religious marketing, which demonstrates just how strongly intertwined Hindu religious marketing has become with Hindu nationalist politics.[89] Acclaimed philosopher of science and religion Meera Nanda has also written extensively on the effects of globalization on Hindu marketing, and its inherent ties to right-wing Hindu nationalism. Her book, *The God Market*, is a more recent account of Hindu religious marketing in India, and demonstrates clearly how many of McKean's assertions from the early and mid-1990s have been perpetuated into the 2000s and onwards.[90]

It is Fr. Lawrence's opinion that through his many ventures he is building God's Kingdom and as such, he utilizes those methods that seem best suited for the region and that have already been implemented by many of his Hindu counterparts across the country. He explains:

> Actually, St. Thomas Mount was historically a popular place, but the devotion, as such, was not very big. In fact, I don't know whether I told you, when I went there as [an] assistant [priest], my first sermon was, 'If this would have been in the hands of Hindus, by this time this would have become a temple like Tirupati or Sabarimalai, so popular, but in the hands of Catholics, this Mount has become a lovemaking park, like a desert. Now, nobody goes there to pray and so on.[91]

Later in our interview, Fr. Lawrence stresses how necessary it is for the Church to maintain his marketing vision, in order to attract more visitors to shrines like San Thome and St. Thomas Mount. He states, "And also a lot of dignitaries come from all over. When those kind[s] of people come, you should use a little publicity and so on. See, how the Hindu temples have become popular, it is because of these dignitaries going and so on, you know. So, why can't San Thome['s] Archbishop do that?"[92] In other words, the Church should utilize mass media far better and hold press conferences more regularly, especially when someone famous visits a Catholic shrine, in much the same way many Hindu temples take advantage of such opportunities.

Indeed, as McKean's research has demonstrated, India's recent economic growth has opened up a myriad of financial opportunities for Hindu institutions all across the nation, and many of these institutions have successfully found a profitable place within the nation's burgeoning economy. She also states that at the time she published her book in the mid-1990s, it has become more ideologically and financially profitable for Indian political entities to openly support and patronize Hindu religious institutions and even individual gurus.[93] McKean continues by further explaining the many complexities behind the enterprise of Hindu-centered marketing and commercialization in India. She writes:

> Leading gurus, landowning and business families, and representatives of Brahmin panda and pandit interests are key actors in local affairs. These dominant groups, however, are neither mutually exclusive nor are their goals wholly antagonistic. They all strive to maximize the profits of pilgrim traffic in spirituality and ritual: Brahmins own hotels and shops; ashrams earn income like hotels by housing pilgrims; merchants in the bazaar, like gurus in their ashrams, sell religious objects.[94]

Additionally, McKean also explores how, through the association and sponsorship of the Hindu nationalist movement, Hinduism becomes something of a monolithic brand that can be advertised and commodified nationally and internationally.

In Nanda's research, we see that much of what McKean observed in the 1990s has steadily become normative, and thus, more deeply rooted into India's socio-religious economic policies. What Nanda is especially concerned about is the explicit triangular relationship between the Indian state, local businesses, and Hindu institutions. According to Nanda, there are two primary areas in which the Indian government and local businesses come together with regard to providing aid for Hindu religious institutions. The first is in the education and training of Hindu priests and gurus, and the second is in the acquisition of land for the expansion and building of religious edifices and facilities.[95] She states, "In both of these areas, the interests of the state, big businesses, and temples are becoming one and the same. This is turning temples into profit-making centres for the state economy and private businesses, and turning the state and businesses into accessories of the cultural-political agenda of the temples."[96] As Nanda concludes, the primary consequence of such an arrangement is the "deeper penetration of distinctively Hindu institutions into the public sphere where they end up substituting for secular educational and health services which the state is obligated to provide for all its citizens."[97] In other words, the state government has gradually become more complicit in its support of Hindu institutions, where initially it strove to maintain a secularly-motivated distance. Nanda also notes the Hindu right's growing reliance on

Hindu gurus, something that McKean explicitly examined, as a primary mode for promulgating Hindutva within contemporary Indian society, especially the new middle class. She explains, "Supporters of Hindutva, incidentally, are fully aware of the usefulness of the new gurus for their cause .... What drives Hindus are either venerated temples or individual preachers and 'living saints.' They are to Hinduism what evangelical preachers are to Christianity."[98] Clearly, the use of religious marketing in India has become a well-established tool for the propagation of Hindu temple and ashram culture, as well as Hindu nationalism.

For obvious reasons, Fr. Lawrence and other Church administrators have very little interest in promoting Hindu nationalism but, much like the Hindu institutions analyzed by McKean and Nanda, they hope to cultivate a larger local and international audience with regard to St. Thomas's Indian legacy. Thus, Fr. Lawrence and other Church officials have purposefully broadened their target audience for such shrines as San Thome and St. Thomas Mount to include not only pilgrims and potential converts, but also tourists and local history enthusiasts.

It should be noted that both McKean and Nanda, in their respective books, are extremely critical towards the commodification and marketing of Hinduism, especially in light of right-wing Hindu nationalist agendas. From their writings, it is hard to determine whether or not their disdain encompasses religious marketing in general or if it is specific to the Indian socio-political context. I believe it is best to maintain an objective lens when analyzing religious marketing in any context, and therefore my utilization of McKean and Nanda's scholarship does not presuppose my general agreement with their opinions. This issue is also apparent due to my focus on Catholic shrines, given that Protestant Christians have criticized for centuries the Church's long history of worldly enterprise, which is typically associated with the selling of indulgences. Perhaps by not being critical of this topic my book could be construed as a positive analysis on Catholic marketing and commodification. However, I am merely presenting the perspectives of Fr. Lawrence and other Church administrators who clearly see religious marketing as a necessary evangelizing tool within the modern-day context of urban Hindu Chennai.

As we can see, Fr. Lawrence's emulation of Hindu marketing strategies also led to some new challenges. While local Church patrons may have some sway over the construction of any given church structure, the final decision-making is left to the Church hierarchy and in many cases to the parish priest. Fr. Lawrence noted to me on several occasions the bureaucratic hurdles he has had to face due to disagreements between himself and some of his well-to-do congregants. Many of these disagreements were a result of Fr. Lawrence's marketing vision, which embraces India's economic liberalization, but in another sense comes close to emulating what some Hindu institutions have already implemented.[99] By itself, emulation of Hindu marketing models is not problematic. However, this association may have upset some congregants due to the fact that many Hindu religious institutions in India have direct ties to right-wing Hindu nationalist political entities, many of whom openly utilize anti-Christian rhetoric and espouse anti-Christian policies. Detractors of Fr. Lawrence have claimed that his utilization of such marketing strategies denotes mismanagement of funds, or worse still is a possible sign of internal corruption on the part of the Church administration.[100] Fr. Lawrence certainly does not see it this way, and noted how his detractors only represented a very small band of individuals, who, if anything, were only attempting to flaunt their social position and government connections.[101] In the end, Fr. Lawrence successfully navigated this challenge by simply forging ahead.

Other theoretical considerations: framing post-post-colonialism, popular Christianity, and indigeneity

This book utilizes a number of theoretical notions in order to better structure and explain the revivalist strategies currently being implemented by the Church in Chennai. Over the course of this project's development, I have looked to several theories that have been traditionally employed in the study of India and Indian Christianity. However, as this project took on a more cohesive form, I chose to discard many of these standard theories pertaining to the historical development of Indian religions, and it seemed that many of my findings were able to stand on their own by simply being put forward as demonstrative evidence and answers to my many analytical questions. I ultimately only used those theoretical notions that best suited a project focused primarily on the subject of religious marketing at Indian Catholic shrines and Hindu nationalist ideology within Indian politics. Thus, as stated previously, I chose to purposefully avoid those theories, typically under the umbrella of post-colonial theory, which focus on the historical and socio-political ramifications of colonial and post-colonial constructs that are commonly utilized within the scholarly study of India today.

The aftermath of World War II (1939–1945) would see the dissolution and inevitable independence of many of Europe's long-established colonies, thus heralding the beginning of the so-called post-colonial era, which one could argue is still underway. India finally gained its long-coveted independence from British rule in 1947. During that time, Christianity's presence in India was viewed by many of the new nation's anti-imperialist factions and early Hindu nationalists as a forced intrusion into India's religious landscape. This growth of post-colonial rhetoric emphasized the Christian missionary establishment and disregarded the indigenous Indian Christian ethnic minorities and those Indian Christians who freely converted to Christianity. Wendy Doniger, a renowned Sanskritist, is very much aware of this prevailing attitude and places the fault on both academic scholars of South Asia and Protestant Christian theologians, both of whom had their own reasons for ignoring the legacy of Indian Christianity during the greater part of the twentieth century.[102] According to Doniger, the scholarly neglect of Indian Christianity was due to the fact that many early scholars of religion were more entranced by the exotic other, such as Hinduism and Buddhism, and thus did not consider localized expressions of Christian belief as exotic or ancient enough to warrant serious study. Furthermore, many Protestant theologians and missionaries also neglected and distorted the legacy of both indigenous and Catholic forms of Indian Christianity because such communities were either deemed not Christian enough to warrant empathy, or too anomalous within a Protestant missionary scheme.[103] With the early development and shift towards post-colonial theory in Western academia, many of these attitudes would persist and be perpetuated into the present.

In an indirect way, the persistence of the Hindu right has also complicated the scholarly use of post-colonial theory when discussing Indian Christianity. The larger issue at hand is that much of the rhetoric utilized by the Hindu right regarding Indian Christian converts appears to be borrowed, to an extent, from these prevailing attitudes in post-colonial theory. As Doniger notes, influential post-colonial theorists Michel Foucault and Edward Said, and many of the scholars they would inevitably inspire, viewed religion, especially Christianity, as simply an imperialistic means for achieving political power.[104] In other words, post-colonial theory relegated Indian Christians to the status of victims who had no control over the construction of their new and foreign religious identities, and thus failed to take into consideration the possibility that such "victims" may have had more of a hand in guiding their own religious destiny. This perspective is also prevalent in Hindu right ideology, and is a driving force behind the development of Hindu reconversion programs within the nation.[105]

Doniger suggests that in order to traverse the pitfalls of applying post-colonial theory to Indian Christianity, one must utilize a method of writing "that views the Indians who were subject to Christian missions neither simply as victims nor simply as resistors (against Hinduism or Islam, as was once argued of those who did convert, or against the Christians, said of those who did not convert), but rather as active agents."[106] Doniger applies the term "post-post-colonialism" to describe this theoretical movement that supposedly "rebelled against the first rebels, attempting to rescue the colonized from the still insulting position of victims to which early post-colonialism had consigned them. It sought to excavate and restore the integrity of voices of resistance, and it found them, sometimes preserved in obscure sources that had been overlooked, sometimes embedded like a fifth column within the records of their oppressors."[107] Fortunately, most scholarship on Indian Christianity today has come to accept the uniqueness of Indian Christian identity and has begun to shift focus away from the missionaries and onto the missionized themselves.

In many ways, it is due to this association with the Hindu right that post-colonial theory has come under fire by many scholars within academia.[108] With this in mind, post-post-colonialism can also be understood as post-colonial theory tailored to explain Hindu right extremism in light of India's national identity coming to terms with its own diverse political and religious history. This project echoes the above sentiments by analyzing the tactics and language of the Hindu right parallel to post-colonial theory and presents Indian Christians as active agents in their own religious destinies.

This is not to say that the language of post-colonialism is entirely without merit. For example, it is an interesting fact that many Hindus in South India regularly visit Catholic shrines in order to worship and venerate Catholic saints. In many ways, this phenomenon can be considered a religious synthesis of sorts between the rituals and symbols of Hinduism and Christianity. One common notion of religious synthesis comes by way of post-colonial theory, which speaks of this religious and cultural phenomenon in terms of "hybridity" or "creolisation." Post-colonial theory understands hybridity as an act of religious synthesis executed by the colonized in order to challenge the colonizer. Thus, hybridity is an anti-colonial strategy whereby the colonized purposefully synthesizes its indigenous traditions and customs with the vocabulary of the colonizer, so as to establish a kind of solidarity against their oppressors.[109] As this book is not about oppressed communities, and it considers the many Hindu visitors to Catholic shrines as active agents in their own religious destiny, this notion of hybridity is ultimately inadequate for my purposes.

Another term that is often applied to the consequences of religious synthesis is "syncretism." Postmodernist anthropologists Rosalind Shaw and Charles Stewart are proponents of the idea that syncretism should be understood and utilized as a non-contentious term that simply denotes the basic process of religious synthesis.[110] They offer the term "anti-syncretism" to denote "the antagonism to religious synthesis shown by agents concerned with the defence of religious boundaries."[111] Undoubtedly, the Roman Catholic Church is a prime example of such "agents" in the world today. However, as my work will demonstrate, the Church in Chennai is currently utilizing evangelization strategies that invite and encourage, to some degree, religious synthesis at its shrines.

This book makes use of the concept of "popular Christianity" because it acts as something of a middle ground between hybridity and syncretism in its understanding of Hindu and Christian religious synthesis in India. As an academic discourse popular Christianity "stands outside institutional prescriptions," and in many ways it can "challenge commonly constructed distinctions and power relations between Hindu and Christian, elite and local, East and West, and indigenous and foreign."[112] Thus, the idea of focusing on the "popular" aspects of Christianity helps to better acknowledge the independent religious agency of its subjects, and does not treat its participants as unwilling members of an oppressed modern-day anti-colonial movement. Instead, popular Christianity, or popular Catholicism in this instance, focuses on the personal experiences of its adherents as they navigate the eclectic landscape of religious piety in India to fulfil their own spiritual needs. South Asianist and former Catholic priest Selva Raj writes:

> Popular Catholicism, which guides and defines the religious life and practices of Catholics in India, constitutes a vibrant strand of Indian Catholicism. Prominent in ritual manifestations, popular Catholicism in India contains several features that distinguish it from Catholicism elsewhere. A noteworthy feature of this popular Catholicism is that the usual distinctions between the Hindu, Muslim, primeval, and Christian traditions, as well as the normative boundaries between official and popular religion, become significantly blurred.[113]

It is due to these blurred lines that terms like syncretism and hybridity are far too rigid in their assessment of contemporary religious synthesis and the personal motivations behind such phenomenon. Even the Church itself understands the significance of the adjective "popular" when used to describe this form of local piety, because it understands that regardless of possible deviations from doctrine, it is still a movement "of the people."[114]

After looking at many contemporary studies on Indian Christianity, it is clear that a great deal of them focus on the appropriation of several Catholic saints by Hindu devotees, most prominently St. Mary (the mother of Jesus) along with various other saints that have achieved localized popularity.[115] Once again, this is due to the appeal of studying hybridized forms of Christianity and Hinduism by modern scholars weaned on post-colonial theory. Thus, many of these works tend to focus on ritual from the bottom-up perspective, since rural ritual expression tends to more readily demonstrate hybridity. While this emphasis on village, folk, and popular Christianity has contributed much to the field, it has neglected those centers of Christianity in India that do not exhibit the characteristics of Hindu/ Christian hybridity, such as the three sacred sites associated with St. Thomas located in Chennai, Tamil Nadu.

Major sites such as these are equally important to the research of Christianity in India because it is through this urban context that Roman Catholic policy and procedures are disseminated to rural villages and missions throughout India. The many ways in which the indigenous Catholic hierarchy in Chennai utilizes the history, symbols, and rituals of their local culture is significant in that it still manifests a uniquely Indian, Christian, and Tamil mode of operation. Within the urban context of Chennai, the symbols and heritage of local Roman Catholic Indians become a significant point of reference for better understanding the politics of religious renewal and revival within a country where Christianity has only a minority status.

This is one of many reasons as to why I purposefully chose not to closely engage in detailed descriptions of Indian Catholic ritual taking place at San Thome or elsewhere in Chennai, and instead, focus on the development of Catholic infrastructure and policy within this urban context. Again, I believe that my theoretical agenda serves to emphasize the originality of my project's perspective, as well as to highlight its unique contribution to the study of Indian Christianity.

Thus, this project argues that local Church administrators actively and purposefully promote these revivals because they recognize the advantages of promoting St. Thomas's historical, political, and religious legacy as a means to validate an indigenous Indian Christian identity. However, Church leaders are waylaid by the Saint's lack of popular Christian and Hindu support, which is more prevalent at shrines devoted to St. Mary and St. Anthony. While this project is not centered around "popular" Christianity per se, it does take into account how Church administrators have, in recent times, softened their attitudes towards such forms of worship, especially with regard to the larger context of Catholic renewal in Chennai. In this context we are seeing the utilization of a shrine-based evangelization strategy that aims to better attract and potentially evangelize those Hindus already visiting Catholic shrines of their own accord.

Another complex issue that this project confronts is the socio-religious and political concept of indigeneity, especially in how it is perceived and utilized by religious communities in modern-day India. Typically, the term indigeneity or the concept of an indigenous movement denotes local Christian movements that are neither mainstream nor associated with European missionization, but instead are solely the product of local appropriation and acceptance into the Christian faith. Roger Hedlund, a historian of South Asia whose research focuses on the history of Church missions in India, argues that church traditions such as the Roman Catholic Church and those Protestant denominations that were eventually subsumed into the Church of North India (CNI) and South India (CSI) cannot be called indigenous churches because they were largely the product of foreign missionary efforts. Instead, indigenous Indian movements are typically found in "the so-called fringe sections largely (not exclusively) of Pentecostal, Charismatic or Evangelical origin," which "has its own structures and cultural expressions which are frequently outside the orbit of the traditional Churches."[116] While I agree with the spirit of Hedlund's explanation, it is ultimately limited by the fact that it does not take the notion of popular Christianity into account. By looking through the lens of popular Catholicism, certain aspects of Indian Catholic ritual and devotion can be understood as "cultural expressions which are frequently outside the orbit of the traditional Churches" as per Hedlund's explanation, but still remain within the confines of the Catholic institution as a legitimate expression of Catholic piety.[117]

At the forefront of the Church's efforts at indigenization in India, and elsewhere around the world, are its two most prolific evangelization models: "inculturation" and liberation theology, whose main purposes are to appropriate and utilize local indigenous customs alongside Catholic faith, belief, and practice.[118] However, I believe that it is important to make and emphasize a clear distinction between the global Catholic Church, which is officiated by its hierarchy in the Vatican, and the national and local Church in India, which is overseen by a diverse Indian clergy at all levels of the hierarchy that is more or less responsible for the majority of Catholic affairs within its own dioceses and parishes. Thus, what we see at shrines such as San Thome and St. Thomas Mount is the local Church's active attempt to propagate and legitimize its own indigenous Christian origin and identity through the historical legacy of St. Thomas the Apostle and his death and burial in ancient Mylapore (Chennai).

More specifically, St. Thomas's Indian legacy has become the key foundation for the Indian Church's claim for a universally legitimate indigenous Indian Christian origin. Also, part of what Fr. Lawrence and the Church in Chennai have attempted to promote is that St. Thomas's Indian legacy encompasses both pre-colonial and colonial era missionization, which includes the Portuguese annexation of Mylapore and their subsequent renovation and revival of St. Thomas's tomb. Today, this legacy of renovation and revival is maintained through the Church's efforts to further promulgate St. Thomas's story and hopefully attract new converts to the Catholic faith. Thus, contemporary Catholic renewal in Chennai can be seen as both Catholic indigenization and as a "true *indigenous* church movement," because it is a church movement initiated and executed by an indigenous Indian Catholic hierarchy and laity.[119] Thanks, in part, to the reforms of Vatican II, the present-day Indian Church is now several decades removed from an era where mostly European clergy would missionize and administer to its Indian congregation.

Much of the Church's justification for indigenization comes as a response to the politicized rhetoric of India's Hindu right, especially to the ideology of Hindutva. At its inception, Hindutva narrowly redefined the meaning and significance of Indian indigeneity to only encompass those religious systems that originated out of India's soil to the purposeful exclusion of Islam and Christianity, which are now seen by Hindutva advocates as being foreign transplants into the Indian nation, and thus, inauthentic Indian religions. Of course, the Indian Church cannot abide by this rhetoric, and has responded in kind through various political and socio-religious actions. Indeed, San Thome and St. Thomas Mount have become centers for political action, rallying behind the legacy of St. Thomas in order to better educate and validate Christianity's place as an authentic and indigenous expression of Indian religiosity and faith.

One final way in which this project confronts the issue of indigeneity involves the personal sentiments of my Indian Catholic informants, many of whom, I suspect, see their own indigenousness not as something entirely determined by their religion, but by their Tamil Indian heritage and ancestry. For instance, Mr. Zander, a retired government official and long-standing member of San Thome's congregation, stated, "Because my fore-fathers, some one or two generations back, they became Christians. I'm a Christian because of my forefathers."[120] Mr. Zander's words exemplify a common sentiment among the Tamil Catholics I met; that their identity as Catholics stem from an understanding that they or their "forefathers" were once Hindu, and that fact alone makes them Indian and indigenous. Thus, by extension, the new religion of which they are willfully a part of also becomes a part of their indigenous identity, an identity that is simultaneously Hindu, Catholic, Tamil, and Indian.

Outline of subsequent chapters

The following chapters each discuss a specific renewal and revivalist strategy that serves to inform the overarching process of Catholic renewal in Chennai. Chapter 2 of this book analyzes how the Church in Chennai has utilized and shaped the historicity of St. Thomas in order to validate Indian Christian indigeneity and market St. Thomas's Indian legacy among Christians and non-Christians alike. It explores how the Apostle's death and burial has become the Tamil Church's new myth of origin.

Chapter 3 analyzes several Hindu right criticisms of the St. Thomas tradition through a close reading of some of the Church's harshest critics. These condemnations against both the Catholic Church and the St. Thomas legend are ultimately the product of recent trends in Hindu nationalist rhetoric, more specifically, the socio-religious and political ideology of Hindutva. This chapter also examines how the Church's St. Thomas revival has been influenced by Hindu nationalist rhetoric, and it outlines the steps the Church has taken at some of its shrines to both quell and repudiate Hindu right criticisms.

Chapter 4 focuses solely on the 2004 renovation of San Thome Cathedral. During this renovation, various marketing strategies were utilized in order to revive local devotion and national interest in the site. I argue that Fr. Lawrence Raj, San Thome's parish priest at that time and the project's instigator and driving force, effectively created a St. Thomas "faith brand" from which to solidify and enhance the Apostle's Indian legacy. Fr. Lawrence also endeavored to preserve the heritage and historical significance of the old Portuguese cathedral and tomb site as a monument to St. Thomas's local legacy.

Chapter 5 pursues this same analysis, but also serves to further contextualize San Thome's renovation amid the backdrop of the greater Catholic renewal throughout Chennai. Initially, this chapter will demonstrate how Fr. Lawrence's St. Thomas brand has been perpetuated at St. Thomas Mount, and marketed in almost the exact same way as at San Thome. Clearly, the revivals at San Thome and St. Thomas Mount are part of a greater Catholic renewal in Chennai, which is, above all else, focused on the evangelization and missionization of the Indian people and the preservation of the current Catholic community. Drawing upon evidence taken from some of Chennai's smaller Catholic shrines, this chapter assesses the impact of "popular" Catholic devotion and its influence on the Church's current shrine-based strategy as well as the future prospects for Catholic renewal in South India. Additionally, I will showcase several specific facets and strategies that have come to characterize Catholic shrinal development in Chennai, and will serve to determine the extent to which shrinal marketing, evangelization, and community preservation have come to define the greater Catholic renewal in Chennai.

Methodology and final thoughts

My methodological approach to this project was simple. Through the combined utilization of ethnographic field work and library research, I hoped to gain the best possible understanding of contemporary Catholic renewal and revival in and around the sacred shrines of St. Thomas in Chennai, India. My field work involved living in Chennai for nearly six months, and conducting interviews with key members of the Chennai Catholic community, as well as collecting any related local media pertaining to St. Thomas in India. As such, my research uses several sources that are unique to the Church in Chennai and the three sacred sites associated with St. Thomas. I also took many photographs, and was a participant observer at many of the Catholic festivals and services I attended during my time in Chennai.

As this was my first attempt at field research in a foreign land, I did my best to make positive first impressions with all my potential informants, especially with those individuals belonging to the Church hierarchy. For the most part, I was successful in engaging with many interesting and knowledgeable Indians and Indian Roman Catholics throughout my time in Chennai. I found most of the individuals I talked to at Catholic shrines throughout Chennai to be very open to my lines of inquiry, and usually they did their best to answer my various questions, either formally or informally. Undoubtedly, I was probably viewed by many such individuals as evidence of their respective shrine's growing international reputation, or, at the least, as a possible conduit for providing another level of advertisement for their shrines, and for Indian Christianity in general.

In some cases, I did run afoul of the language barrier, which was due to the fact that I am not fluent in the Tamil language, which limited my ability to engage with certain individuals. However, due to the nature of my project, which focuses on these shrines at an administrative level, I was able to narrow down my required list of informants to include mainly members of the Church hierarchy and administration, many of whom are highly educated and fluent in English.

On a final note, I would like to point out that many of the texts and publications that I came across in Chennai were initially written in English and not in Tamil. It would seem that it is common practice for the Church in India to publish materials in English. It is clear that the Church espouses universality and treats English as a *lingua franca* in today's modern world, seeing as English is an official language of the Indian nation. Ultimately, I believe that there exists in India a pervasive attitude that assigns greater prestige to a text and its author for a work that is written and published in English over any other local language. This may just be an assumption on my part, but seeing the many English language publications coming out of both religious and political institutions throughout India, it seems a fair observation. However, a good percentage of Church publications were also available as either a Tamil translation or as a subsidiary Tamil-language publication, which demonstrates the Church's desire to broaden its approach to marketing.

As we will see in the following chapter, I will utilize many of these local texts and other published materials in order to demonstrate the Church's recent willingness to better market St. Thomas in Chennai and elsewhere. The significance of many of these texts is how they present St. Thomas's Indian legacy as a legitimate and validating force for the present-day Church, especially with regard to Indian Christian indigeneity and Tamil Christian origins, but more importantly, as part of the greater Catholic renewal in Chennai.

Notes

1 Office of the Register General & Census Commissioner, India, "Census of India 2011: C-1 Population by Religious Community," http://www.censusindia.gov.in/2011census/C-01.html (Accessed October 8, 2015).
2 BBC News, "Factfile: Roman Catholics around the world," http://news.bbc.co.uk/2/hi/4243727.stm (Accessed December 5, 2012). See also: World Christian Database, http://www.worldchristiandatabase.org/wcd/default.asp (Accessed October 23, 2015).
3 See: N. Gerald Barrier (ed.), *The Census in British India: New Perspectives* (New Delhi: Manohar Publications, 1981).
4 Kumar Suresh Singh, "Introduction," in *People of India*, ed. Kumar Suresh (Calcutta, Anthropological Survey of India, 1992), 211.
5 World Christian Database, http://www.worldchristiandatabase.org/wcd/default.asp (Accessed October 23, 2015).
6 Robert Eric Frykenberg, *Christianity in India: From Beginning to the Present* (New York: Oxford University Press, 2008), 463.
7 Ibid, 463–464.
8 Michael Bergunder, *The South Indian Pentecostal Movement in the Twentieth Century* (Cambridge: Wm. B. Eerdmans Publishing Co., 2008), 18.
9 Leslie Brown, *The Indian Christians of St. Thomas* (Cambridge: Cambridge University Press, 1982), 11.
10 Ibid, 65.
11 James Kurikilamkatt, *First Voyage of the Apostle Thomas to India: Ancient Christianity in Bharuch and Taxila* (Bangalore, India: Asian Trading Corporation, 2005), 5–18. See also: Brown, *The Indian Christians of St. Thomas*, 43.

12 George Mark Moraes, *A History of Christianity in India: From Early Times to St. Francis Xavier: A. D. 52–1542* (Bombay: P. C. Manaktala and Sons Private Ltd, 1964), 25–27. For a complete English language translation of the *Acts Thom.* see: A. F. J. Klijn (ed.), *The Acts of Thomas: Introduction, Text, and Commentary* (Leiden: Brill, 2003).

13 Brown, *The Indian Christians of St. Thomas*, 45.

14 Jacob Vellian, *Syrian Church Series Volume XVII: Knanite Community: History and Culture* (Kerala: Jyothi Book House, 2001), 45–57. For a concise summery of the *Thomma Parvom* see: A. M. Mundadan, *History of Christianity in India Volume I: from the Beginning up to the Middle of the Sixteenth Century* (Bangalore: Theological Publications in India, 1984), 30–32. For a summary of the *Thomma Parvom* and *Margam Kali* see: Brown, *The Indian Christians of St. Thomas*, 49–51.

15 Stephen Neill, *A History of Christianity in India: The Beginnings to AD 1707* (Cambridge: Cambridge University Press, 1984), 33.

16 Ibid, 35.

17 John Keay, *A History of India* (London: Harper Collins Publishers, 2000), 121.

18 Ibid, 121–123. See also: Brown, *The Indian Christians of St. Thomas*, 59–63.

19 For a simplified map of established trade routes c. 300 BCE–500 CE see: Jonathan Mark Kenoyer and Kimberly Heuston, *The Ancient South Asian World* (New York: Oxford University Press, 2005), 150.

20 Kurikilamkatt, *First Voyage of the Apostle Thomas to India*, 41–66.

21 Neill, *A History of Christianity in India*, 27–28. See also: Kurikilamkatt, *First Voyage of the Apostle Thomas to India*, 69–72, 74–88. See also: Brown, *The Indian Christians of St. Thomas*, 47.

22 Kurikilamkatt, *First Voyage of the Apostle Thomas to India*, 181–184. See also: Neill, *A History of Christianity in India*, 28.

23 Kurikilamkatt, *First Voyage of the Apostle Thomas to India*, 173–174.

24 A.C. Perumalil, *The Apostles in India* (Patna: Xavier Teachers' Training Institute, 1971), 98–101. See also: Brown, *The Indian Christians of St. Thomas*, 52–53. See also: Kurikilamkatt, *First Voyage of the Apostle Thomas to India*, 173–174.

25 Brown, *The Indian Christians of St. Thomas*, 52–54.

26 P. J. Podipara, *The Thomas Christians* (Bombay, India: St. Paul Publications, 1970), 22. See also: Kurikilamkatt, *First Voyage of the Apostle Thomas to India*, 174. See also: Duncan Forbes, *The Heart of India* (South Brunswick and New York: A. S. Barnes and Company, 1968), 174.

27 Brown, *The Indian Christians of St. Thomas*, 59.

28 Kurikilamkatt, *First Voyage of the Apostle Thomas to India*, 180–188. See also: Neill, *A History of Christianity in India*, 50–51, 64, and 190.

29 Neill, *A History of Christianity in India*, 43. See also: Mundadan, *History of Christianity in India Volume I*, 75–76, and 95.

30 Kurikilamkatt, *First Voyage of the Apostle Thomas to India*, 188–189.

31 Ibid, 205.

32 Mundadan, *History of Christianity in India Volume I*, 78–79.

33 Neill, *A History of Christianity in India*, 42. See also: Jacob Kollaparambil, *The Babylonian origin of the Southists among the St. Thomas Christians* (Rome: Pont. Institutum Studiorum Orientalium, 1992).

34 Neill, *A History of Christianity in India*, 49.

35 Don Sebastian, "Did Thomas the Apostle visit South India?" http://www.dnaindia.com/dnaprint.asp?newsid=1066746 (accessed June 30, 2008).

36 Corinne G. Dempsey, *Kerala Christian Sainthood: Collisions of Culture and Worldview in South India* (Oxford: Oxford University Press, 2001), 5–8.

37 Ibid, 6.

38 Neill, *A History of Christianity in India,* 111–112.
39 Ibid, 112–113.
40 Moraes, *A History of Christianity in India,* 237.
41 Joseph Thekkedath, *History of Christianity in India Volume II: From the Middle of the Sixteenth Century to the End of the Seventeenth Century* (Bangalore: Theological Publications in India, 1982), 256–257.
42 M. N. Pearson, *The New Cambridge History of India: The Portuguese in India* (Cambridge: Cambridge University Press, 1987), 119.
43 Stephen A. Missick, "Mar Thoma: The Apostolic Foundation of the Assyrian Church and the Christians of St. Thomas in India," *Journal of Assyrian Academic Studies* Vol. XIV, No. 2 (2000): 50.
44 Pearson, *The New Cambridge History of India,* 119. For a more detailed account of what happened at the Synod of Dampier, see: Brown, *The Indian Christians of St. Thomas,* 32–42. See also: Podipara, *The Thomas Christians,* 138–142.
45 For a more detailed account of the schisms and divisions that befell the Thomas Christian community after the Synod of Dampier see: Frykenberg, *Christianity in India,* 358–375.
46 Ibid, 347.
47 A. M. Mundadan, *Indian Christians: Search for Identity and Struggle for Autonomy* (Bangalore: Dharmaram Publications Dharmaram College, 2003), 146–147.
48 Ibid, 162–164.
49 Neill, *A History of Christianity in India 1707–1858,* 274.
50 Keay, *India,* 413.
51 Thekkedath, *History of Christianity in India Volume II,* 205–208. See also: Neill, *A History of Christianity in India 1707–1858,* 95.
52 Neill, *A History of Christianity in India 1707–1858,* 279
53 Frykenberg, *Christianity in India,* 352.
54 Ibid, 355–356.
55 Mundadan, *Indian Christians,* 168.
56 Frykenberg, *Christianity in India,* 357.
57 Ibid.
58 Ibid, 356.
59 Ibid, 357.
60 Ibid, vii.
61 Roger E. Hedlund, *Quest for Identity, India's Churches of Indigenous Origin: The "Little Tradition" in Indian Christianity* (Chennai: MIIS/ ISPCK, 2000), 196.
62 Indira Narayanan and Susheela Raghavan, "Geography," in *Madras/Chennai: A 400-Year Record of the First City of Modern India: The Land, The People & Their Governance,* ed. S. Muthiah (Chennai: Palaniappa Brothers, 2008), 3.
63 Similar arguments are made by both C. J. Fuller and Joanne Punzo Waghorne in their respective books. See: C. J. Fuller, *The Renewal of the Priesthood: Modernity and Traditionalism in a South Indian Temple* (Princeton and Oxford: Princeton University Press, 2003). See also: Joanne Punzo Waghorne, *Diaspora of the Gods: Modern Hindu Temple in an Urban Middle-Class World* (New York: Oxford University Press, 2004).
64 Podipara, *The Thomas Christians,* 7.
65 Interview with Fr. Lawrence Raj, Chennai, June 15, 2009.
66 Manohar Samuel, "Christianity," *Madras/Chennai: A 400-Year Record of the First City of Modern India: The Land, The People & Their Governance,* ed. S. Muthiah (Chennai: Palaniappa Brothers, 2008), 162–168.
67 Waghorne, *Diaspora of the Gods,* 76–77.
68 Samuel, "Christianity," 166.

69 S. Muthiah, *Madras Rediscovered* (Chennai: East West, an imprint of Westland Limited, 2008), 119.

70 Joseph Vazhuthanapally, *The Biblical and Archaeological Foundations of the Mar Thoma Sliba* (Kottayam, Kerala: Oriental Institute of Religious Studies India Publications, 1990), 8–9.

71 See: J. Edwin Orr, *The Re-study of Revival and Revivalism* (Pasadena, CA: School of World Mission, 1981), i–viii.

72 Ibid, ii–iv.

73 Susan Bayly, *Saints, Goddesses and Kings: Muslims and Christians in South Indian Society, 1700–1900* (Cambridge: Cambridge University Press, 1989), 257–262.

74 Muthiah, *Madras Rediscovered,* 123–126.

75 S. J. Anthonysamy, *A Saga of Faith: St. Thomas the Apostle of India* (Chennai: National Shrine of St. Thomas Basilica, 2009), 109–113.

76 Ibid, 125–129.

77 Quoted in Sashi Kala Chandran, "Down Memory Lane with Fr. Lawrence Raj," *Sweet Fruits of God's Harvest on Earth: Rev. Fr. Lawrence Raj Sacerdotal Silver Jubilee Commemorative Souvenir,* ed. Fr. Lawrence Raj Silver Jubilee Souvenir Committee. (Chennai: Fr. Lawrence Raj Silver Jubilee Souvenir Committee, 2007). As of the publication of this book Fr. Lawrence has completed his tenure at St. Teresa's and has since been assigned to a new parish within the Archdiocese of Madras-Mylapore.

78 Interview with Fr. Lawrence Raj, Chennai, June 15, 2009. See also: "Poignant handing-over and taking charge," *Voice of St. Thomas* 1, 5 (July–September 2007): 25.

79 Field Notes, Chennai, July 29, 2009.

80 Sashi Kala Chandran, "Down Memory Lane with Fr. Lawrence Raj."

81 Interview with Fr. Lawrence Raj, Chennai, June 15, 2009.

82 Interview with Mr. Zander, Chennai, August 5, 2009.

83 Fuller, *The Renewal of the Priesthood*, 39–40.

84 Mary E. Hancock, *The Politics of Heritage from Madras to Chennai* (Bloomington, IN: Indiana University Press, 2008), 1–22.

85 Ibid, 12.

86 Mara Einstein, *Brands of Faith: Marketing Religion in a Commercial Age* (London and New York: Routledge, 2008).

87 Ibid, 1–15.

88 See: Fuller, *The Renewal of the Priesthood.* See also: Waghorne, *Diaspora of the Gods.*

89 See: Lise McKean, *Divine Enterprise: Gurus and the Hindu Nationalist Movement* (Chicago: University of Chicago Press, 1996), 1–42.

90 See: Meera Nanda, *The God Market: How Globalization is Making India More Hindu* (Noida, Uttar Pradesh: Random House India, 2009), 1–11.

91 Interview with Fr. Lawrence Raj, Chennai, December 15, 2010.

92 Ibid.

93 McKean, *Divine Enterprise,* 5.

94 Ibid, 13.

95 Nanda, *The God Market,* 113.

96 Ibid.

97 Ibid, 114.

98 Ibid, 101.

99 For more scholarship on established Hindu marketing models in and outside India see: Tulasi Srinivas, "Traditions in Transition: Globalisation, Priests, and Ritual Innovation in Neighbourhood Temples in Bangalore," *Journal of Social and Economic Development* 6, 1 (Jan.–June, 2004): 57–75. See also: Vineeta Sinha, *Religion and Commodification: 'Merchandizing' Diasporic Hinduism* (New York: Routledge, 2011).

100 See: Forum for Catholic Unity, "Corruption Charges Against the Archbishop of Madras-Mylapore," *Metamorphose* (October 2009). This article exists as a downloadable document that can be found at the following website: http://www.ephesians-511.net/. The direct downloadable link is as follows: http://ephesians-511.net/docs/ARCHBISHOP_OF_MADRAS_MYLAPORE-CORRUPTION_CHARGES_AGAINST_THE.doc.
101 Interview with Fr. Lawrence Raj, Chennai, December 15, 2010.
102 Wendy Doniger, "Foreword: The View from the Other Side: Postpostcolonialism, Religious Syncretism, and Class Conflict," in *Popular Christianity in India. Riting Between the Lines*, eds Selva J. Raj and Corinne G. Dempsey (Albany, NY: State University of New York Press, 2002), xi–xii. See also: Jonathan Z. Smith, *Drudgery Divine: On the Comparison of Early Christianities and the Religions of Late Antiquity* (Chicago: University of Chicago Press, 1990).
103 Doniger, "Foreword," xi.
104 Ibid, xii. To be fair, Edward Said was, by birth, an Arab Protestant Christian. In one of his final and lesser known works he conceded that a post-colonial community, like Arab Protestants, could exemplify "an experience of imperialism that is essentially one of sympathy and congruence, not of antagonism, resentment, or resistance. The appeal by one of the parties was to the value of a mutual experience." I believe a similar sentiment is present within the Indian Catholic communities in Chennai today. See: Edward W. Said, *Culture and Imperialism* (New York: Alfred A. Knopf, Inc., 1993), 40.
105 See: Christophe Jaffrelot, *Religion, Caste and Politics in India* (New York: Columbia University Press, 2011), 144–169.
106 Doniger, "Foreword," xii–xiii.
107 Ibid, xii.
108 Richard M. Eaton, "(Re)imag(in)ing Otherness: A Postmortem for the Postmodern in India," *Journal of World History* 11, 1 (Spring 2000): 63–64.
109 Ania Loomba, *Colonialism/ Postcolonialism* (London and New York: Routledge, 2004), 173–174.
110 Rosalind Shaw and Charles Stewart, "Introduction: problematizing syncretism," in *Syncretism/ Anti-Syncretism: The Politics of Religious Synthesis*, eds Charles Stewart and Rosalind Shaw (London and New York: Routledge, 1994), 1.
111 Ibid, 7.
112 Selva J. Raj and Corinne G. Dempsey, "Introduction," in *Popular Christianity in India. Riting Between the Lines*, eds Raj, Selva J. and C. Dempsey (Albany, NY: State University of New York Press, 2002) 1–2.
113 Selva J. Raj, "The Ganges, the Jordan, and the Mountain: The Three Strands of Santal Popular Catholicism," in *Popular Christianity in India: Riting Between the Lines*, eds Selva J. Raj and Corinne G. Dempsey (Albany, NY: State University of New York Press, 2002), 39.
114 Pope Paul VI, *Evangelii Nuntiandi*, http://www.vatican.va/holy_father/paul_vi/apost_exhortations/documents/hf_p-vi_exh_19751208_evangelii-nuntiandi_en.html (Accessed February 2, 2013).
115 Corinne Dempsey investigates the cults of St. George and St. Alphonsa within the context of colonial and postcolonial Kerala as case studies for hybridized Hindu and Christian religious identities. Dempsey, *Kerala Christian Sainthood*. Corinne G. Dempsey, "Lessons in Miracles from Kerala, South India: Stories of Three "Christian" Saints," in *Popular Christianity in India: Riting Between the Lines*, eds Selva J. Raj and Corinne G. Dempsey (Albany, NY: State University of New York Press, 2002), 115–139. Margaret Meibohm's PhD dissertation for the University of Pennsylvania is probably the most in-depth study to date on the highly popular shrine dedicated to Our Lady of Health in Vailankanni, Tamil Nadu. This Marian shrine is easily the most visited and

venerated Catholic shrine in India. Margaret Meibohm, "Cultural Complexity in South India: Hindu and Catholic in Marian Pilgrimage" (Ph.D. dissertation, University of Pennsylvania, 2004). Selva J. Raj has written on the Tamil Catholic use of traditional South Indian vow rituals, among other things, specifically at shrines dedicated to St. John de Britto, St. Anne, and St. Anthony. Selva J. Raj, "Transgressing Boundaries, Transcending Turner: The Pilgrimage Tradition at the Shrine of St. John de Britto," in *Popular Christianity in India: Riting between the Lines*, eds Selva J. Raj and Corinne G. Dempsey (Albany, NY: State University of New York Press, 2002), 85–111. Selva J. Raj, "Shared Vows, Shared Space, and Shared Deities: Vow Rituals among Tamil Catholics in South India," in *Dealing with Deities: The Ritual Vow in South Asia*, eds Selva J. Raj and William P. Harman (Albany, NY: State University of New York Press, 2006), 43–64. Selva J. Raj, "Public Display, Communal Devotion: Procession at a South Indian Catholic Festival," in *South Asian Religions on Display: Religious Processions in South Asia and in the Diaspora*, ed. Knut A. Jacobson (London and New York: Routledge, 2008), 77–91. Selva J. Raj, "Serious Levity at the Shrine of St. Anne in South India," in *Sacred Play: Ritual Levity and Humor in South Asian* Religions, eds Selva J. Raj and Corinne G. Dempsey (Albany, NY: State University of New York Press, 2010), 21–36. David Mosse has written several articles based on his ethnohistorical fieldwork in rural Southeastern Tamil Nadu. He is primarily concerned with the escalation of caste conflict within the Roman Catholic ritual system between low-caste and high-caste converts, and the Church's eventual solution to ease said tensions. His case study revolves around the village Church festival of St. James. David Mosse, "Honour, Caste and Conflict: The Ethnohistory of a Catholic Festival in Rural Tamil Nadu (1730–1990)," in *AltÈritÈ et IdentitÈ. Islam et Christianisme en Inde*, eds Jackie Assayag and Gilles Tarabout G. (Paris: Ehess, 1997), 71-120. David Mosse, "Idioms of Subordination and Styles of Protest among Christian and Hindu Harijan Castes in Tamil Nadu," *Contributions to Indian Sociology* 28, 1 (1994): 67–106. David Mosse, "The Politics of Religious Synthesis: Roman Catholicism and Hindu Village Society in Tamil Nadu, India," in *Syncretism/ Anti-Syncretism: The Politics of Religious Synthesis*, eds Charles Stewart and Rosalind Shaw (London and New York: Routledge, 1994), 85–107. Paul Younger devotes two consecutive chapters in his book, *Playing Host to Deity*, to two separate South Indian festivals dedicated to St. Mary. Paul Younger, *Playing Host to Deity: Festival Religion in the South Indian Tradition* (Oxford: Oxford University Press, 2002), 109–124.

116 Roger E. Hedlund, *Quest for Identity, India's Churches of Indigenous Origin: The "Little Tradition" in Indian Christianity* (Chennai: MIIS/ ISPCK, 2000), 3.

117 Ibid, 3.

118 Sebastian C. H. Kim, *In Search of Identity: Debates on Religious Conversion in India* (New Delhi: Oxford University Press, 2005), 109–131.

119 Hedlund, *Quest for Identity*, 2.

120 Interview with Mr. Zander, Chennai, August 5, 2009.

2   Reviving the history of St. Thomas

Martyrdom and burial as a new myth of origin for Indian Catholics in Chennai

Introduction

In analyzing recent shrinal revivals in Chennai, it is clear that the local Catholic administration has in the past maintained a minimalist approach in acknowledging and perpetuating St. Thomas's religious legacy. Only within the last ten years has the Church in Chennai developed new strategies to actively market and revive devotion to St. Thomas at his associated sites. It has done so with the intention of educating both local and global audiences about St. Thomas's religious and historical worth to Christianity in India. Additionally, the Chennai Church has taken steps to shape Tamil Catholic identity around the person of St. Thomas by emphasizing the Apostle's intimate connection with the region.

This chapter considers the context and strategies associated with the revival of devotion to St. Thomas in Chennai. The key revivalist strategies discussed here pertain to the way that the three St. Thomas shrines have used various media tools for disseminating information about St. Thomas. Other strategies include the use of more local and intimate venues, such as monthly devotionals, parish festivals, and church sermons or homilies. Ultimately, it is the hope of Church administrators that the increased output of published media such as books, magazines, pamphlets, CDs, and other such paraphernalia, as well as the greater day-to-day emphasis on St. Thomas's presence in festivals and homilies, will serve to further popularize the three St. Thomas sites as noteworthy Chennai heritage sites, global Catholic pilgrimage centers, and major tourist destinations within India.

As well as discussing the strategies used to revive devotion to St. Thomas, this chapter will also investigate the historical realties that have led to a lack of devotion towards St. Thomas on the part of Catholic Tamils. As Fr. Lawrence and other local Indian Catholics often told me, the St. Thomas story is not very well known in India, let alone the rest of the world. More surprisingly, it is not even well known among most Tamil Roman Catholics living in Chennai or elsewhere in South India. Church administrators in Chennai aim to address this ignorance and bring St. Thomas's popularity more in line with the level of devotion enjoyed by other Catholic saints such as St. Mary, the mother of Jesus, whose popularity in South India is quite staggering. It is also a matter of pride for the current Church in Chennai that the sacrality of these three sites be upheld as befits an Apostle of Jesus Christ, something that had been lacking in previous years.

Coupled with the goal of increasing popular devotion to St. Thomas, Church administrators in Chennai also aim to raise the Apostle's national reputation from his current status as just another saint to that of a religious progenitor emblematic of all Indian Christians. In other words, they hope to raise St. Thomas's profile to the same level of reverence and acceptance as shown by the Syrian Christian communities of Kerala. This regional veneration for St. Thomas is due to the fact that for many Malayalee Christians their religious ethnic identity as Thomas Christians hinges on the historical validity of the Apostle's voyage to India and the belief that he converted and baptized their ancestors all those centuries ago.

Tamil Christians have no such connection to St. Thomas, save for the tradition that the Apostle was martyred and buried in ancient Chennai. Therefore, I will argue in this chapter that the recent emphasis on the death and burial of St. Thomas in Chennai has effectively created a new myth of Christian origin in Tamil Nadu. This new perspective creates for all Tamil Christian communities in the region a direct connection to the person of St. Thomas on par with the Keralite claim for an ancient ethnic and communal Christian ancestry. Thus, the Catholic Church in Chennai is interpreting the past in order to shape its present revival, but also utilizing its present social and political context in order to shape its past.

St. Thomas forgotten: the Apostle's lack of presence in Tamil Nadu

This section will move back and forth between Tamil Nadu's past and present in order to discuss several of the historical and socio-religious factors that have contributed to St. Thomas's low profile in Tamil Nadu. As I have mentioned above, outside of Kerala, St. Thomas is not very well known in India. In terms of popular worship, Tamil Hindus who regularly visit Christian shrines hardly ever do so with the Apostle in mind. I interviewed one Catholic Tamil who had been a parishioner at San Thome for over thirty years, and whose testimony regarding the knowledge of St. Thomas in Chennai is startling. According to Mr. Zander, "Most of the parishioners, even the parishioners, not only Christians in Chennai... most of the parishioners, they didn't know the importance of the tomb of St. Thomas there. To be very frank, even certain parishioners [of San Thome], they don't know there is a tomb there. Really! Really! Only the pilgrims who come from abroad and other people know."[1] Mr. Zander noted that it is mainly Keralite Christians who make the pilgrimage to these sites, as well as some international visitors who are already aware of the tomb's significance.

Church leaders are troubled that San Thome's very own parishioners do not know their own parish's history. However, this lack of awareness partly stems from the Church's own lack of focus on this history in earlier times. In confessing his earlier lack of awareness, Mr. Zander also highlighted the Church's own lack of attention to St. Thomas:

> To be very frank, since 1974 I am here. You won't believe, only two, three years back I went up to St. Thomas Mount. See, very ignorant, we [are] down here. We don't know much of the thing ... priests and other people, they don't take steps to ... enlighten [us in] mass about the importance of St. Thomas Mount, about its history ... that is why I never studied about St. Thomas's history in my school or college ... only a couple of years back only I went up to St. Thomas [Mount] to see the church. I was also not interested, nobody bothered to enlighten me. This is the case ... we are not able to tell about St. Thomas, spread about St. Thomas, in Chennai ... when they [visiting pilgrims] ask me, I am not properly enlightened to explain to them. Suppose I am as a parishioner, I am standing there, they ask me some stories. I should be prepared to explain to them.[2]

Fr. Lawrence made similar remarks pertaining to the lack of shrinal promotion on the part of the Church, as well as St. Thomas's low profile in Tamil Nadu. He claimed that:

> Even in India, even in Tamil Nadu, they don't know much about St. Thomas. This is one of the saddest thing[s]. I have gone and preached all over, I said, "having an Apostle, having a saint, how blessed we are!" But none of us know about it. Which is something sad, that is because the Church has neglected very badly, they have not promoted the devotion to St. Thomas. Kerala, yes, they are very much devoted, but not in Tamil Nadu. Now, I, in fact, in the ... the early eighties when I was [assigned to] St. Thomas Mount, I have become the new leader ... [for] all these matters ... about the importance of these places, three places in Madras, and how they have been neglected.[3]

As Fr. Lawrence claims, during his brief stint at St. Thomas Mount, he became motivated to take a leading role in the preservation of the St. Thomas tradition in Chennai. Seeing firsthand the lack of local awareness with regard to the St. Thomas sites, Fr. Lawrence considered that an information campaign would be necessary. He saw the wisdom in utilizing various media as one aspect of his 2004 renovation project at San Thome. This would help educate the local populace, and raise St. Thomas's profile all across India.

One factor in St. Thomas's low visibility is related to administrative structure, since the city's three St. Thomas sites had always operated independently of each other. Mr. Zander stressed that each site was more or less concerned with its own operations, and that there was no united front in preserving St. Thomas's legacy. This larger issue was another dimension Fr. Lawrence hoped to address during the 2004 revival. His initial plan was to organize joint festivals between the three sites, which should have been relatively easy since they all fell under the jurisdiction of the Archdiocese of Madras-Mylapore. However, in 2003, just a year prior to the renovation of San Thome, St. Thomas Mount was removed from that Archdiocese and placed under the jurisdiction of the Diocese of Chingleput. To paraphrase Fr. Lawrence, this move made any hope for a joint revival "impossible," since each diocese is essentially an autonomous bureaucratic entity.[4] Fr. Lawrence was clearly dismayed at this turn of events, and summed it up as a poor decision on the part of the Archbishop of Madras-Mylapore, especially at such a crucial point in time.

Historical factors in St. Thomas's low profile in Tamil Nadu

Historically speaking, several other factors have limited the spread of St. Thomas's popularity in Tamil Nadu. In recent times, the most immediate factor has simply been the progression of modernity due to the end of the colonial era and the growth of a new Indian nation. As discussed in Chapter 1, by the early 1500s the Portuguese had appropriated Mylapore (now a suburb of modern-day Chennai) along with the tomb of St. Thomas, where they established a trading port and settlement.[5] From this vantage point, the Portuguese set out to cultivate and preserve the St. Thomas tradition, which would later become synonymous with their overarching missionary agendas. Susan Bayly has written extensively on religious conversion and the intermingling of religious communities during India's colonial period. She notes the great lengths to which the Portuguese crown strived to establish and maintain the cult of St. Thomas in Mylapore, all in order to solidify their power in South India and elevate their prestige as Christian benefactors.[6]

However, with the rise of British colonialism and the subsequent decline of the Portuguese, the maintenance of a cult of St. Thomas also declined. In general, the Roman Catholic Church persevered under British dominion and into Indian independence, and the three St. Thomas sites of Chennai became some of the last vestiges of Portuguese authority in Tamil Nadu. By 1887, the Vatican had transferred all of its ecclesiastical authority over to a completely Indian Church hierarchy.[7] In 1952 Mylapore saw its last Portuguese bishop, and after this it fell solely on the shoulders of the newly amalgamated Archdiocese of Madras-Mylapore and its indigenous Indian hierarchy to oversee the preservation of St Thomas's local legacy, if they were so inclined.[8]

Of course, for many of Chennai's Roman Catholics, the St. Thomas sites are cherished parts of their local cultural heritage. However, due to the religious and social upheavals that occurred in India following its independence in 1947 and into the modern day, heritage preservation was simply not an immediate priority for the Roman Catholic Church during that era.[9] Only recently have Church administrators in Chennai seriously set out to revive interest in St. Thomas locally and abroad.

Lack of ethnic communal lineage in Tamil Nadu

Another factor that has stunted the growth of St. Thomas's profile in Tamil Nadu is the lack of cultural and ethnic ties associated with the Saint, such as those found in Kerala. As already noted in Chapter 1, Christianity in Kerala and the Malabar Coast was much more successful than in Tamil Nadu and the Coromandel Coast.[10] Most of the traditions concerning the success and longevity of the Syrian Christian communities in ancient Kerala come from the Syrian Christians themselves by way of oral tradition and communal memory.[11] The key assertion is that ancient Kerala was a relatively peaceful and religiously tolerant region due to its on-going harmonious and successful trade with foreign merchants, which ultimately attracted Indian Christian immigrants and refugees from other, less tolerant, parts of India, such as the Coromandel Coast.[12]

All of this helps to explain why the Keralite Christians are the most numerous and knowledgeable pilgrims who regularly visit the three St. Thomas sites in Chennai. Fr. Lawrence was quick to point this fact out to me. He said, "You see, the people who come from abroad and from Kerala, they know the importance of these places, so they regularly come. They make their visit [to the three sites] compulsory when they come to the city ... our people, the so-called Tamil people, they don't have much devotion to St. Thomas. I don't know whether it is the failure of the bishops and the clergy. I used to feel bad about it always."[13] Mr. Mark from Kerala made a similar claim, stating that, "where part of his remnants are buried there in San Thome, there's Little Mount, and St. Thomas Mount, all these places are really ... spots where the Keralites, Malayalees like to go to mass on Sundays. That's where they go, like to kind of really meet the person of St. Thomas there."[14]

Not all of my Tamil Catholic informants were so amicable in their tone when discussing the Thomas Christians. Tamil informants often felt that visiting Malayalee Christians came across as arrogant with regard to their special connection with the person of St. Thomas. As Mr. Zander put it, "Particularly ... Keralites, they alone [say] that St. Thomas is their own Apostle ... ah, St. Thomas belongs to Keralites only, they used to argue, because, see, he came and landed there [ancient Kerala], he started ... the first church[es] there."[15] Sr. Merrill, a nun who works at the tomb shrine at San Thome told me about a complaint made by a Malayalee pilgrim who disliked the reproduction of Caravaggio's painting *The Incredulity of Saint Thomas* that was hanging in the foyer. The pilgrim disagreed with this particular portrayal of the "Doubting Thomas" story and felt obliged to share his concern at its lack of authenticity.

As it stands, the pride that brings many Keralite Christians to Chennai is not prevalent among Tamil Roman Catholics. Fr. Lawrence and other Church administrators hope that a well-organized revivalist strategy and time will eventually promulgate an equivalent pride, indicative of a strong socio-religious identity pertaining to the three locally controlled St. Thomas shrines.

Clearly, well before the arrival of the Portuguese, Indian Christian communal ties to the Mylapore and greater Tamil regions were at some point severed. The tomb of St. Thomas in Mylapore was not completely abandoned or forgotten, but organized pilgrimage to the site did become rarer. Thus, by the time the Portuguese arrived in India, with their myriad of Catholic saints, Mylapore and the Coromandel Coast had little to no Christian presence, while the Malabar Coast still had within its lands a number of venerable Syrian Christian communities. As such, for Portuguese missionaries and traders, the Coromandel Coast was practically untilled soil patiently awaiting the seeds of Roman Catholicism and European commerce.

Other popular Catholic saints within Tamil Nadu's religious landscape

One final socio-historical factor that serves to emphasize the lack of regional awareness and popular devotion to St. Thomas in Tamil Nadu is the existence of several other locally popular Catholic saint cults that have established themselves deep within Tamil Nadu's eclectic religious landscape. While it is hard to ascertain whether the existence of such cults have contributed to St. Thomas's low profile, I have observed that Church administrators have seen the benefits of underscoring St. Thomas's close connection to such personalities, especially with the figure of St. Mary. However, it can be inferred from the many conversations I had with Tamil Catholics that these various local Christian saint cults have grown to overshadow the St. Thomas tradition. This same observation can also be inferred from the large amount of scholarship on popular Christianity in Tamil Nadu that make little to no mention of St. Thomas.[16]

Even in Kerala, St. Thomas is not "popular" in the same sense as St. Mary or St. Anthony in modern-day India. Susan Bayly has noted that the cult of St. Thomas was once deeply ingrained within Keralite Syrian Christian religious life.[17] However, this no longer seems to be the case in Kerala today. Corinne Dempsey explains that, "St. Thomas is also, without doubt, one of the most important saints to Kerala Christians, if not *the* most important. Unlike St. George, St. Sebastian, and St. Gregorios, however, Thomas is currently not so much a cult saint as he is an emblematic patron saint. In this way his function is much like Alphonsa's in her capacity to carve and justify a unique Kerala Christian identity."[18]

This is also true for St. Thomas in Tamil Nadu, but to a lesser extent and limited to only those communities with long-standing ties to any one of the three Chennai shrines associated with him. As Fr. Lawrence explained, the Thomas Christians of Kerala maintain "a lot of identity with St. Thomas and that has got a lot of influence, also, on the people. But ... here [in Tamil Nadu] ... of course, as I told you already ... I don't know what sort of influence it has got on the people. Of course, we all say ... the [Christian] faith was brought by St. Thomas, in that way, we have that in the amount of devotion and connections to St. Thomas and so on. And from the beginning, they did not give much importance to that, so that kind of identity ... I don't think it was emphasized."[19] In other words, for those Tamil Catholics who know the history of St. Thomas in India, he at least serves as an "emblematic patron saint," even if there is no ethnic or communal justification in his having visited India as we see with the Thomas Christians of Kerala.

On my final visit to Chennai in 2010, I had the opportunity to have supper with Fr. M. Arulraj the parish priest of Little Mount. According to him, the three most popular Christian cults in Tamil Nadu are, in order of their popularity, St. Mary, St. Anthony, and baby Jesus. My Malayalee informant made observations about several other popular saints in Tamil Nadu, especially those who have very little presence in Kerala. Mr. Mark explained, "St. Francis Xavier and St. John de Britto and St. Ignatius [of Loyola], these are the real pillars of Tamil Nadu Christians. There [in Kerala] it's St. Thomas and they don't know much about St. Francis Xavier, St. John de Britto, and St. Ignatius [of Loyola]."[20] A Tamil Catholic fellow I met up with on several occasions corroborated Mr. Mark's words and firmly added that while many Malayalee Christians consider themselves to be the Christians of St. Thomas, the historical equivalent in Tamil Nadu is that many Tamils consider themselves to be the Christians of St. Francis Xavier (b. 1506 – d. 1552).[21] St. Francis Xavier was a Spanish Jesuit who carried out missionary work throughout South India, mainly in regions that had a Portuguese colonial presence, and is credited with almost single-handedly organizing and rejuvenating the Catholic missionary enterprise in sixteenth-century India, which is why he is often referred to as the second Apostle to India.[22]

For Fr. Lawrence, who has become invested in promoting the St. Thomas tradition in India, popular cults like those previously mentioned are sources of exasperation. In one of my interviews with Fr. Lawrence, he clearly expressed to me his personal frustration in the matter:

> Vailankanni [shrine of St. Mary] is so popular, St. Anthony is so popular, St. Francis Xavier is so popular. But St. Thomas, while the Apostle of India was instrumental in bringing the Faith to this country, is not

visible. Even the celebration of St. Thomas's feast on July 3rd is nothing
excit[ing], yeah. So, when you have the car procession for Our Lady,
you will see the big crowds ... and, of course, for some of our Catholics,
they don't know much about it; Hindus, also, for they also don't know
much about it.[23]

Fr. Lawrence's words serve to emphasize two important aspects of popular
Tamil (South Indian) religious culture and pluralism. First, they stress the
overwhelming popularity of St. Mary, specifically at the Our Lady of
Vailankanni Basilica shrine located far south of Chennai in the Nagapattinam
district of Tamil Nadu. Second, they highlight the great number of Hindus
who consider themselves the devotees of Mother Mary, whose presence at
Christian sacred sites are indications of a shrine's prestige.

While it is impossible to prove without statistical or numerical data, it is
assumed by scholars of South India, as well as by many of the Catholic
Indians I spoke with, that the majority of visitors and pilgrims that visit
Christian sacred sites and attend festivals in India are Hindus.[24] The
Catholic Church, unlike many Protestant groups in India, have allowed a
certain leeway with local customs, while many Hindus are very willing to
accept the vast array of Christian saints into their pantheons and daily
worship. More specifically, the Church understands the above phenomenon
as merely "popular religiosity" or "popular piety," because it is seen as
being of the people, which is why it is doctrinally tolerated to some
degree.[25] As stated before, the most astonishing example of this phenomenon is St. Mary, whose manifestation at Vailankanni has steadily grown in
popularity since its occurrence during the colonial era. Vasudha Narayanan,
a professor of religion whose work focuses on the varied traditions of Tamil
Hindu culture, states, "I would argue that Mary as Vailankanni is not just
a Christian deity but a Tamil and (more recently with her appeal to the
Bombay pilgrims) an Indian deity because she is worshipped in her *particular* [emphasis in original] manifestation at Nagapattinam, and she favors all
devotees, not just those who convert to Christianity or who are Christian
by faith."[26] In other words, St. Mary, and to a lesser extent St. Thomas,
have become tantamount to Indian Hindu deities, further establishing
Christianity and its many denominations as a mainstay of India's religious
landscape.

Given the issues with respect to the marketing of St. Thomas as a significant devotional figure, it is clear that St. Thomas is up against some rather
stiff competition in Tamil Nadu, and even taking into consideration the
recent revivals, not much has changed. However, the main reason for
Fr. Lawrence's frustration with regard to Vailankanni's popularity is
certainly not Christian/ Hindu hybridity or any fear of syncretism, but that
the two thousand year legacy of St. Thomas's martyrdom and tomb site are
virtually unknown in Tamil Nadu. Fr. Lawrence states, "Yeah, it is more
historical. See, we ... we say, 'The tomb is the womb of Christianity in

India.' It is because of St. Thomas, Christianity came to India. So therefore, the cathedral of San Thome becomes more ... far more important. And also this Vailankanni shrine and so on, became very famous only now ... of late, actually after [19]70s and so on."[27] Fr. Lawrence claims that Vailankanni's mass appeal only spread to Chennai and other parts of Tamil Nadu fairly recently due to a serendipitous Tamil-language film made about the Catholic shrine in the 1970s.[28] Thus it is no surprise that the Church in Chennai would adopt a revivalist strategy that includes highlighting and disseminating the main advantage St. Thomas has over his competition: a living historical and pre-colonial legacy that dates back to the first century CE.

New revivalist strategies at San Thome and elsewhere: recent publications concerning St. Thomas and his martyr's legacy

Church administrators in Chennai, such as Fr. Lawrence, have used various revivalist strategies to rectify the lack of knowledge regarding St. Thomas's local and national legacy. Namely, they have adopted a revivalist strategy that entails a wider use of mass media publications that can better serve to educate and inform the local populace about St. Thomas's Indian legacy, and with time, eventually reach a wider national and international audience. As Fr. Lawrence has remarked, it falls to the clergy to better spread the word about the Apostle's deep connection with the lands of South India.

Since San Thome's renovation took place as early as 2004, it is here where this revivalist strategy received its first implementation. During the time of Fr. Lawrence's tenure at San Thome, the Cathedral published several histories in both book and documentary form, a new quarterly magazine, a couple of special souvenir booklets, various pamphlets and brochures, devotional and informational CDs and DVDs, and a slew of other paraphernalia. This section will focus on those publications and discourses that have come out of San Thome since 2004, and will only briefly touch upon those materials that have come out of St. Thomas Mount and Little Mount in recent years. St. Thomas Mount's revival is still underway and is clearly utilizing many of the same revivalist strategies that were initiated at San Thome, in the hopes of mirroring its immediate successes. This will be covered in greater depth in Chapter 5.

Alongside this greater use of print and audio media, we are also seeing a greater emphasis placed on St. Thomas in the form of monthly devotionals, annual festivals, and other such events that provide the clergy with a public platform to discuss St. Thomas within the local community. As I argue, one of the main goals for the Chennai Church is to instil in Tamil Catholics feelings about the legacy of St. Thomas that are on par with Syrian Christian devotion to the Apostle in Kerala. In other words, by presenting St. Thomas's death and burial in ancient Chennai as a significant part of Tamil Christian heritage, these events become a pre-colonial and indigenous origin story for all of Tamil Christianity, making Tamil Christian identity something equivalent to the Thomas Christian identity of Syrian Christians in Kerala.

Through a close reading of many of these publications, a number of common themes become apparent that demonstrate how the Church is attempting to solidify St. Thomas's legacy within the region. First, many of these publications emphasize the antiquity and historicity of the three St. Thomas shrines in Chennai. Second, they present St. Thomas's martyrdom as a crucial event that directly connects the Apostle's blood to the soil of India. Third, and to a lesser extent, they propagate regional narratives and traditions regarding the Apostle's missionary activities in ancient Mylapore.

The significance of St. Thomas historicity

As stated previously in Chapter 1, the only historically validated fact regarding St. Thomas's journey to India is that a man living in the first century CE could realistically travel from Jerusalem to India by way of pre-existing land and sea routes.[29] Although this fact stands alone, for many pious historians this is foundation enough to continually return to the historicity of the St. Thomas tradition and build upon it using the many other strands of historical plausibility that exist.

For many Church administrators and historians, the historical validity of the St. Thomas story is clearly a significant issue for them, and an important aspect of Catholic renewal in Chennai, since the authenticity of these three sites hinges on the belief that St. Thomas visited and died in India. While faith and fervor usually do not require the validation of historical research in order to persevere, the situation in Chennai concerns the general lack of such faith with regard to St. Thomas. Thus, the goal of many Church administrators such as Fr. Lawrence is to instil this faith into the people, for whom a historical account can provide a useful tool. However, if one were to visit any one of these three sites, the story of St. Thomas that he or she would be told would lack the scholarly depth provided by a highly researched historical analysis. As Brother Joe, a former tour guide at San Thome and now the current groundskeeper at Little Mount, related to me:

> So, I explain to them that he [St. Thomas] came to India, first to Kerala in 52 AD, he landed at a place called Cranganore, he built seven churches in Kerala and he preached and prospered for some 18 years there. Then by the Coromandel Coast he came to Mylapore in 68 AD. And he was preaching in Mylapore in a small chapel and he was preaching to the people. There was a man named Rajah Mahadevan, who being a Hindu, he derides St. Thomas for preaching the new religion, Christianity of Christ. He wanted to kill him, and St. Thomas ran to Mylapore and came to the area of Little Mount, the jungle he partly

came. So he hid himself in the cave, and he used to go to the Big Mount, from here about 3 kilometers, used to go there on top of the Mount, he used to walk, pray there, and he used to come and stay and preach to the people. Later on, when Rajah Mahadevan knew that he is hiding in the Little Mount cave, so he sent his men to catch him. When they are trying to catch him, he escaped from here to St. Thomas Mount. There, while he was praying before the cross, the men who chased him to St. Thomas Mount, pierced him with a lance, killed him AD 72 on 18th of December. The same people took the body, buried in the chapel where he built it. Now the tomb of St. Thomas is there in the present cathedral under the main altar. And the body became a dust; the bones are taken away to [Italy].[30]

All the actual historical nuances involved in "proving" St. Thomas's journey are not crucial to a believer. For most believers, the truth of the matter revolves around the places he visited, where he was killed and buried, the Christian communities he left behind, and the miracles that are still occurring in his name.

For those Indian Christians who are aware of the St. Thomas tradition, it is not a matter of history so much as it is a matter of faith and religious identity, especially for the Thomas Christians of Malabar, and possibly for those Tamil Catholic communities in and around the three sacred sites of Chennai. However, histories about St. Thomas are still vital for the sake of education and apologetics, mainly for those Indian Christians still unaware of the St. Thomas story, and especially for the three sacred sites themselves which can utilize such texts as an accessible means to disseminate the Apostle's importance to a wider national and international audience.

Since 2000, a number of different histories have been published that discuss at length the historical validity of St. Thomas's life and missionary work in first-century India. Unsurprisingly, the majority of these works have come out of India, and have been written by members of the Indian Christian clerical and lay community.[31] Here I am only interested in those histories that directly pertain to the three St. Thomas sites in Chennai. Many of the works I am familiar with are either inaccessible or unknown to the Church in Chennai, which is probably why it has had to rely on commissioning and publishing its own accounts of St. Thomas's connection to local history. It can also be presumed that the Church in Chennai would only support those histories that coincide with its vision of the St. Thomas story and that help to advance its specific socio-political and religious agendas. Thus, these locally-written histories play an important role for Chennai's St. Thomas shrines, because they attempt to historically verify the Apostle's legacy, which in turn, serves to educate the local populace about St. Thomas and hopefully instil in them a greater sense of pride and esteem for the progenitor of their faith.

Self-published histories from the three
St. Thomas shrines of Chennai

The first full-length study of St. Thomas in India was *India and the Apostle Thomas*, which was written by A. E. Medleycott who was the Vicar Apostolate of the Diocese of Trichur in Kerala prior to its publication in 1905. Later, a number of other Catholic historians would also contribute various books and articles on the subject of St. Thomas.[32] Of most interest to me are those works that were written and published specifically for the three St. Thomas sites in Chennai. The earliest of these works was *In the Steps of St. Thomas*, which was written by Herman D'Souza, a Catholic priest and, at the time, rector of St. Thomas Mount. First published in 1952, its aim was to provide tourists and pilgrims with a guidebook to the Christian sites in the area.[33] To this day, both Medleycott and D'Souza's books are still being published at San Thome under the auspices of the Cathedral's own publishing house Disciples of St. Thomas (DOST). According to DOST's webpage on San Thome's website they, "help the church and clergy with their talents, experience and resources. They obey the local parish priest and organize their activities in consultation with the parish priests/bishops. They are the defenders of faith and take pride in identifying as the Right Arm of the Church."[34] Since 2008–2009, at San Thome specifically, they also initiated a project with the explicit goal of digitizing and preserving all historical records pertaining to St. Thomas and Indian Christianity in their possession.[35]

In 2004, San Thome Cathedral, through the DOST, published its very own historical analysis of St. Thomas with a second edition in 2009. This book, *A Saga of Faith* by local Catholic priest S. J. Anthonysamy, was commissioned by Fr. Lawrence in preparation for the completion of San Thome's 2004 renovation project.[36] In 2010, St. Thomas Mount published its own copy of D'Souza's *In the Steps of St. Thomas*, which serves their needs since it was originally written for pilgrims specifically visiting the Mount. More significantly, in July of 2010, St. Thomas Mount also published a small booklet entitled *St. Thomas Mount-Chennai-South India: The Spot of the Heroic Martyrdom of St. Thomas the Apostle and the Cradle and Glory of the Indian Church*.[37] This detailed and thorough work covers a decent amount of information in only 28 short pages that act as both a history and tour guide, as well as providing an overview of St. Thomas Mount's liturgical offerings. This work is a more readily accessible alternative to D'Souza's more extensive historical narrative. Not to be left out, Little Mount eventually commissioned its own booklet, *Brief History of St. Thomas and Little Mount*. This booklet was written by a knowledgeable member of the parish and was also published in 2010.[38] However, these works by themselves should be considered only something of a necessary first step in initiating the larger strategy of promulgating St. Thomas's ancient legacy into the mainstream.

Working somewhat chronologically, the following section will serve to analyze these works and other such media derivatives, including magazine publications and CDs, which have come out of San Thome's revival. During the time of the Cathedral's renovation, we can also see how the legacy of St. Thomas's Indian mission and martyrdom have been employed in order to add further weight to this revival, and present St. Thomas as the founder of the Indian Christian faith that was ultimately solidified through his death and burial.

San Thome's 2004 renovation souvenir booklet

It is apparent that the restoration of San Thome Cathedral, which took place from June 2003 to December 2004, was the most significant event to initiate the recent St. Thomas revivals in Chennai. The Cathedral's success during this time would inspire and motivate St. Thomas Mount to launch its own restoration projects and revivalist endeavors later in 2007. Little Mount would also do its part, but to a far lesser extent, due to its limited space and resources.

Clearly, the successful completion of San Thome's renovation and the addition of a new underground tomb shrine was a cause for great celebration for the local Catholic community in and around Chennai. The blessings for the new tomb chapel, museum, and auditorium were all held as special public events. Another public function was held around this time, which acted as a release party of sorts for Anthonysamy's *A Saga of Faith*, as well as for other media releases about St. Thomas, such as a Tamil language book on the Apostle, devotional albums in both audio cassette and CD formats, and later a twenty- minute documentary on DVD detailing the Cathedral's restoration work. In order to memorialize all of these events, the Cathedral published a substantial souvenir booklet simply entitled *Souvenir San Thome Historic Event 2004*.[39] The bulk of its content is made up of advertisements from local businesses and organizations, as well as a great number of congratulatory letters and well-wishes from prominent members of society, such as local politicians and high ranking clergy. Also included is a small section of articles devoted to the history of St. Thomas and his connection to Chennai, or as the booklet says, "to provide material that will nourish your mind and heart."[40] This section includes articles by several noteworthy Church historians, namely Joseph Thekkedath, A. M. Mundadan, and S. J. Anthonysamy.

One significant inclusion into the souvenir booklet was a transcript of the homily given by the Apostolic Nuncio of India for San Thome's December 12, 2004 consecration ceremony, over which he presided. The Apostolic Nuncio discussed at some length the historical importance of the San Thome Cathedral and concluded:

This Cathedral has a very special significance for the whole Catholic world. After St. Peter's Basilica in Rome, built over the tomb of St. Peter, together with this of my diocese of origin, Santiago de Compostela, [these] are the only Basilicas built over the tomb of an Apostle. Santiago built over the tomb of St. James and this over [the tomb] of St. Thomas. The historicity and apostolic character of this place should be a matter of great pride and joy to all of us, and especially to you, the people of the Archdiocese of Madras-Mylapore.[41]

The office of Apostolic Nuncio is essentially the Vatican's ambassador to India, and thus, carries a lot of weight within the Catholic community. It is something of a happy coincidence that the Apostolic Nuncio at the time, Pedro López Quintana, was originally from the diocese that is the location for the tomb of St. James at Santiago de Compostela. Since 2004, San Thome has eagerly fostered this unique connection with two of Christendom's most visited and celebrated shrines, St. Peter's in Rome and St. James's in Spain, as a way to underscore its own neglected significance. In this way, San Thome can also make the claim of being a church of global importance on par with St. Peter's and St. James's, and thus validate St. Thomas's position, alongside Peter and James, as one of the earliest leaders and founders of the Christian faith.

Another important section of the souvenir booklet included a compilation of congratulatory-remarks, prose pieces, and poetry written and submitted by members of the local community. Many were in Tamil, but there were some written in English. One noteworthy entry was a poem written by Grace Victor, a member of San Thome's congregation. This poem is interesting because it strongly conveys the Church's greater revivalist message about St. Thomas's deep connection to India and the local Christian community. This poem is entitled "Blessed are the Santhomites!" and in it we find several references to St. Thomas's connection to the soil of India, as well as a general case being made for St. Thomas's intensely regional significance. For example, the first two stanzas in their entirety read:

> Oh! The soil of Santhome!
> We salute you and felicitate you.
> For you bear the foot prints,
> Of the great son Thome
> Who sailed two thousand miles,
> And more to reach you.
> Arms embracing the cross,
> Heart imprisoning mother Mary,
> Loads and loads of love for sharing,
> He reached you, to present you HOPE.
> Dear Santhomites!

What would our life have been,
But for this son of the soil,
We would not have known our CREATOR.
Would not have known our Saviour and his spirit,
And not the least, the maternal love of Mary.
This son of the soil,
Who knelt down beside Christ,
To run his fingers through his master's side,
But carried his love to us.[42]

The first stanza is addressed to the "soil of Santhome," which also seems to signify St. Thomas's tomb site, as well as the Indian land for which St. Thomas "sailed two thousand miles" to reach. This stanza is essentially proclaiming to the soil of San Thome how fortunate it was to have been visited by St. Thomas, and most importantly, it addresses St. Thomas's lasting impression on the soil of India left by his "foot prints."

The second stanza is then addressed to all the "Santhomites," in other words, the local community of Christians who are connected to San Thome through the legacy of St. Thomas and his tomb. In this stanza, St. Thomas's connection to the Indian soil becomes more overt as he is now referred to as the "son of the soil." As the son or child of the Indian soil, St. Thomas has essentially become Indian and indigenous. This poem also highlights St. Thomas's connection to St. Mary, which is a direct reference to the South Indian tradition that St. Thomas carried with him to India a number of relics pertaining to the Virgin, as well as the belief that he experienced a vision of her at Malayattoor hill in Kerala.[43] Undoubtedly, this mention of St. Mary is also meant to allude to her significant popularity in modern-day Tamil Nadu.

In the last half of the poem, not reproduced here, Grace Victor utilizes her own perspective in order to proclaim to her audience, the Santhomites, all the gifts they have received due to the legacy and reality of St. Thomas's Indian mission, which includes "life," "hope," and the "KEY stone of wisdom." In this way, it is not hard to see how St. Thomas is being elevated to a foundational figure, and is thus a "KEY stone" in more than just one way. This idea is taken further in the final stanza of the poem, which is written from the perspective of all Santhomites as they address and ask for intercessions from St. Thomas himself. The poem ends with the author asking St. Thomas to specifically help all Santhomites with issues of faith. The last line of the poem, "Our Lord and Our God," is a direct quote from the New Testament (John 20:28) taken from the moment when St. Thomas overcomes his doubt regarding the resurrection of Jesus and makes this faith proclamation.[44] In other words, it is through St. Thomas's doubt that all Santhomites find their faith. In this way, all Santhomites are unified in their Christian faith, the faith that was brought to them by St. Thomas, and as the "son of the soil," St. Thomas has been transformed into an indigenous saint and progenitor, epitaphs that are solidified through his mission and martyrdom in India. However, the poem does not explicitly make a case for St. Thomas's martyrdom as being tantamount to a local myth of origin. Instead, it sets the groundwork for an implicit argument by alluding to the Apostle's spilled blood on Indian soil, as well as highlighting the legacy of his tomb site at San Thome.

One final aspect of this poem is that it was purposefully included in San Thome's souvenir booklet. As a limited edition souvenir, this booklet was specifically aimed at the local community, and was probably put together in order to inform and educate the congregation. More significantly, however, it was more a matter of instilling pride than of mere information. As such, the tomb of St. Thomas at San Thome becomes important because it signifies the martyrdom of St. Thomas in India, the melding of St. Thomas's blood to the Indian soil. And with St. Thomas's martyrdom the faith of the Indian Christian community becomes validated, because it is through the Apostle's death that he has become the "son of the soil." Thus, St. Thomas is perceived as an indigenous, as well as the earliest, founder of the Christian faith in India, especially in the Chennai region of Tamil Nadu, where his blood-stained soil can be physically found.

"Song of India"

Because the 2004 souvenir booklet was a limited edition, San Thome needed other publications and mediums in order to sustain the messages found in the booklet. One solution to this issue was the commissioning of a brand new song about St. Thomas that could be played throughout the year at special church events. Fortunately, 2006 was an auspicious year for San Thome because it marked the 400th anniversary of the Mylapore Diocese (1606–2006). During this special year, Fr. Lawrence commissioned a collection of devotional Tamil Christian songs to be locally composed and released on a special CD.

The song in question was aptly titled "Song of India" (translated from Tamil) and was a part of this new CD, for which it was specifically written, in honor of and about St. Thomas. As a medium, it was clear that such a song had never been utilized in this way for the specific task of memorializing the legacy of St. Thomas in Chennai. During my many visits to San Thome, I was able to hear this song performed live on several occasions, most notably at the July 3rd festival, as well as during various other services that pertained to St. Thomas throughout the year. The song has evidently become a standard of San Thome's church choir repertoire. A portion of the translated lyrics are as follows:

> May my journey continue in your path.
> May my feet flourish in your grace.
> So that India would be saved, he shed his holy blood on the soil.

So that we are saved – today.
We need to be pure.

You [St. Thomas] did not believe until you touched Jesus' wounds.
After touching, you did not abandon him as long as you lived.
You traveled around the entire country in order to tell us about Jesus' love.
Standing firm as a witness, giving [your] life, you ascended and remain
as a pillar in this holy assembly.[45]

Once again, the person of St. Thomas is connected to the land of India, as both the saviour and "protector of this holy land," and the key element to this salvation is the fact that St. Thomas "shed his holy blood on the soil." This imagery is contextualized within St. Thomas's Indian mission where he "traveled around the entire country," and finds fulfilment in the Apostle's martyrdom where he gives up his life as a witness to his faith. As we see from the previous poem and in other examples to follow, St. Thomas's faith proclamation is also highlighted in this song in order to hark back to the famous "Doubting Thomas" incident (John 20: 24–29).

Clearly, the imagery of this song is meant to convey the progress of St. Thomas's journey of faith and how he would eventually bring this faith to India, and even after his death, both the Apostle's spirit and the faith he brought with him still "remain as a pillar in this holy assembly," by which is obviously meant San Thome Cathedral. In other words, the significance of St. Thomas's martyrdom has forever transfixed his spilled blood onto the soil of San Thome, and by extension, all of India. Thus, when the author proclaims, "We need to be pure," this, in the context of the second stanza, strongly implies that St. Thomas's blood purified or sanctified India as a whole. This is an interesting idea as this allusion is typical of many Hindu deities, who shed their blood in order to transform land into holy sites.[46] This assertion could be construed as a challenge to the religious validity of Hinduism, or possibly a jab at the political ideologies of the Hindu right. Therefore, St. Thomas's legacy transfixes the Christian religion onto the soil of India through his martyr's blood, which purifies the land and its people, as well as solidifying the Apostle's deep connection to India as the founder of its Christian faith. As a marketing medium, this memorable and catchy song is a pragmatic idea and tool. Songs like this are useful because they can be played whenever the occasion offers an opportunity, thus consistently reminding San Thome's Tamil Catholic parishioners about the importance of St. Thomas's life and death to India and to their local Christian heritage.

S. J. Anthonysamy's "A Saga of Faith"

Since the 2004 souvenir booklet discussed earlier was intended as a limited release item, its short history section can be viewed as a general primer for the mass release of Anthonysamy's *A Saga of Faith*, which is also advertised in this booklet, strategically placed as the last page of the history section.[47] *A Saga of Faith* was written, initially in English, for a general audience and thus possesses an accessibility that can be measured by its straight-forward narrative and simply written prose, especially when compared to more scholarly and detailed histories about St. Thomas.[48] Additionally, none of these other histories were available to the local community. *A Saga of Faith* provides another layer of accessibility by virtue of being a local publication, and as Anthonysamy even states about his book, "It is mostly a popular presentation and does not claim to have a scientific character about it."[49] In my opinion, compared to many of the other books on St. Thomas, *A Saga of Faith* is easily the most accessible historical reconstruction of St. Thomas's mission to India.

Anthonysamy is explicit in both the book's purpose and audience, and we can assume that this accessibility was ultimately intentional. As Anthonysamy explains, "And it was his [Fr. Lawrence's] proposal to bring out a write-up on St. Thomas and his mission in India on this occasion [San Thome's re-christening] ... in order to help numerous pilgrims and visitors to have a better knowledge of the Apostle, and thus help to enhance their Christian faith."[50] Clearly, the main purpose of this book was to be used as a tool for evangelization and spiritual education for the Cathedral's many visitors, which included non-pilgrims. Anthonysamy states, "May the saga of St. Thomas the Apostle have its impact on all the readers of this book and increase their faith in our Master and Lord, Jesus Christ."[51] Again, in the preface to the book's second edition, Anthonysamy remarks, "It is a happy sign that the Indian readers are catching up with the life of their Apostle .... May all such literature only help in the building up of a deep Christian faith in our land."[52] In the first quotation, Anthonysamy recognizes "all" his potential readers, and in the latter, he is explicitly making allusions to the intended goal for the Catholic evangelization of India.

Within the book's primary material, Anthonysamy examines all the important historical sources that still survive to this day, such as *The Bible, The Acts of Thomas,* South Indian oral tradition, the Church Fathers, and colonial era sources, with the final section devoted to the ecclesiastical history of the three St. Thomas sites, from the earliest Portuguese administrators to the present context of an all-Indian indigenous Catholic hierarchy.[53] Anthonysamy most likely utilized Herman D'Souza's *In the Steps of St. Thomas* as a point of reference for his own historical analysis. Like Anthonysamy, but fifty years earlier, D'Souza wrote his book with accessibility in mind, since a guide book of this nature did not seem to exist before his time.[54] Most importantly, Anthonysamy devotes an entire section of his book, as well as parts of the appendices, to local traditions and legends concerning St. Thomas's time in ancient Mylapore, especially those stories relevant to the three sacred sites of Chennai.[55]

A Saga of Faith can be seen as San Thome's flagship publication on the historicity of St. Thomas, instead of the venerable *In the Steps of St. Thomas*; there are two reasons for this. First is the significance of its author, Fr. Anthonysamy, who is a local priest of the Archdiocese of Madras-Mylapore and an accomplished Biblical scholar with a solid reputation as a columnist and professor within Chennai's Catholic community.[56] Second, and more significantly, *A Saga of Faith* offers an up-to-date historical survey of Chennai's three St. Thomas sites, including material on Fr. Lawrence's 2004 renovation of San Thome and the remodeling of St. Thomas's tomb as the newest chapter in San Thome's nearly two-thousand-year-old history, or as Anthonysamy puts it, "a new milestone in the great Saga of Faith."[57]

As such, *A Saga of Faith* also serves to emphasize the significance of St. Thomas's tomb being located in Tamil Nadu, as well as to highlight San Thome's place as a church of global importance. At one point, Anthonysamy writes, "St. Thomas, one of the twelve apostles of Jesus Christ certainly evokes sentiments of pride among us Indians, particularly those of us from Kerala and Tamilnadu," and again, "the sense of elation that had been part of the life of Catholics in the old Diocese of Mylapore and presently the Archdiocese of Madras-Mylapore over the possession of the tomb of the Apostle does not fail to provide us with a dimension of credibility about Thomas here in India."[58] In both the preface and final chapter of the book, Anthonysamy makes mention of San Thome's auspicious connection to the famous St. Peter's Basilica. He declares, "The most important of the sites associated with the Apostle Thomas in India, nay in the whole world is no doubt his tomb. In fact there are only two churches built directly over the tombs of the apostles."[59] Interestingly, he mentions St. Peter's, but overlooks Santiago de Compostela. Regardless, the point remains that San Thome is equal in stature to St. Peter's due to its deep apostolic legacy.

Another key theme of Anthonysamy's book is the allusion to Indian Christian indigeneity that is found throughout this book. However, this theme is better explored in the following subsection, which will look at the individual chapters of *A Saga of Faith* that were reprinted in San Thome's quarterly magazine. On a final note, by the time I made my first trip to Chennai in early 2009, *A Saga of Faith* was out of print, and as such, could no longer be purchased at the Cathedral gift store. I eventually brought this fact to Fr. Lawrence's attention, and he seemed very surprised by this information. Fr. Lawrence's response to this news seemed to indicate that *A Saga of Faith* sold out sometime after Fr. Lawrence was transferred out of San Thome in 2007 and that, for whatever reason, his successor had held off ordering a new edition. Before this even happened, Fr. Lawrence had realized that more cost effective and long-term publications were needed in order to maintain interest in the St. Thomas shrines, as well as to make the dissemination and preservation of the St. Thomas story more sustainable in the years to come.

"Voice of St. Thomas" magazine: articles of faith

During the anniversary year of 2006, Fr. Lawrence established *Voice of St. Thomas* (*VoST*), a quarterly magazine devoted to the person of St. Thomas and to the promotion of Catholic spirituality in Chennai. As Fr. Lawrence stated:

> It *[VoST]* is exclusive of St. Thomas. It is not like other magazines, because other magazines, they deal with the politics, they speak about Vatican, they speak about the Church, and so many things up there. But here, normally, we don't lead into all those kind of things. It is more concentrated on San Thome church, and the life of St. Thomas and also all things connected with St. Thomas, and also Our Lady of Mylapore. So it is … it is more a … a spiritual kind of magazine.[60]

During our interview, Fr. Lawrence also explained to me the impetus for developing such a magazine. He reiterated the point that local devotion to St. Thomas was lacking, and that he also wanted to foster San Thome's international reputation, since the Cathedral received many foreign visitors. Simply, he wanted to generate more publicity at home and abroad, and the publication of a magazine would offer locals and foreign visitors "something solid," or a "manageable standard" that was more than just a "newsletter," which they could take home with them, and, with the benefit of a subscription, keep up to date on church news and events at San Thome.[61]

The greater hope, as conveyed to me by the then current parish priest of San Thome, who was also the *VoST* editor at the time, is that people will take the magazine or other pamphlets and pass them around. Many copies of *VoST* are handed out for free, especially to locals, in order to generate and maintain interest within Chennai and elsewhere.[62] As such, *VoST* serves as a quarterly reminder of the what, where, and why of St. Thomas's significance to Indian Christianity and the events surrounding his person that regularly take place at San Thome and his other shrines. For instance, every issue has listed regular mass timings and monthly days for specialized devotional masses held for St. Thomas and Our Lady of Mylapore, as well as a calendar of special events for the following four month period. A couple of issues even included a special St. Thomas quiz, which was intended to test the reader's knowledge about the Saint's history.[63] There is also a testimonials section included in almost every issue, where pilgrims and members of the local community testify to having their petitions answered thanks to the power of St. Thomas's tomb. However, it is the history of St. Thomas that is the most substantive information presented in this magazine. There are articles discussing many of the local legends surrounding St. Thomas in Mylapore, as well as articles that spotlight many of the other famous shrines associated with the Apostle outside of Chennai, such as those found in Kerala. This magazine has proven to be a great source of data for this project because its articles serve as a strong indicator of those specific facets of St. Thomas devotion that the administrators at San Thome wish to promulgate and foster among the local Catholic community.

St. Thomas Mount also published its own parish magazine, which began distribution in July of 2010.[64] The name of the Hill Shrine's magazine, *The Voice from the Hill* (*TVH*), closely mirrors San Thome's *Voice of St. Thomas*. The most significant differences between these two publications are that *TVH* is published monthly, rather than quarterly, and is published in both English and Tamil versions. San Thome's *VoST* was, from its inception, an English language publication. Recently, however, the Cathedral has started printing a companion Tamil language magazine.

With regard to content, San Thome's *VoST* is much more concerned with the issue of St. Thomas's historicity than *TVH* due to its position as the seat of the Archdiocese of Madras-Mylapore. For instance, the inaugural issue of *VoST* was a double-length issue that functioned as an introduction, once again, to the history and legacy of St. Thomas in India and his three shrines in Chennai. Its content greatly mirrored everything discussed in both the souvenir book and *A Saga of Faith*.[65] Beginning with the second issue, *VoST* started serializing excerpts from *A Saga of Faith* in order to better promote the book, as well as to emphasize St. Thomas's historical importance to its readers.[66] Due to the change in format, the editorial board of *VoST* is able to go back into the text and emphasize key passages or sections that best highlight and interpret St. Thomas's character for a mainstream Christian audience. For instance, issues five and six discuss St. Thomas's "valiant" character.[67] Anthonysamy paints a portrait of St. Thomas that depicts the Saint as a "valiant" Apostle who would bravely die alongside Jesus. Anthonysamy even uses the famous "Doubting Thomas" story to demonstrate this point. Why then would a "valiant" man doubt the resurrection of the Lord? As Anthonysamy responds, "here too he [St. Thomas] was honestly representing the prevalent sentiments of his time; but, what is again more important is that it is Thomas who makes a total reversal of the sentiment of doubt with his excellent attitude of faith and total surrender to Jesus. Here again, the Apostle has shown his valiant personality."[68]

In another instance, where St. Thomas's martyrdom is being discussed, a particular passage from the excerpt is typeset and re-quoted for emphasis on the top left corner of the article. Specifically, "The soil which was stained with the blood of the saint was reverently placed in a pot and was also buried along with the body. That seems to have been a great mark of respect to the blood shed by the saint."[69] This passage is also highlighted in bold in the main body of the article. This passage is important to note because it emphasizes the specific image of the martyred Apostle's blood staining the soil, which is a reoccurring motif prevalent in many of San Thome's publications and physical representations of the St. Thomas story.

To recall a line from the St. Thomas song mentioned above, "So that India would be saved, he shed his holy blood on the soil."[70] Once again, San Thome has utilized its own publication material in order to validate its own antiquity and connect St. Thomas's blood with the Indian soil, thus presenting St. Thomas's martyrdom as the foundation for Indian Christianity.

Homilies and themes from the Feast of St. Thomas presented by "VoST"

The greatest opportunity for San Thome and the other St. Thomas sites to emphasize the cultural and spiritual importance of St. Thomas's Indian legacy is during the celebration of the Feast of St. Thomas, which is held on July 3rd of every year. At San Thome specifically, the Feast of St. Thomas is celebrated over a ten-day festival, usually starting in late June and finishing sometime after July 3rd. The highlights of the St. Thomas festival are the two main car processions that are held on separate days. The first is dedicated to St Thomas and involves a statue of the Saint carried in a large golden teak chariot, which is driven from one end of San Thome High Road to the cathedral courtyard. The second car procession is dedicated to the Holy Eucharist, but this time the chariot carries a participant bishop who, in turn, carries a golden monstrance that contains the exposed transubstantiated host.[71] However, the most prolific event during these festivals is the Catholic mass, which is held each day and led by a special visiting priest or bishop who has tailored their sermon to match the over-arching particular theme of that year's festival.

St. Thomas Mount also celebrates the Feast of St. Thomas in grand style, although it is typically only a three day affair. Since Little Mount is a part of the Madras-Mylapore Archdiocese, its community participates alongside other parishes at San Thome's festival. The time I spent in Chennai allowed me to observe San Thome's July 3rd festival of 2009. A consistent theme that runs through several of these festivals is reconciling the notion that the Indian Christian faith was brought by the Apostle who is often associated with the negative moniker "Doubting Thomas." However, this issue is easily overcome by presenting St. Thomas the doubter as a living symbol for the rejuvenation of faith. It is often pointed out by the local clergy that St. Thomas's response, or spirit-cry, upon seeing the resurrected Jesus for the very first time was to fall on his knees and proclaim, "My Lord and My God!" (John 20:28). As one bishop's homily put it, "the shortest and deepest profession of faith in the New Testament was Thomas' – My Lord and My God."[72] Thus, St. Thomas's doubt is quickly transformed into a permanent expression of faith and belief. As another homily put it, due to the wisdom of Thomas's proclamation of faith, "The total surrender of St. Thomas has infused faith in us."[73] With this in mind, another homily from the same year discussed, "The Paradox: Doubt in order to believe."[74] As we can see, what could easily be a criticism of St. Thomas's character is instead interpreted in a positive light that can be applied to everyone.

This interpretation is taken even further by the local clergy, who ultimately turn it into a communal point of pride. The article discussing the 2010 festival gives a very telling introduction to that year's celebrations. It begins:

> "Doubting Thomas," is a very commonly used phrase in the English language to a person who refuses to believe something without proof and it is unfortunate that our patron saint St. Thomas, the Apostle is remembered well for his doubting, but he was also capable of devotion and courage. It is his devotion to our Lord and his courage that brought him beyond the shores to the tip of the world, India to literally carry out Jesus' great commission given to the apostles …. The people of the National Shrine of St. Thomas are blessed and privileged to celebrate the feast of this great man who dared to go to the ends of the world to preach the good news …. We are privileged as we have received the '*Faith*' [emphasis in original] directly from one of Christ's beloved apostles.[75]

While the characteristic of St. Thomas's doubt is often highlighted by the clergy, these festivals emphasize other important characteristics of the Saint that can be gleaned from the traditions surrounding him. The above quotation also refers to St. Thomas's "devotion" and "courage," traits he must have possessed if he truly made the voyage to India all that time ago. According to the article, even the Archbishop himself "stressed how St. Thomas's coming to India had resulted in so much good for the country. Our faith had actually bloomed on the blood of St. Thomas, so we have to cherish and foster it and consider ourselves blessed and fortunate that one of the apostles of Christ had actually travelled all the way to India to spread the good news."[76] Obviously, the Feast of St. Thomas is also an excellent time to reflect on his martyrdom, specifically the image of blood from which Christianity "bloomed," and what his sacrifice can represent to a religious minority who are consistently threatened by religiously motivated violence.

In addition to St. Thomas's doubt and spirit-cry there is also Jesus' famous response to St. Thomas's supposed lack of faith, "Blessed are those who have not seen and yet believe" (John 20:29). This Bible quotation is also known as the ninth beatitude and was the primary message of San Thome's 2006 St. Thomas day festival. This particular festival also celebrated the four-hundred year anniversary of the Diocese of Mylapore, which was later amalgamated into the current Archdiocese of Madras-Mylapore. The *VoST* article that covered this event makes it clear that St. Thomas's doubt ultimately brought about a "faith awakening" in the form of Jesus' ninth beatitude. The article explains, "This faith awakening was the purpose of the fervent celebration of the Seven Sacraments of Catholic life, for each novena day. Thus, every stage of life [during the festival days] was renewed, from Baptism to the Sacrament of Healing."[77] Once again, St. Thomas's role as a rejuvenator of faith is expressed in light of his doubt over Jesus' resurrection.

It is the Pope's prerogative to decree that any year-long period of time be given a special designation on behalf of some significant Catholic issue. For instance, 2009 was the Year of Priests, and as such, Catholic parishes all over the world would have utilized this decree as a point of continual discussion in order to emphasize the significance of this chosen topic to the Catholic community at large. It was no different at San Thome, where the topic of priestly life came to dominate that year's festivities. Of course, this also provided the opportunity to connect the life and message of St. Thomas with the role of Catholic priests today. While St. Thomas was far less discussed than those issues relating to the priesthood, it was clear that St. Thomas represented the foundation for that year's theme. As one of the Twelve Apostles, St. Thomas was one of the first Christian priests and, undoubtedly, a great one. The *VoST* article states, "It was indeed fitting and right as St. Thomas the Apostle was one of the Twelve Priests ordained by Jesus Christ, that the saint's Feast day and the preceding nine Novena days should highlight themes for Year of Priests."[78] However, not every decreed year poses a topic that can easily be tied to the Apostle, such as the 2010 festival, which fell on the Year of the Youth, and the 2008 festival, which fell on the Year of St. Paul.

In the 2008 festival, while St. Paul was mentioned to some extent, the real focus of the festival was indeed St. Thomas, perhaps more so than usual. Each of the festival's nine novena days was dedicated to one aspect of St. Thomas. More specifically, each aspect represented a certain way in which the history and message of the Apostle could be interpreted and applied in the present day. As such, each day's celebrant prepared his homily with respect to that day's St. Thomas theme. For instance, "St. Thomas, the fount of wisdom" highlighted St. Thomas's wisdom in declaring Jesus Lord and God, and how St. Thomas's faith can give everybody faith. "St. Thomas, Protector in God's Presence" established the Apostle's connection to the Blessed Sacrament, and that just as the Eucharist represents Jesus' sacrifice, so should Christians be willing to sacrifice themselves as St. Thomas did in India.[79]

Many of the other epitaphs used to describe St. Thomas during the 2008 festival are more or less self-explanatory. These include, "St. Thomas Friend of the Poor," "St. Thomas Apostle of Truth," St. Thomas Servant of People," and "St. Thomas Source of Courage." The theme used for the day of the car procession was "St. Thomas – the Forerunner of Our Faith," in which the celebrant described St. Thomas and St. Paul as the "apostles of the Good News, especially to the Gentiles," since both saints "travelled extensively."[80] Once again, the topic returned to St. Thomas's spirit-cry of "My Lord and My God," and how this confession of faith represented the "deep courageous faith of St. Thomas" that all Christians should strive towards.[81]

The final novena day was celebrated by none other than Fr. Lawrence, the Cathedral's previous parish priest who, by this time, was very well known for his renovation efforts at San Thome and other local churches. His homily focused on the day's theme, "St. Thomas: Patron of Our Parish." As the article states:

> St. Thomas lived as he professed and his followers should have the same faith commitment in life. This faith commitment should be expressed through action. St. Thomas led his companions when he said, "come we will go and die with Him." The people of the parish should be committed and get involved in serving the parish. Fr. Lawrence gave his personal testimony of his faith in the Patron Saint as the former Parish priest of the Cathedral and undertook boldly the task of renovating and building a special shrine to St. Thomas. It was not an easy task on many counts, particularly the criticism and opposition that he had to face, but everything was accomplished as planned because of faith and commitment.[82]

It seems very fitting that Fr. Lawrence would point to the recent renovation of San Thome as evidence for the power of St. Thomas's faith, as well as for the power of having faith in St. Thomas, which, as he pointed out, is successfully at work in the world today. As such, Fr. Lawrence touts his recent accomplishments in order to validate the sacrality of the tomb site as a way to motivate San Thome's parishioners into vigilantly preserving St. Thomas's historical legacy in India.

As we can see, the most effective method for disseminating the message of St. Thomas is through actively promoting the Saint at mass and other public events. Even though the Feast of St. Thomas is only held once a year, both San Thome and St. Thomas Mount have officially designated every third day of each month a special day of devotion to St. Thomas as a way to consistently remind the people about his significance and preserve his traditions.

In 2011 San Thome had five web TV cameras installed in the Cathedral's main hall, tomb chapel, and outdoor stage. With the use of this mass media technology, masses and other church events from the Cathedral can be viewed by anyone in the world via live webcast, and older programmes can be viewed on demand via high-speed streaming.[83] San Thome, for some time now, has maintained a parish website, and within the last five years or so it has progressively become more sophisticated in its layout and navigation, thus demonstrating the Cathedral's commitment to reaching larger audiences worldwide, as well as its acknowledgment of the usefulness of more technologically advanced marketing tools.[84] So, if the people cannot go to mass, the mass can now go to the people.

San Thome's tourist pamphlets: local legends in the present day

During my time in Chennai, I acquired as much material published by San Thome as I could find. Unsurprisingly, I found very little that had been published from before the 2004 renovation. Prior to my visit to Chennai, I had been able to acquire San Thome's first museum guide booklet from 1985, which was the year San Thome first established an official museum for its small collection of artefacts. I mention this old museum booklet because it appears that, prior to 2004, San Thome had very little self-published material.[85] In 2004, a new museum was constructed as part of the overall renovation of San Thome, initiating the publication of a range of new visitor guides.[86] These post-2004 publications consisted of two individual pamphlets and a single booklet, all of which were reasonably well-produced.[87]

However, by 2009, all of the above materials appeared to be leftovers from a number of years ago, and thus, were somewhat out-dated, but still of interest for my purposes. It was obvious that the Cathedral was pooling its current resources in order to maintain a single inexpensive pamphlet that could offer a summarized version of the Cathedral's key history and current services. This is evident in the fact that the Cathedral designed its most recent English language pamphlet as a template for all of the multi-language versions that were to follow. As of my second trip to Chennai in 2010, this particular pamphlet had been translated and released in English, Hindi, Tamil, Malayalam, Italian, German, French, and Telugu – the major language demographics of the Cathedral's visitors.[88]

The pamphlet's information and design is credited to the Disciples of St. Thomas, as well as to a man by the name of Simon Chumkat, who, according to Fr. Lawrence was an influential member of San Thome's congregation.[89] This pamphlet uses unequivocal language in stating the historical facts and traditions about St. Thomas. Its cover states, "St. Thomas, one of the twelve apostles of Jesus Christ, came to India in A.D. 52, died as a martyr in A.D. 72 and was buried at Mylapore, San Thome, Chennai, India. The Basilica is built over the Tomb of St. Thomas."[90] As with the rest of the brochure, there is no mention of any controversy or doubt about the legacy of St. Thomas; it is simply presented as a matter of fact and tradition.

This pamphlet is folded into six sections, including the cover and back, with the inner four sections containing the most information. The pamphlet's content includes various snippets of the Cathedral's history, but is primarily focused on several legends concerning the Apostle's time in Mylapore. If we read only these sections, we see an intriguing narrative emerge that creates a roadmap linking St. Thomas's past deeds in Mylapore with the fruition of his labors in modern-day Chennai. Once again, the pamphlet's message is meant to signify St. Thomas's progenitorship of the Christian faith in Tamil Nadu by emphasizing the antiquity and significance of his tomb site, as well as his intimate relationship with the local region.

Reading the pamphlet's main section from right to left, the first story details how St. Thomas managed to miraculously secure a giant log for the construction of Mylapore's very first Christian church. According to legend, a huge log washed up on the shore and ended up blocking the mouth of an important river, causing problems for the local populace. The king of the region and his men were unable to remove it themselves, so St. Thomas stepped in to help. The pamphlet states, "St. Thomas came, spent a few minutes in silent prayer, touched the log with the Girdle of [the] Virgin Mary and asked the men to pull it. They pulled it without any difficulty. Pleased by this the king offered the land where the log was first sighted, for the construction of a church. Thus the first church of Mylapore took shape."[91] Much like the paragraph from the cover of the pamphlet, this section is also presented in a matter-of-fact manner. As we can see, this particular tradition shows how St. Thomas utilized his holy powers in order to gain the favor of the king and ultimately construct the first Christian church in Mylapore, which would later become the Apostle's tomb and much later the current site of the San Thome Cathedral.

The next flap focuses on the Pole of St. Thomas and its supposed role in protecting the Cathedral and its grounds from the tsunami that struck Chennai on December 26th, 2004. Fortunately, the Cathedral survived the tsunami with little to no physical damage, even though several adjacent areas were flooded and destroyed.[92] Many of the locals considered this a miracle brought about not only by the fact that the Cathedral is the site of St. Thomas's tomb, but also by reference to the legend of the St. Thomas pole. As the pamphlet explains, "Legend has it that St. Thomas erected this pole as a mark to prevent the sea from encroaching the land, thus saving the life of the people living near the shore. Faithful believe that it may be the same pole that stands behind the basilica. St. Thomas made this pole from the legendary log that was washed ashore which was gifted by the king for building the church."[93] Anyone visiting San Thome today can find this "miraculous" wooden pole only a few feet away from the rear of the cathedral grounds where it is supported by a block of concrete (Figure 2.1).

From a marketing perspective, this tsunami miracle provided the Cathedral a prime opportunity to showcase its spiritual legacy literally days after the completion of its renovation. Apart from the pole's significance as a relic of St. Thomas, the miraculous nature of this event also provided San Thome with a considerable amount of positive media attention, which was reported by many news outlets such as *The Hindu* and *The New Indian Express* as a welcome piece of good news to help counterbalance the tsunami's devastating toll.[94] Interestingly, there is no substantial data on the Pole of St. Thomas prior to the 2004 tsunami, which implies that it was an

Figure 2.1 The Pole of St. Thomas, located to the right of and behind the Cathedral museum.

Photo: T. C. Nagy.

obscure and almost forgotten tradition, or more cynically, that it was constructed after the fact in order to justify and explain San Thome's recent good fortune. As the brochure relates, the Pole of St. Thomas was carved from the same giant log that was used for the construction of the original church and tomb site, thus continuing the narrative started by the first pamphlet flap. By linking the modern-day tsunami miracle to two separate legends concerning the Apostle and the origin of the first Christian church in Mylapore, the Church is establishing St. Thomas's regional legacy and continued presence in contemporary Chennai. In other words, the miracles of the present are due to the miracles of the past, a belief that can be maintained through the continued preservation of the current cathedral and tomb site, and now the almost forgotten Pole of St. Thomas as well.

In the third page of the pamphlet the narrative is maintained by introduc-
ing a back-story to the initial legend of the miraculous log. Recall that
St. Thomas used the Girdle of St. Mary in order to get the giant log out of
the river's mouth. As such, this third section focuses specifically on the
legend of St. Mary's Girdle, which has its origins in ancient Syrian and other
Western oral and written traditions. As the pamphlet states, "According to
[the] tradition of Edessa (now in Syria), [the] Blessed Virgin Mary dropped
her girdle to St. Thomas at the time of her assumption to heaven and
St. Thomas always wore the same tied around his waist. While transferring
the Apostle's relics to Edessa, the merchant who was doing so, also carried
a portion of the Girdle of [the] Virgin Mary which was buried along with
[the] saint's body."[95] As the first story established, St. Thomas had the
Girdle of St. Mary in his possession during his time in Mylapore, and was
ultimately buried with it. Thus, in accordance with Syrian tradition,
St. Thomas's relics were removed from India and transported to Edessa at
some point in time, as was a part of the Girdle. Along with continuing the
over-arching narrative, this obscure Western legend also denotes
St. Thomas's close relationship with St. Mary, a relationship that is also
maintained in Indian Christian tradition.

As the fourth and final informational flap of the tourist pamphlet implies,
St. Thomas's tale does not end with his death and burial, but is continued
through the preservation of his relics and tomb site at San Thome and elsewhere. This page is divided into three headings, with only the first two
being of relevance to the overarching narrative. The second heading reads
"Relics of St. Thomas," and states, "St. Thomas day is celebrated on [the]
3rd of July in memory of the martyrdom. Blood soaked earth and the lance
that killed were brought to Mylapore and buried along with his body."[96]
We see again the direct connection being made between St. Thomas's
martyrdom and the blood-soaked earth of India.

Another facet to this discourse is the fact that San Thome does not have
in its possession any significant portion of the Apostle's skeletal remains,
which is why the Cathedral tends to focus on St. Thomas's blood and the
red soil that is found in his tomb site. The flap's first heading, which is
entitled "Tomb of St. Thomas," is not so much about San Thome's underground tomb chapel or its history, but is an explanation as to why the
Cathedral no longer has in its possession any of St. Thomas's skeletal
remains. It begins, "The tomb was opened the first time to take some earth
to cure the son of ruling king Mahadevan," who was the same king that
allowed St. Thomas to use the giant log towards building Mylapore's first
Christian church.[97] The pamphlet goes on to explain, "Between A.D. 222
and A.D. 235 a greater portion of St. Thomas' remains was removed to
Edessa in Asia Minor. Later this was moved to Chios in [the] [M]editerra-
nian and finally it was rested in Ortona, a small town on the [A]driatic
coast of Italy in the province of Abruzzo."[98] Once again, Indian Christian
traditions about St. Thomas are linked with Western ones in order to

establish a narrative continuity between them, and by referencing the ancient Mylapore king one last time, the significance of St. Thomas's tomb and relics is connected to the three previous legends, thus completing the pamphlet's strategically structured narrative about the Apostle's physical and spiritual ties to the region.

The bulk of the material that is presented in this pamphlet is mythohistorical in character. While historical information is scattered throughout, it is noticeably less than that found in the Cathedral's other recent publications. Obviously, these brochures are mainly aimed at local, national, and international pilgrims, and possibly tourists, who are religiously minded. As such, this particular presentation is not so much concerned with providing historical data or employing historiography, but is instead attempting to forge a direct spiritual link and narrative between St. Thomas's Western Christian tradition and his Indian Christian legacy. Once this link is established, it provides a validation of sorts for both San Thome's spiritual power and its legitimacy as the tomb site of one of the Twelve Apostles of Christ. When coupled with the supposedly miraculous present-day event regarding the tsunami and St. Thomas's pole, the Church is able to confer tangibility to their claims. For San Thome, the best-case scenario is that it is now more difficult for Christians the world over to ever doubt that a holy Apostle of Christ was originally buried upon the shores of San Thome beach.

Assessment of initial success

Fr. Lawrence, in our first interview, commented to me on the sad state of the three St. Thomas shrines prior to 2004. He briefly discussed St. Thomas's low profile in Tamil Nadu, but quickly added, "And slowly, generally, it started picking up, and out of this restoration [San Thome in 2004], I think somewhere that the news went all around. Because so many magazines were publishing at that time, and so many newspapers were writing daily, and now you can see lot of [an] international crowd coming, tourism, especially during this tourist season."[99] Of all our talks and interviews, this last statement is probably the closest assessment Fr. Lawrence ever gave concerning the outcome of his revivalist project. Fr. Lawrence was hesitant to call any aspect of San Thome's revival an unqualified success. While he would admit that there had been an improvement (even five years on from the renovation, when our interview was conducted) he would not speculate on the growth and longevity of San Thome's shrinal reputation going forward. For one thing, Fr. Lawrence was dubious about the effectiveness of print media. Speaking with regard to the *VoST* magazine Fr. Lawrence explains:

> I don't say it was very successful because initially we did not concentrate on the subscriptions, so initially we were just trying to distribute the copies ... one big problem with our people, what I have seen, they

don't have the habit of reading ... so, for example, if you take the *New Leader*, that is supposed to be a national Catholic magazine. It is going out for the past so many years, but then the subscriptions are very few, a few thousands. And we have one in Tamil Nadu ... that is a Tamil magazine. So, hardly they are able to sell only ten thousand copies all over Tamil Nadu, for including all the institutions, churches, everything. So, that shows how people are not so much interested in reading all these things. And that's same thing with this magazine, also.[100]

If Fr. Lawrence's generalization about Tamils not being in the "habit of reading" is remotely true, then the bulk of San Thome's printed media, including books, is also limited to a more narrow audience. Recall that Anthonysamy's *A Saga of Faith* was out of print by the time I visited Chennai in 2009, and the fact that a second edition was not soon forthcoming would imply that there was no immediate demand for it.

When I interviewed San Thome's current parish priest and *VoST* editor, I asked him if he thought *VoST* was doing well. He replied, "Yes, because when I came here, around a hundred copies were being sold, but now it is more than seven-hundred, seven-hundred copies are going out all over the country."[101] From this interview, as well as from looking at current issues of *VoST*, there is clearly more initiative on getting subscriptions, which is something Fr. Lawrence admitted to having lacked during his time as editor. On the other hand, 700 issues is hardly a wide distribution amount, even relatively speaking, which is probably why greater emphasis is placed on the St. Thomas festival and devotional days, where the priest or bishop can readily proclaim the message of St. Thomas and the significance of his local shrines to anybody who attends mass or any of the special programs. In other words, festivals and other special services reach a far larger local audience than published reading material, in either the English or Tamil language.

Chapter summary

As this chapter has demonstrated, San Thome's primary message regarding the life and times of St. Thomas revolves round the issue of Indian Christian indigeneity and Tamil Catholic identity. San Thome's many publications on the history of St. Thomas repeatedly emphasize several key features of St. Thomas's legacy: (1) he was one of the Twelve Apostles of Jesus; (2) even though he doubted it at first, he was a witness to the resurrection of the Lord; (3) he missionized South India; (4) he had a close spiritual relationship with Mother Mary; (5) he was martyred and buried in Mylapore; (6) he is the religious and spiritual progenitor of Christianity in India past and present. Together, these six features illustrate a St. Thomas who represents India's ancient and direct connection to first-century Christianity and its founder. They also highlight the Apostle's even deeper connection to the soil of India, especially in modern-day Chennai where the sites of his death and burial are kept alive by the Tamil Catholic communities who watch over them. San Thome's message is clear, that the St. Thomas of Keralite and European tradition is the same St. Thomas who was killed and buried in the land of the Tamils. Thus, St. Thomas is not only the cornerstone of Keralite Christian identity, but also a myth of origin that solidifies Tamil Catholic identity and Indian Christian indigeneity in general. The obvious contradictory fact is that St. Thomas was not born in India or ethnically Indian; however, through his missionization, martyrdom, and burial in India, along with the communal memorialization of his deeds, St. Thomas is transformed into an authentic Indian saint. This once again reaffirms Robert Frykenberg's point that the figure of St. Thomas is pivotal to the study of Indian Christianity, and as I have added, for better recognizing Indian Christianity's unique post-post-colonial positionality within modern-day India's eclectic socio-religious landscape.

Clearly, a unique Tamil Catholic identity is being constructed here that is closely linked to the legacy of St. Thomas, and much like many post-colonial/ post-post-colonial identities, its foundation is a past that is "being continually fashioned by the events, perceptions and interests of the present."[102] In other words, it is the socio-religious and political context of the present day that is instigating the Church administrators in Chennai to fashion a past that historically validates the Tamil Catholic association with the martyred St. Thomas. As the following chapter will discuss, there are many reasons, both social and political, that keep the Church's rhetoric on indigeneity somewhat stifled, if not cautionary. As we will see, the discourse of indigeneity and St. Thomas's blood also speaks directly to a larger issue currently facing the Indian Christian community today, the legitimacy of their religious identity in the face of India's current political climate and Hindu right ideology. Thus, the Church in Chennai has been forced to develop revivalist strategies that take into consideration the rhetoric of Hindu nationalism, in order to both defend itself and to challenge such discourses intellectually and politically.

Notes

1 Interview with Mr. Zander, Chennai, August 5, 2009.
2 Ibid.
3 Interview with Fr. Lawrence Raj, Chennai, June 15, 2009.
4 S. J. Anthonysamy, *A Saga of Faith: St. Thomas the Apostle of India* (Chennai: National Shrine of St. Thomas Basilica, 2009), 145.
5 A. M. Mundadan, *History of Christianity in India Volume I: From the Beginning up to the Middle of the Sixteenth Century* (Bangalore: Theological Publications in India, 1984), 425–426.

6 Susan Bayly, *Saints, Goddesses and Kings: Muslims and Christians in South Indian Society, 1700–1900* (Cambridge: Cambridge University Press, 1989), 261–262.

7 A. M. Mundadan, *Indian Christians: Search for Identity and Struggle for Autonomy* (Bangalore: Dharmaram Publications Dharmaram College, 2003), 168.

8 "Archdiocese of Madras-Mylapore: History," http://www.archdioceseof madrasmylapore.org/about_us.php (accessed October 10, 2008).

9 Sebastian C. H. Kim, *In Search of Identity: Debates on Religious Conversion in India* (New Delhi: Oxford University Press, 2005), 38–40.

10 Stephen Neill, *A History of Christianity in India: The Beginnings to AD 1707* (Cambridge: Cambridge University Press, 1984), 42. See also: Jacob Kollaparambil, *The Babylonian Origin of the Southists among the St. Thomas Christians* (Rome: Pont. Institutum Studiorum Orientalium, 1992). Mundadan, *History of Christianity in India Volume I*, 78–79.

11 See: Stephen A. Missick, "Mar Thoma: The Apostolic Foundation of the Assyrian Church and the Christians of St. Thomas in India," *Journal of Assyrian Academic Studies* XIV, 2 (2000): 33–61.

12 James Kurikilamkatt, *First Voyage of the Apostle Thomas to India: Ancient Christianity in Bharuch and Taxila* (Bangalore, India: Asian Trading Corporation, 2005), 180–188. See also: Neill, *A History of Christianity in India*, 43, 50–51, 64, and 188–190. See also: Mundadan, *History of Christianity in India Volume I*, 75–76.

13 Interview with Fr. Lawrence Raj, Chennai, December 20, 2010.

14 Interview with Mr. Mark, Chennai, July 23, 2009.

15 Interview with Mr. Zander, Chennai, August 5, 2009.

16 See: Corinne G. Dempsey, *Kerala Christian Sainthood: Collisions of Culture and Worldview in South India* (New York: Oxford University Press, 2001). See also: Corinne G. Dempsey, "Lessons in Miracles from Kerala, South India: Stories of Three "Christian" Saints," in *Popular Christianity in India: Riting between the Lines*, eds Selva J. Raj and Corinne G. Dempsey (Albany, NY: State University of New York Press, 2002), 115–139. See also: Selva J. Raj, "Shared Vows, Shared Space, and Shared Deities: Vow Rituals among Tamil Catholics in South India," in *Dealing with Deities: The Ritual Vow in South Asia*, eds Selva J. Raj and William P. Harman (Albany, NY: State University of New York Press, 2006), 43–64. See also: David Mosse, "The Politics of Religious Synthesis: Roman Catholicism and Hindu Village Society in Tamil Nadu, India," in *Syncretism/ Anti-Syncretism: The Politics of Religious Synthesis*, eds Charles Stewart and Rosalind Shaw (London and New York: Routledge, 1994), 85–107.

17 Bayly, *Saints, Goddesses and Kings*, 276–280.

18 Dempsey, *Kerala Christian Sainthood*, 180n. 9.

19 Interview with Fr. Lawrence Raj, Chennai, June 15, 2009.

20 Interview with Mr. Mark, Chennai, July 23, 2009.

21 Joseph Thekkedath, *History of Christianity in India Volume II: From the Middle of the Sixteenth Century to the end of the Seventeenth Century* (Bangalore: Theological Publications in India, 1982), 1.

22 Neill, *A History of Christianity in India*, 134–165. See also: Cardinal Crescenzio Sepe, *St. Thomas, Apostle 1,950 Years Ago; St. Francis Xavier 450 Years Ago*, http://www.catholicculture.org/culture/library/view.cfm?recnum=4580 (Accessed January 18, 2012).

23 Interview with Fr. Lawrence Raj, Chennai, December 20, 2010.

24 Paul Younger, *Playing Host to Deity: Festival Religion in the South Indian Tradition* (Oxford: Oxford University Press, 2002), 107–124. However, the categories of Christian and Hindu, especially in the context of a Catholic festival in India, are not necessarily as clear cut as my statement suggests. See also: Selva J. Raj and Corinne G. Dempsey, "Introduction," in *Popular Christianity in India. Riting between the Lines*, eds Raj, Selva J. and C. Dempsey (Albany, NY: State University of New York Press, 2002) 1–2. On the other hand, my Tamil Catholic informants were very clear in distinguishing themselves from their Hindu neighbors. Additionally, Indologist Matthias Frenz has published recently (in English) a couple of articles discussing in depth the subject of Hindu / Christian hybridity at Vailankanni Shrine. See: Matthias Frenz, "The Virgin and Her 'Relations': Reflections on Processions at Catholic at a Catholic Shrine in Southern India," in *South Asian Religions on Display: Religious Processions in South Asia and in the Diaspora*, ed. Knut A. Jacobson (London and New York: Routledge, 2008), 92–103. Matthias Frenz, "The Illusion of Conversion: Śiva meets Mary at Vēlānkanni in Southern India," in *Asia in the Making of Christianity: Conversion, Agency, and Indigeneity, 1600s to the Present*, eds Richard Fox Young and Jonathan A. Seitz (Leiden: Brill, 2013), 373–401.
25 See: Pope Paul VI, *Evangelii Nuntiandi*, http://www.vatican.va/holy_father/paul_vi/apost_exhortations/documents/hf_p-vi_exh_19751208_evangelii-nuntiandi_en.html (Accessed February 2, 2013). See also: International Theological Commission, *Faith and Inculturation*, http://www.vatican.va/roman_curia/congregations/cfaith/cti_documents/rc_cti_1988_fede-inculturazione_en.html (Accessed August 19, 2012).
26 Vasudha Narayanan, "Afterward: Diverse Hindu Responses to Diverse Christianities in India," in *Popular Christianity in India. Riting Between the Lines*, eds Raj, Selva J. and C. Dempsey (Albany, NY: State University of New York Press, 2002) 265.
27 Interview with Fr. Lawrence Raj, Chennai, June 15, 2009.
28 Ibid.
29 See: Eleanor Nesbitt, "South Asian Christians in the UK," in *South Asian Christian Diaspora: Invisible Diaspora in Europe and North America*, eds Knut A. Jacobsen and Selva J. Raj (Farnham: Ashgate, 2008), 20.
30 Interview with Brother Joe, Chennai, June 11, 2009.
31 See: Kurikilamkatt, *First Voyage of the Apostle Thomas to India*. See also: Anthonysamy, *A Saga of Faith*. See also: Benedict Vadakkekara, *Origin of Christianity in India: A Historiographical Critique* (Delhi: Media House, 2007). See also: Jacob George, *The Trails of St. Thomas: 2000 Years of Christianity in India* (Charleston, SC: Create Space Inc., 2014).
32 See: Henri Hosten, *Antiquities from San Thome and Mylapore, the Traditional Site of the Martyrdom and Tomb of St. Thomas the Apostle* (Calcutta: Baptist Mission Press, 1936). Alberto Pereira de Andrade, *Our Lady of Mylapore and St. Thomas the Apostle* (Madras: San Thome, 1956). Kurikilamkatt, *First Voyage of the Apostle Thomas to India*. Vadakkekara, *Origin of Christianity in India*.
33 Herman D'Souza, *In the Steps of St. Thomas* (Chennai: Diocese of Chingleput, Apostolic Hill Shrine of St. Thomas, 2010), 9.
34 Disciples of St. Thomas, http://www.santhome.org/ (Accessed February 5, 2011).
35 Herman D'Souza, *In the Steps of St. Thomas* (Chennai: National Shrine of St. Thomas Basilica, 2009), back cover.
36 Anthonysamy, *A Saga of Faith*.

37 P. John Bosco, *St. Thomas Mount-Chennai-South India: The Spot of the Heroic Martyrdom of St. Thomas the Apostle and the Cradle and Glory of the Indian Church* (Chennai: Apostolic Hill Shrine of St. Thomas, St. Thomas Mount, 2010).

38 M. Nevis Victoria, *Brief History of St. Thomas and Little Mount* (Chennai: Centurion, 2010).

39 *Souvenir San Thome Historic Event 2004* (San Thome Cathedral, Chennai, Tamil Nadu, India: San Thome Cathedral Basilica, 2004).

40 Ibid.

41 Pedro López Quintana, "Homily of the Apostolic Nuncio: On the Occasion of the Consecration of the Renovated San Thome Cathedral, Archdiocese of Madras-Mylapore December 12, 2004," in *Souvenir San Thome Historic Event 2004* (San Thome Cathedral, Chennai, Tamil Nadu, India: San Thome Cathedral Basilica, 2004).

42 Grace Victor, "Blessed are the Santhomites!" in *Souvenir San Thome Historic Event 2004* (San Thome Cathedral, Chennai, Tamil Nadu, India: San Thome Cathedral Basilica, 2004).

43 Today, this is the site of the Church of Malayattoor, which is located near the village of Malayattoor, Kerala. St. Thomas is believed to have stopped here on his way to Mylapore. At the time of this book's publication, the Church of Malayattoor is the only officially recognized Roman Catholic International Shrine in India. Interview with Fr. Lawrence Raj, Chennai, December 15, 2010.

44 Victor, "Blessed are the Santhomites!".

45 James Carvalho and Francis Carvalho, "Song of India," in *At the Feet of St. Thomas*. Translated by Rick Weiss. Chennai: National Shrine of St. Thomas Basilica, 2004.

46 See: David Shulman, *Tamil Temple Myths: Sacrifice and Divine Marriage in the South Indian Śaiva Tradition* (Princeton, NJ: Princeton University Press, 1980), 90–110.

47 *Souvenir SanThome Historic Event 2004*.

48 For example, see: Mundadan, *History of Christianity in India Volume I*. See also: A. C. Perumalil, *The Apostles in India* (Patna: Xavier Teachers' Training Institute, 1971). See also: D'Souza, *In the Steps of St. Thomas*. See also: Kurikilamkatt, *First Voyage of the Apostle Thomas to India*. See also: Vadakkekara, *Origin of Christianity in India*.

49 Anthonysamy, *A Saga of Faith*, xi.

50 Ibid, x–xi.

51 Ibid, xi.

52 Ibid, xii.

53 Ibid, xiii–xv.

54 D'Souza, *In the Steps of St. Thomas*, 9.

55 Anthonysamy, *A Saga of Faith*, 87–103, 137–140, 149–157, and 175–176.

56 Ibid, back cover.

57 Ibid, 129.

58 Ibid, ix.

59 Ibid, x.

60 Interview with Fr. Lawrence Raj, Chennai, June 30, 2009.

61 Ibid.

62 Interview with Fr. Charles, Chennai, July 8, 2009.

63 Disciples of St. Thomas, "What do you know about St. Thomas?" *Voice of St. Thomas* 1, 12 (April–June 2009): 17. And: Disciples of St. Thomas, "St. Thomas Quiz-II," *Voice of St Thomas* 2, 6 (October–December 2010): 18–19.

64 *The Voice from the Hill* 1, 1 (July 2010).

65 *Voice of St. Thomas* 1, 1 (July–September 2006).

66 S. J. Anthonysamy, "A Saga of Faith Part I," *Voice of St. Thomas* 1, 2 (October–December 2006): 14–15.

67 S. J. Anthonysamy, "A Saga of Faith Part I," *Voice of St. Thomas* 1, 5 (July–September 2007): 12–13. S. J. Anthonysamy, "A Saga of Faith Part V," *Voice of St. Thomas* 1, 6 (October–December 2007): 12–13.

68 Ibid, 13.

69 S. J. Anthonysamy, "A Saga of Faith Part XV," *Voice of St. Thomas* 2, 5 (July–September 2010): 10–11.

70 James and Francis Carvalho, "Song of India."

71 For a general overview of the general characteristics of Catholic processions in India see: Frenz, "The Virgin and Her Relations," 92–94.

72 Vimala Padmaraj, "Living the Faith: A Touching Account of the Feast of Saint Thomas AD 2007," *Voice of St. Thomas* 1, 5 (July–September 2007): 15.

73 Josephine Joseph, "Festivity to Honour the Apostle of India," *Voice of St. Thomas* 1, 9 (July–September 2008): 16.

74 Ibid, 17.

75 Sashi Kala Chandran, "Feast of St. Thomas-The Apostle," *Voice of St. Thomas* 2, 5 (July–September 2010): 14.

76 Ibid, 14.

77 Vimala Padmaraj and J. Josephine, "Celebrating the Ninth Beatitude," *Voice of St. Thomas* 1, 2 (October–December 2006): 10.

78 Ibid, 12–13.

79 Josephine Joseph, "Festivity to Honour the Apostle of India," 16–17.

80 Ibid, 17.

81 Ibid.

82 Ibid.

83 "Web Television from Basilica," *Voice of St. Thomas* 2, 9 (July–September 2011): 10.

84 San Thome Church, http://www.santhomechurch.com/ (Accessed February 8, 2009). San Thome's live webcasts can be found at: Santhome Church TV, http://www.santhomechurch.tv/a/ (Accessed February 8, 2009).

85 Travel writer Charlie Pye-Smith visited San Thome Cathedral around 1997, as recorded in his travelogue *Rebel and Outcasts*. He was fairly unimpressed by what he saw at San Thome and St. Thomas Mount, citing the Roman Catholic Church's caretakership as detrimental to the St. Thomas tradition. With regard to printed material, he notes a leaflet he picked up at the Cathedral's entrance that contained information on the Cathedral structure, as well as the general history of St. Thomas's tomb. He also notes purchasing some booklets from the museum, but does not name any of them. See: Charlie Pye-Smith, *Rebel and Outcasts: A Journey Through Christian India* (London: Viking, 1997), 202–206.

86 A. J. Adaikalam, *The St. Thomas' Cathedral Museum* (Madras: San Thome, 1985).

87 See: Simon Chumkat, *St. Thomas: Monuments in Chennai, India* (Chennai: IRIS SOFTEK). See also: *San Thome Cathedral Basilica: A Quick Introduction* (Chennai: San Thome Cathedral Basilica). See also: *San Thome Cathedral Basilica: Rich in History, Steeped in Faith* (Chennai: San Thome Cathedral Basilica).

88 *National Shrine of St. Thomas Basilica* (Chennai: National Shrine of St. Thomas Basilica, 2009).

89 Interview with Fr. Lawrence Raj, Chennai, June 30, 2009.

90 *National Shrine of St. Thomas Basilica* (Chennai: National Shrine of St. Thomas Basilica, 2009), cover page.

91 Ibid, 1.
92 Interview with Fr. Lawrence Raj, Chennai, June 15, 2009.
93 *National Shrine of St. Thomas Basilica*, 2.
94 Simon Chumkat, "The Miraculous Pole," *Voice of St. Thomas* 1, 6 (October–December 2007): 10–11.
95 *National Shrine of St. Thomas Basilica*, 3.
96 Ibid, 4.
97 Ibid, 5.
98 Ibid.
99 Interview with Fr. Lawrence Raj, Chennai, June 15, 2009.
100 Interview with Fr. Lawrence Raj, Chennai, June 30, 2009.
101 Interview with Fr. Charles, Chennai, July 8, 2009.
102 H. L. Seneviratne, "Identity and Conflation of Past and Present," *Identity, Consciousness and the Past: Forging of Caste and Community in India and Sri Lanka*, ed. H. L. Seneviratne (New Delhi: Oxford University Press, 1997), 19.

3   The influences of Indian political ideologies on Catholic revivalist strategies in Chennai

Introduction

As the previous chapter demonstrated, Church administrators at San Thome and St. Thomas Mount have utilized various forms of published media in order to increase local awareness about St. Thomas's Indian legacy and to foster a deeper connection between the Apostle and Tamil Catholic identity and indigeneity. However, the Church in Chennai's utilization of the St. Thomas story in order to emphasize Indian Christian indigeneity barely scratches the surface regarding the greater socio-political context from which the St. Thomas sites in Chennai have launched their recent revivals. This chapter will analyze the development of India's current socio-political landscape, paying particular attention to the rise of Hindu nationalism and how its rhetoric of Hindutva has influenced contemporary Catholic renewal in Chennai.

Today, the Catholic Church in India views the ideology of Hindutva as being synonymous with the anti-Christian rhetoric and violence that has plagued the Indian Christian minority for the last decade or so. I argue that a number of the revivalist strategies adopted by Church administrators in Chennai have been initiated as a response to, or in light of, the intolerant elements of Hindutva in order to quell, confront, and challenge the Hindu nationalists who criticize the Indian Christian community using this ideology.

Catholic renewal in Chennai is best discussed within the contemporary political contexts of both national and regional politics in India. At the national level, India's ruling Congress Party currently adheres to a platform of secular democracy in the face of the rising tide of right-wing Hindu nationalism. At the local and regional level, Tamil Nadu has, for a long time, been socially and politically unreceptive to Hindu nationalism, however, this is slowly changing. The Catholic Church and the St. Thomas tradition have not escaped the scrutiny of local Hindu right groups in Chennai, and thus, the Church has had to plan accordingly with regard to their recent renewal and revivalist activities. This chapter will discuss those revivalist strategies developed as a response to Hindu right accusations and polemics. It will also demonstrate how some of these strategies have been utilized by the Church in Chennai in order to confront issues such as communal violence and spiritual decline.

This chapter is divided into two main sections. The first discusses the rise of Hindu nationalism, and the subsequent persecution of Indian Christian communities in India. This socio-religious and political context highlights the relevance of St. Thomas's legacy of martyrdom and sacrifice to contemporary Indian Christianity. The second will discuss and analyze the writings of two outspoken Hindu nationalists, Ishwar Sharan and Sita Ram Goel, focusing on their specific criticisms of the Catholic Church and its proliferation of the St. Thomas tradition in India. This section will also look at some revivalist strategies employed by the Church in Chennai that specifically represent either a mindfulness of Hindu right criticisms or are a response and challenge to Hindutva.

Hindu nationalism: political entities and ideologies

The rise of Hindu nationalism has had a profound effect on India's current political landscape, and its influence has impacted upon the way the Catholic Church in India has had to conduct itself with regard to missionization and renewal. Hindu nationalism's contemporary character as an Indian political movement and ideology emerged during the late nineteenth century, but only solidified once the drive towards India's independence gained momentum during the early twentieth century. During this timeframe, various pro-Hindu organizations sprang up in order to weigh in on issues overlooked by the dominant and secular Indian National Congress Party (INC). The most dominant and long-lasting of these groups, the Rashtriya Swayamsevak Sangh (RSS or National Volunteer Corps), was founded in 1925 and is still going strong today.[1] Not long after Independence, the RSS lost practically all of its political support due to the fact that Mahatma Gandhi's assassin was a former member. In order to facilitate a Hindu nationalist presence within India's newly established political system RSS leadership established a new political party in 1951, the Bharatiya Jana Sangh.[2] The Jana Sangh mixed moderate populist political strategies with more aggressive Hindu right policies. The two strategies never meshed well, however. By 1980, the Jana Sangh had disappeared and been supplanted by the newly-formed Bharatiya Janata Party (BJP or Indian People's Party), which maintained its ties to the RSS while adopting a moderate political platform.[3]

The RSS eventually established several other offshoot organizations as well. Today, all of these various groups are collectively called the Sangh Parivar (Family of Associations) and maintain strong ties to the RSS. For this project, however, only one other member of the Sangh Parivar is relevant, the Vishva Hindu Parishad (VHP or World Council of Hindus), which was created in 1964. The VHP was formed out of the combined efforts of the RSS and several Hindu religious leaders, and was tasked with organizing the various Hindu religious sects into something more structurally consistent and uniform.[4]

Today, the RSS, BJP, and VHP are the most influential and prominent Hindu nationalist organizations in India. Working in concert, the VHP acts as the religious branch of the Sangh Parivar, the BJP as the political wing, and the RSS serves to train new members in the teachings and ways of their particular brand of Hindu nationalist thought. Christophe Jaffrelot, perhaps the most prolific scholar on the subject of Hindu nationalism, characterizes the RSS as a "Hindu nationalist sect," because it combines a western para-military style and structure with traditional Hindu rituals and values.[5] At the core of the RSS's teachings, and across the entirety of the Sangh Parivar, is the ideology of Hindutva or Hinduness, which encompasses the ideals for the ethnic, religious, and cultural identity for a proper Hindu nation.[6] As we will see, the ideology of Hindutva would ultimately set the course for the way Hindu nationalism would come to view and interact with India's Christian communities and institutions.

The origins of Hindutva and its development as a political ideology

The term "Hindutva" was first used in 1923 by the anti-British revolutionary Vinayak Damodar Savarkar in his book *Hindutva: Who is a Hindu?* By the time he wrote this pivotal work, his political focus had already shifted away from anti-British sentiment and towards a more hostile anti-Muslim position. In *Hindutva*, Savarkar argued that a strong singular Hindu nationalist identity needed to be established in order to combat the Muslim threat to India.[7] Savarkar's work represents the most influential treatise on Hindu nationalist identity and remains the ideological core for the modern-day Sangh Parivar. After independence, several Hindu nationalist thinkers refined Savarkar's notion of Hindutva into the more populist ideology it is today.

Jyotirmaya Sharma, a respected political philosopher, identifies six key features of Hindutva thought that are shared between Savarkar and his literary predecessors. First, Sharma identifies the need for a single universal Hinduism based mainly on upper-caste traditions and shorn of any low-caste derivatives or deviations. Second, the idea that Hinduism needs to reclaim its masculinity and war-like aggression, which was lost due to India's long history of slavery and colonialism. Third, that Hinduism was, in fact, the mother religion, from which all other world religions originated and that these, as such, can only be mere shadows of Hinduism. Fourth, that Hinduism and the Hindu nation will always be under threat from disruptive elements, both foreign and internal. Fifth, that Hinduism's theology begins and ends with the Vedas and Upanishads, which are the purest links to India's golden age. The sixth and final ideal is the adoption and utilization of strong, aggressive, and uncompromising rhetoric as a decisive tool against the enemies of Hinduism.[8]

These six characteristics of Hindutva are still prevalent ideological hallmarks of the Sangh Parivar's greater political agenda, which also provides them with the socio-historical and religious justification for persecuting Muslims and Christians within India's borders, regardless of ethnicity. As Jaffrelot states, "Indian culture was to be defined as Hindu culture, and the minorities were to be assimilated by their paying allegiance to the symbols and mainstays of the majority."[9] In other words, while Indian Christians and Indian Muslims within any given state or region may share the same ethnicity as Indian Hindus, they do not share in Hindu culture, and thus are to be considered second-class citizens because by being non-Hindus they cannot be true Indians.

Savarkar himself promoted this line of thinking that specifically singled out Muslims and Christians as impediments to the Hindu nation. Savarkar explains:

> We [Hindus] are one because we are a nation, a race and own a common Sanskrit (civilization) in the case of some of our Mohammedan [Muslim] or Christian countrymen who had originally been forcibly converted to a non-Hindu religion and who consequently have inherited along with Hindus, a common Fatherland and a greater part of the wealth of a common culture … are not and cannot be recognized as Hindus. For though Hindusthan [India] to them is Fatherland as to any other Hindu yet it is not to them a Holyland too. Their Holyland is far off in Arabia or Palestine. Their mythology and Godmen, ideas and heroes are not the children of this soil.[10]

As Savarkar asserts, even though non-Hindu Indians can still claim a lineage of traditional Indian culture they are no longer able to view or accept the Indian land as their religious "Holyland" or center, due to their association with foreign Western religions. In other words, while a "true" Indian (Hindu) will look to India as both his homeland and Holyland, a Muslim or Christian Indian will only look to India as a homeland, and ultimately place their religious loyalties with foreign sacred centers like Mecca, Jerusalem, and Rome. Thus, the assumption can be drawn that all Muslims and Christians would naturally place their foreign Holylands above the Indian nation, and thus disrupt national unity through their divided civil loyalties. It is easy to see how this idea is applicable to the Church in India, due to its strong ties with Rome.

Since its inception, the targeted "enemies" of the Hindu nationalist movement have primarily been Muslims and Christians, but mainly Muslims because of their larger population in India. These two groups are seen as foreign elements that have transplanted themselves into India by way of conquest and thus, cannot be considered indigenous to the soil of

Mother India. This kind of rhetoric and demonization is most greatly exemplified in the events surrounding the demolition of the Babri Mosque in the city of Ayodhya in December of 1992, an incident that highlights the BJP's steady rise in popularity and political influence.

Even during the height of their power the BJP maintained their moderate platform and never implemented any of the more extreme Hindu nationalist agendas, such as sanctioning the building of a new Rama temple on the site of the Ayodhya Babri Mosque. While the BJP has always been committed to Hindutva, its relatively moderate stance has created some tension with the RSS and VHP. The BJP was finally ousted from power in 2004 by the INC; this led many within the Sangh Parivar to further question the reliability of the BJP's moderate politics, which only served to widen this division. In addition to the BJP's adoption of a moderate platform came a softening of its anti-Muslim rhetoric, since the potential for further political fallout, should another incident similar to the Ayodhya affair take place, could spark the possible dissolution of the BJP's hard-earned political alliances.[11] The rest of the Sangh Parivar seems to have realized this as well. This move away from more explicit anti-Muslim rhetoric has allowed for the Sangh Parivar to shift its primary focus onto India's Christian communities, which is evident from the recent increase in anti-Christian sentiment coming out of India's contemporary Hindu right movement.[12]

Hindu right anti-Christian rhetoric and violence in India

Over the years, the Sangh Parivar has clearly expressed its growing concerns regarding Christianity's continued presence in India. Reiterating Savarkar's perspective on the issue, the Sangh Parivar has criticized Indian Christians for their ties to foreign Western institutions, such as American missionary societies or the Catholic Church in Rome. These ties allegedly ultimately compromise the Indian Christian community's loyalty to the Indian nation, thus making them less than ideal citizens, if not impediments to national unity. As Walter K. Andersen and Shridhar D. Damle explain:

> RSS writers allege that Christian values have tended to distance Christians culturally from the national mainstream in some parts of the country. From this proposition, a subproposition is deduced: because some Christians do not consider themselves culturally Indian, they do not experience a sense of community with other Indians. One could phrase the proposition in the more esoteric terms of the belief system: because Christians are culturally different, they have separated themselves from the "national soul".[13]

In other words, due to the global character of Christianity, many Indian Christians see themselves as belonging to a community that goes beyond just the Indian nation. In essence, by choosing to belong to this global

Christian community they have made the choice to leave behind the greater Indian community.

At the forefront of most anti-Christian rhetoric in India is the issue of religious conversion. The Sangh Parivar has two major concerns regarding Christianity's presence in India and Christian theology in general. First is the Christian project to proselytize and missionize wherever it goes; second is their fear that Christian missionaries are thus unabashedly luring Hindus away from their traditional heritage. In doing so, Christians are seen as conspiring against the Hindu nationalist ideal for a culturally and religiously united Hindu nation. Additionally, they criticize the fact that many missionary endeavors and Christian institutions in India are financially backed by outside powers. Hindu nationalist Ishwar Sharan states:

> The Christian Church in India is still a 17th century colonial Church financed from abroad. It has a sophisticated international support system in place (and this is especially true of the newer American evangelical Churches). It is very arrogant and corrupt, a quasi-independent state that is coddled and pampered by the Indian government and media alike. It is answerable to nobody, which is reason enough for a responsible national government to order a white paper investigation into its finances and activities.[14]

In other words, missionaries have a seemingly endless supply of money in order to carry out the agendas of their foreign patrons, which many Hindu nationalists believe to be the utter transformation of India into a Christian nation.[15]

Christianity's global community, combined with its inherent desire to promulgate its faith has made many Hindu nationalists afraid of what a growing Christian population in India could mean for the future of Hinduism and the Hindu nation. Chetan Bhatt, a sociologist and human rights activist who has written extensively on Hindu nationalism, highlights that "Underlying the VHP and the RSS orientation to Christianity was a narrative of a global Christian conspiracy, orchestrated by an alliance between the Pope and Catholic Church in Rome and American Christian fundamentalists."[16] The idea of a "global Christian conspiracy" is one of the more extreme fears held by the Hindu right regarding Christian missionary efforts. This fear has led to the additional belief that the Indian Christian population has grown exponentially in India within the last thirty years and continues to do so to the detriment of Hindu religion and culture.[17] Initially, Hindu nationalists were primarily concerned over the conversion of Hindus to Islam, since Islam was the larger of the two minority communities, but Christian missionaries eventually took center stage. In fact, one of the founding purposes for the formation of the VHP was to contend with Christian missionary activities alongside their main objective of streamlining the Hindu religion.[18]

After the Ayodhya incident forced the Sangh Parivar to tone down its anti-Muslim rhetoric, its efforts were effectively refocused on a more outspoken anti-Christian stance. This eventually came to a head in the late 1990s as the BJP's influence strengthened once more. As Jaffrelot points out, the Sangh Parivar's basic anti-Christian discourse was more or less a reproduction of the anti-Muslim discourses it had utilized in the past.[19] With anti-Christian sentiment already stirred up in various states, the initial fear of a wider Christian conspiracy was further compounded by a number of events. For example, in 1998, Sonia Gandhi, an Italian-born Catholic, would rise to become the leader of the INC and stand in opposition to the BJP during that year's election. In 1999, Pope John Paul II made his second and final visit to India. Additionally, several Evangelical Christian missionary societies declared special proselytizing campaigns for the run up to the auspicious year 2000.[20] These events combined with the Sangh Parivar's ideological xenophobia would further motivate its members to more drastic measures towards halting the spread of Christianity in India.

Even before some of the above events took place, members of the Sangh Parivar had already undertaken to thwart and reverse any instances of mass conversion to Christianity in the country, especially within the "tribal" areas of India, where the ritualized strategy of "reconversion" was adopted and utilized by the Sangh Parivar to varying degrees of success.[21] Another, more politicized strategy, which became widespread after the year 2000, was the passing of special anti-conversion laws. These laws varied from state to state, but more or less represented the same thing: government-supported restrictions on religious conversion. These laws were passed in the name of safeguarding individuals and communities from the lures and temptations offered by missionaries, and were mainly adopted in states where the BJP and the Sangh Parivar held the most sway.[22]

For example, in late 2002 the Tamil Nadu state government passed an anti-conversion bill called The Tamil Nadu Prohibition of Forcible Conversion of Religion Ordinance.[23] The Tamil political party that was in charge of the government at this time was the All India Anna Dravida Munnetra Kazhagam party (AIADMK), which was led by the intermittently popular Jayalalithaa Jayaram. When this bill was passed, she and the AIADMK fully supported and were allied with the BJP, which explains why she attempted to pass this anti-conversion bill, as well as an additional law that attempted to ban animal sacrifices within Hindu temples.[24] Both of these laws are representative of the BJP's adherence to Hindutva, with its explicit goals of preserving Hindu culture, as well as the streamlining of Hindu rituals and practice. However, both policies were widely unpopular in Tamil Nadu, so in 2004 when the BJP was ousted by the INC as the ruling national party, Jayalalithaa took this opportunity to officially repeal both of these laws.[25]

Traditionally, Hindu nationalist groups like the BJP have never been popular in Tamil Nadu. However, in recent times, due to the decline of traditional Tamil political philosophies and anti-Brahmanism coupled with a growing awareness of globalization, more and more Tamils have come to support the Hindu nationalist movement.[26] Hindu nationalist groups, such as the Hindu Munnani, have been able to increase their popularity in Tamil Nadu by tailoring their political rhetoric through the appropriation of traditional Tamil symbols and sensibilities, which have allowed them to create a more "Tamil-friendly Hindutva" from which to garner state-wide support.[27] However, as C. J. Fuller attests, regarding the general state of Hindu nationalist support in Tamil Nadu, "people's general sympathy for Hindu nationalism is strongly affected by their own interests in their own locality, and is not driven by unqualified enthusiasm, let alone religious fanaticism. For the most part, Hindu nationalists (like other political activists) succeed when they align their campaigns with local interests and exploit local divisions, and they fail when they do not."[28] As exemplified in Tamil Nadu, Hindu nationalism and the ideology of Hindutva have developed into a more moderate socio-political movement than elsewhere in India, and due to this "normalization," as Fuller calls it, more Tamils are less likely to view Hindu nationalist groups as religious extremists.[29] Unfortunately, this is not the case in other parts of India today.

Several other organizations under the Sangh Parivar umbrella rose to national prominence in the late 1990s. Two groups in particular, the Hindu Jagran Manch (HJM or Forum for Hindu Awakening) and the Bajrang Dal (Hanuman's Army), played a significant role in orchestrating later anti-Christian protests and localized violence against Christian communities. Chetan Bhatt notes these two groups as being more representative of a "Hindu supremacist ideology" that stands apart from the typical Hindutva ideology of their parent organizations.[30] Bhatt identifies the Bajrang Dal as being particularly unruly and militant, so much so that even the RSS has decried the Bajrang Dal's membership a nothing more than "riff raff."[31]

With all these elements in place, the outbreak of anti-Christian violence in the north was perhaps predictable, especially in those Indian states where the BJP and RSS had the most political and social influence. As Jaffrelot explains, even though the BJP were committed to the ideals of Hindutva, they also had to distance themselves from the rest of the Sangh Parivar, especially in matters that could result in communal violence. Jaffrelot states:

> Thus while the BJP leaders more or less maintained their moderate line, the RSS and VHP leaders adopted by and large the same attitude vis-à-vis the Christians as the one they had developed vis-à-vis the Muslims. For this reason, the atrocities in Gujarat and Orissa cannot be regarded as purely local developments. There was probably no centralized master plan against the Christians, initially, but local activists certainly felt more secure after the VHP leaders endorsed their mischiefs.[32]

In order to explain the switch from Muslims to Christians in the Indian states mentioned above, Jaffrelot posits that it was primarily due to the

Christian community being perceived as a "soft target" with fewer numbers. With the BJP now in charge of the local government, it was their responsibility to maintain law and order, and the Sangh Parivar risked compromising their control by inciting the larger Muslim community. The smaller Christian community, if antagonized, could be more easily contained.[33]

As these incidents started garnering international media attention, the BJP and the other more directly involved members of the Sangh Parivar had to take a step back and go on the political defensive. Regardless, members of the BJP and RSS would ultimately use this international scrutiny of Hindu nationalism to further bolster their claims of a global Christian conspiracy out to get them.[34] To this day, anti-Christian rhetoric and acts of anti-Christian violence still permeate, to varying degrees, the Indian landscape where the Sangh Parivar is most influential. Hindutva is thus a socio-political reality that the Catholic Church in India has to contend with on a regular basis. The most recent and shocking outbreak of large-scale communal violence between Christians and Hindus in India took place in the Kandhamal district of Orissa state before spreading to nearby states. This particular episode of rampant anti-Christian violence lasted for more than a year (c. 2007–2008), and resulted in the deaths of hundreds of Christians, as well as several Hindus, and the displacement of more than ten thousand, mainly Christian, refugees.[35] Clearly, Indian Christians today live within a precarious socio-religious and political context, in which the reality of persecution and even death are every-day possibilities.

As we have seen from the above sections, certain Hindu nationalist discourses attempt to attack Christianity and Indian Christian identity both ideologically, through Hindutva, as well as physically, through communal violence. Obviously, the legacy of St. Thomas as missionary, progenitor, and martyr is far more pronounced during such troubled times. Thus, it stands to reason that the Church would see the advantages of reviving and promulgating the story of St. Thomas as an intimate and regionalized symbol of hope and unwavering faith for a people whose very identity and religiosity were under attack.

San Thome responses to anti-Christian violence in India

The anti-Christian violence in Orissa was very fresh in the minds of Indian Christians when I first arrived in Chennai in February 2009. For many of my informants, the violence represented their worst fears come to life. Their anxiety was compounded by the fact that India's general elections were fast approaching in May 2009. There was widespread concern that further violence would be more probable if the BJP defeated the INC and regained the political power it lost in 2004.[36] The violence in Orissa and the fast-approaching general elections even prompted San Thome's quarterly magazine, *Voice of St. Thomas* (*VoST*), to suspend their policy of not publishing overtly politicized articles. In the first two issues of 2009, *VoST* published two forthright articles denouncing the violence in Orissa, and criticizing the BJP for their Hindutva leanings and for turning a blind eye to the disruptive actions of the Sangh Parivar.[37]

The first article is about a rally and demonstration that was held on November 22, 2008 in Chennai that was organized by the Archdiocesan Women's Commission in response to the violence in Orissa, specifically regarding the rape of a Catholic nun. In attendance were the Archbishop of Madras-Mylapore and over 2000 supporters. The report opens:

> When the virulent Hindutva violence engulfed believers in Orissa, especially Kandhamal District and the media wept reports of killings and destruction but not of remedial justice .... But when we learnt about the police who stood mute witness to the barbaric "communal rape" of a Catholic nun, that's when the Christian community in India felt desolately orphaned by the law of our secular land.[38]

The language utilized by the article's author Loreto Xavier clearly places the blame on Hindu right extremism. He describes the violence as "Hindutva violence" and utilizes the term "communal" to describe the nun's rape. The term communal is often invoked by India's intelligentsia to denote religious violence in India, which was typified by the mass riots after Ayodhya. Xavier is clearly conveying the opinion that Hindutva and communal violence are synonymous expressions of Hindu right fundamentalism, as in the Ayodhya case, which he then punctuates by emphasizing India's supposed status as a "secular land."[39]

These criticisms are further broadened in the second article, which is a re-print of a letter written by Julio Ribeiro who was the former Mumbai Commissioner of Police and a nationally prominent Indian Catholic. In his letter, he openly criticizes the BJP and other Hindu nationalist groups for their implicit and explicit contribution to the recent outbreak of anti-Christian violence. He states, "I am sorely disappointed with the BJP for not reining in the VHP and the Bajrang Dal, who like the SIMI and its offshoot, the Indian Mujahideen feel that the best way and only way to attain peace is to kill those who they think are different."[40] He goes on to question the Hindu right claim of missionary coercion and forced conversion. He agrees that such things happened in the colonial past, but not in the modern day. He writes, "For generations, tribals and so-called 'Untouchables' have been kept down. Christian missionaries, with their stress on education and health, have challenged the foundations of this social order. That, I believe, is the cause of the present upheaval," which seems to be the consensus among many of the Catholics in Chennai.[41] While Ribeiro never explicitly mentions Hindutva, he does state, "My ancestors, like those of most Christians in India, were Hindus," which seems to imply that it was on his mind.[42] With the 2009 general elections soon approaching, the machinations of the Hindu right coupled with the fear of further anti-Christian violence were on many Indian Christian minds.

Several of the Indian Christians I talked to in Chennai frankly expressed the uneasiness they felt about the possibility of a new BJP government. For instance, Mr. Mark articulated his doubt over the BJP's supposedly moderate platform, and belief that the ties between the BJP and the rest of the Sangh Parivar were far closer than the party was letting on. He was also adamant that if the BJP ever returned to power it would definitely attempt to rebuild the Rama temple on the site of the demolished Babri Mosque, which would result in even greater communal tensions and most likely widespread violence.[43] Brother Joe from Little Mount believed that if the BJP had its way, Christianity in India would be "destroyed."[44] Sr. Merrill of San Thome shared similar sentiments. Her opinion reflected the common Indian Christian view point I encountered during my time in Chennai that a BJP government would only lead to more "suffering" on the part of the Indian Christian community.[45]

Not surprisingly, the majority of Christians in India supported the INC during the 2009 elections. This is clearly due to its steadfast adherence to secular democracy, its support for minority rights, and its open denunciation of the BJP as a political party whose Hindu nationalist policies only served to promote communal violence and enable Hindu right militancy. To the relief of my informants, as well as the Indian mainstream media, the 2009 general election ended with the INC maintaining control of India's parliamentary government. Upon their convincing victory, a national political magazine splashed the following statement on their cover, "Congress Resurgence: The party re-establishes its all-India presence as people vote for stability and secularism."[46] When I asked Mr. Mark if he thought the INC's victory was a good thing, he ecstatically proclaimed, "Yeah, of course ... obviously, the Congress really is a secular government, whatever you say ... whatever drawbacks it may have, it still supports the allegiance of India, the integrity of India, the BJP does not."[47] Mr. Mark's feelings on the election result was indicative of the collective sigh of relief I noticed from the many Indian Christians I was in contact with in Chennai, and since the INC won the election by a wide margin, the Christian community was not alone in its political desire for tolerance.

However, the threat of Hindu right inspired anti-Christian rhetoric and violence still looms precariously over the Indian Christian community regardless of whatever political party is in power. The political character of the BJP government during the late 1990s and early 2000s, coupled with the anti-Christian violence of that time period, represents the Indian political context from which Fr. Lawrence initiated, in 2004, the renovation of San Thome and the revival of the St. Thomas tradition in Chennai. Additionally, the 2008 outbreak of anti-Christian violence in Orissa should be viewed as part of the political backdrop that shapes St. Thomas Mount's revivalist projects, as well as San Thome's continual efforts to preserve the St. Thomas tradition and raise its profile within India as a true national heritage site and as beacon of hope for all Indian Christians facing persecution and disenfranchisement. As I argue, it is no surprise that the timing of these two respective St. Thomas revivals coincides with two highly publicized outbreaks of anti-Christian violence in India, making it clear that Church administrators like Fr. Lawrence were able to grasp and foresee the political situation and prepare accordingly. Thus, the rise of Hindu nationalism and the proliferation of Hindutva ideology into India's modern-day political landscape have provided the Church in Chennai a profound opportunity and context from which to revive the worship and legacy of St. Thomas in India. In short, when modern-day Indian Christians face a reality where they could be called upon to make the ultimate sacrifice for their identity and faith, the legacy of St. Thomas as founder of the Indian Christian faith and as a martyr, can easily become an inspiring force for perseverance and steadfastness against any doubts. Furthermore, it is possible that many of St. Thomas's attributes, such as those discussed in the previous chapter, for example his courage to travel to India and his valiant nature in the face of death, are able to not only create a visage of an awe-inspiring holy man, but also provide the Indian Catholic community with a personification of tried-and-true Christian masculinity that can contend with Hindutva's controversial notions of Hindu masculinity.

The following section will further explore the specific criticisms leveled at the three St. Thomas sites in Chennai by Hindutva advocates Ishwar Sharan and Sita Ram Goel in order to extrapolate how these specific criticisms underscore the broader anti-Christian rhetoric prevalent in contemporary Hindutva thought and Hindu nationalist politics. This section will also discuss the various revivalist strategies adopted by Church administrators in Chennai as a way to respond, evade, and challenge the rhetoric and criticism of the Hindu right during this last decade of local Catholic renewal.

Sita Ram Goel and Ishwar Sharan: arguments against St. Thomas

Ishwar Sharan is a Canadian convert to Hinduism who has made a name for himself as the leading Hindu advocate against Catholic claims to the three St. Thomas sites, and has done so through a proliferation of published materials, internet articles and live speaking events.[48] The name "Ishwar Sharan" is actually a penname for Swami Devananda Saraswati, the name he is currently known under after having become a Smarta Dasanani sannyasi in 1977.[49] However, he will be referred to by his alias as Ishwar Sharan throughout this book. While the work of Sharan and others like him compile many interesting criticisms against the Church in India and the St. Thomas tradition, these works are rife with hostile rhetoric and conspiratorial accusations. Sharan's basic opinion of the St. Thomas tradition is that it is a "myth" and a "fairy tale and communal virus."[50] For Church administrators like Fr. Lawrence, who are well aware of Sharan's work, such writings can only be described as polemical.

Sharan's essay, *The Myth of Saint Thomas and the Mylapore Shiva Temple*, argues that the Catholic Church fabricated the St. Thomas legend in order to justify their ownership of the St. Thomas sites in Chennai, which he asserts were violently stolen away from local Hindus during the onset of Portuguese colonialism. He then concludes that the Portuguese were responsible for the destruction of the original Kapaleeswara Temple on which the current San Thome Cathedral now stands.[51] What is most fascinating about his book and other such rhetoric is that it, too, demonstrates the propensity for contemporary political and religious groups to manipulate the historical past in order to address present-day issues, while simultaneously claiming that the truths of today originally derived from the traditions of the reclaimed past. For instance, the Hindu right discourse that Christianity's presence in India represents the same old Western imperialism of the colonial era is mainly utilized as a blanket criticism of the fact that many modern-day Christian missionary organizations in India are funded and sponsored by foreign donors in the West. Additionally, an issue like St. Thomas having been killed by Brahmins becomes a point of contention because it is indicative of South India's long-standing history of anti-Brahman sentiment, which has typically run antithetical to Hindu nationalism's staunch Brahmanical establishment.

Furthermore, within India's modern-day political arena, the Roman Catholic Church has become a self-professed champion for social justice in India, a role that does not sit well with many Hindu nationalists, including Sharan. More specifically, the Church's strong promotion and support for Dalit social equality signifies a socio-religious criticism of India's caste system. Even the term "Dalit" is a politically charged and controversial term within the arena of modern-day Indian politics. As the anthropologist David Mosse eloquently explains, "*Dalit* [emphasis in original] is a word of Sanskrit origin meaning 'broken' or 'crushed' and stands for the identity of those inferiorized communities who are today struggling from the humiliation and oppression of untouchability, and who in significant numbers had earlier turned to Christianity in various moves to reject inferiority and build an alternative future for themselves."[52] In other words, it is a moniker of empowerment for a people who have been disenfranchised for a very long time. This controversial political position readily goes against the traditional socio-religious hegemony and organic totality that many within the Hindu right wish to preserve under the auspices of a unified Hindu nation. After all, the religious authority and social status enjoyed by the Brahmins and other high-caste groups in India is intrinsically tied to the acceptance and establishment of the caste system. As we will see, the bulk of Sharan's argument against the St. Thomas tradition is built upon the work of another influential Hindu nationalist writer, Sita Ram Goel, who Sharan describes as being "the only Indian historian working today who has a clear understanding of Christian theory and practice."[53] Likewise, the works of both Goel and Sharan are, at their core, oriented toward the advocacy of Hindutva ideology.

Within Hindu nationalism's over-arching anti-Christian political agenda, the St. Thomas tradition in Tamil Nadu and Kerala has never had the same level of exposure as the more national issues of conversion en masse and foreign missionization. However, this does not mean that the St. Thomas tradition has gone completely unnoticed by the Hindu right. Since the mid-to-late 1980s, the St. Thomas tradition has been on the radar of one of Hindu nationalism's most outspoken writers, Sita Ram Goel (b. 1921 – d. 2003). In 1981, Goel founded the publishing house "Voice of India," and through this institution has written and published a great range of Hindu nationalist literature that "aims at providing an ideological defense of Hindu society and culture."[54] Other notable names in the Voice of India family of authors include such controversial scholars as Ram Swarup, Arun Shourie, and Belgian indologist Koenraad Elst. Sebastian Kim, a respected professor of theology who has written on the topic of Christian conversion in India, notes that Goel and Voice of India are not officially associated with the Sangh Parivar or any other mainstream Hindu nationalist groups, and, in fact, the Sangh Parivar has purposefully distanced itself from Goel due to his "forthright" rhetoric.[55]

Nonetheless, many of the publications to come out of Voice of India have become highly influential resources for the Hindu right's anti-Muslim and anti-Christian campaigns.[56] Historian and theologian Michael Bergunder, who has written extensively on the subject of contemporary South Asian Christianity, states, "Goel may be considered one of the most radical, but at the same time also one of the most intellectual, of the Hindu nationalist ideologues." Bergunder goes on to describe Goel's publishing house Voice of India as, "one of the few which publishes Hindu nationalist literature in English which at the same time makes a 'scientific' claim. Although no official connections exist, the books of Voice of India – which are of outstanding typographical quality and are sold at a subsidized price – are widespread among the ranks of the leaders of the Sangh Parivar."[57] The fact that many of Voice of India's publications are in English demonstrates Goel's desire to reach a wide national and international audience, especially Hindu intelligentsia who have moved out of India. The fact that Voice of India does not maintain close ties to any political organizations seems to help in legitimizing its claim as a neutral apolitical institution dedicated to offering "scientifically" credible information "free of biased information despite their provocative topics."[58] As such, Hindu nationalist scrutiny of the St. Thomas tradition has become far more prevalent than it has ever been before due to a number of Voice of India publications.

Sita Ram Goel's initial ideological goal in establishing Voice of India was to provide credibly researched scholarship that would unequivocally debunk the Aryan Invasion theory.[59] His aim eventually progressed to anti-Muslim publications, and more ardently, anti-Christian works, especially with regard to Christian evangelization, which he considered tantamount to Western imperialism and the major cause of all of India's communal problems. His solution to this problem was to expose, in print, the imperial nature of Christianity and Islam, while simultaneously promoting Hindu culture as a means to rejuvenating Hindu self-confidence.[60] Meera Nanda, in her book about the politics of Hindu marketing and consumerism, makes direct mention of Goel and Voice of India, and is very explicit in her condemnation of his overt political agenda, which she describes as a "theology of hatred."[61]

Goel's earliest analysis of the St. Thomas tradition can be found in his book *Papacy: Its Doctrine and History*, which was written and published in order to protest Pope John Paul II's first visit to India in 1986. In this book, Goel makes his opinion on the matter of St. Thomas very clear. Among other things, Goel argues that the St. Thomas story was nothing more than a "myth" fabricated and perpetuated by the Roman Catholic Church in order to further their imperialistic agendas. He outlines five specific reasons as to why the Catholic Church would have a need to manufacture and maintain such a tradition, but goes no further in his analysis.[62] Several years later, Ishwar Sharan would continue where Goel left off and further analyze the reasons why the Catholic Church still continues to hold firmly onto the St. Thomas legend. Published by Voice of India in 1991, Sharan's book *The Myth of Saint Thomas and the Mylapore Shiva Temple* is loosely organized around Goel's five points of contention against the St. Thomas tradition, which Sharan further refines and expands.[63]

For the sake of brevity, I have compiled Goel and Sharan's arguments against St. Thomas into four basic ideas, which will serve to structure and organize the following section of this chapter. According to Goel and Sharan, the St Thomas tradition: (1) provides Catholic justification for anti-Brahmin and anti-Hindu sentiment because of St. Thomas's alleged martyrdom at the hands of Brahmins, which in turn, provides the Church with a sympathetic martyr figure; (2) allows Christianity to claim an ancient and indigenous Indian heritage as opposed to one that came by way of Western colonialism and imperialism, and additionally, legitimizes Syrian Christian caste identity; (3) provides Christian missionaries, past and present, with an archetypal story of persecution that they can use to justify and cover up their own history of persecution against Hindus, which involved the destruction of Hindu temples to make way for Christian churches; and (4) provides Christian justification for the evangelization of all India.[64]

Goel and Sharan's specific contentions with the St. Thomas tradition are clearly informed by the broader Hindu nationalist ideology of Hindutva, which is easily ascertained by reading the above four criticisms alongside Jyotirmaya Sharma's six ideals of Hindutva, as previously discussed in this chapter.[65] For instance, while Michael Bergunder considers many of the publications to come out of Voice of India well written and researched, it is hard to deny the aggressive and absolutist language utilized by Goel and Sharan in their respective works or elsewhere. As Sharma notes, the sixth ideal of Hindutva is the adoption and utilization of uncompromising rhetoric as a decisive tool against the enemies of Hinduism.[66]

In a later work by Goel, *History of Hindu-Christian Encounters (AD 304–1996)*, he reiterates the points he made about St. Thomas from his previous work. Towards the beginning of this particular chapter he writes:

> No other Christian denomination ... comes anywhere near the Roman Catholic Church when it concerns committing of blatant forgeries and foisting of pious frauds .... The Roman Catholic Church in India has remained true to the tradition. The literature it has produced during the last five centuries is full of lies of the filthiest sort, not only about Hindu religion and culture but also about its own "religion" and role. And this garbage heap is topped by the hoax about the so-called St. Thomas.[67]

As we can see, Goel's basic opinion of the Catholic Church is that it is an establishment built and based on lies and religious machinations, and that of all the Christian denominations in India it is the most viable threat to Hindu culture. His blanket description of its vast output of literature is a "garbage heap" of "forgeries" and "frauds," and that the St. Thomas "hoax" stands at the top of this mess. Additionally, the following chapter of his book is unabashedly titled, "Plea for Rejecting Jesus as Junk."[68]

Sharan's own use of language, especially in *The Myth of Saint Thomas* is far less confrontational than what can be found in Goel's books, and is, in fact, quite eloquent at times. However, Sharan seems to be less formal in his use of language when it comes to different mediums. For instance, in a candid interview that was published online, Ishwar Sharan was very forthcoming with his opinion regarding the future of Christianity and Islam in India. He states:

> The clash of civilizations will continue, indeed, will become more pronounced, unless Christianity and Islam give up their religious bigotry and world-conquering ambitions. This is very unlikely as bigotry and religious imperialism are inherent within their belief systems. These systems have to be reformed, but cannot be reformed because their adherents believe that the religions are divinely ordained .... But it has not happened in the Islamic and Marxist worlds of Asia and will not happen without a fight.[69]

Sharan's above statement and use of language is very revealing. He makes it clear that he believes both Christianity and Islam to be inherently flawed religions. In his opinion, they are both bigoted and megalomaniacal in their agendas, and both in need of serious reform. However, he does not believe that reform is possible due to their propensity towards "religious imperialism," which is certainly meant as an allusion to the Mogul and European colonization of India. Perhaps, what is most alarming, is Sharan's assertion that as things are today in Asia, any serious attempt at dealing with

Christianity or Islam will require "a fight," which certainly implies the need for defensive measures on the part of Hinduism.

To be fair, the use of such strong rhetoric can be understood as a viable response since its impetus could have stemmed from a sincere belief that the Roman Catholic Church or any foreign power was implementing dubious and conspiratorial tactics against Hindu culture and identity. Regardless, from the Christian perspective, such language, no matter the justification, comes across as polemical. More to the point, Sharan and Goel's use of aggressive language is but a smaller indicator of their implicit advocacy of Hindutva and Hindu nationalist agendas. The following subsections will continue the above analysis of Sharan and Goel's writings as they pertain to particular themes in the Church's ongoing endeavors to promote St. Thomas in Chennai and elsewhere.

Sharan and Goel's contestation of St. Thomas's martyrdom as anti-Brahmanical

For the Church in Chennai, the idea that St. Thomas died a martyr's death is a central focus and theme of the Apostle's modern-day Indian legacy; it stands as the ultimate example of the kinds of sacrifices Indian Christians may be called upon to make in India today. While Sharan and Goel's response to this issue is to argue it was all made up, their real concern focuses on how the modern-day Church uses this tale in order to advance their missionary agendas. Specifically, many Hindu nationalists view the Church's newfound role as a champion for Dalit rights as an attack on the Hindu caste system, and as evidence of the Church's implicit anti-Brahmanism. That St. Thomas was killed at the hands, or at the behest, of Brahmins (the uppermost caste) only accentuates the point. As Goel writes:

> [T]he Catholic Church can malign the Brahmins more confidently. Brahmins have been the main target of its attack from the very beginning. Now it can be shown that the Brahmins have always been a vicious brood, so much so that they would not stop from murdering a holy man who was only telling God's own truth to tormented people. At the same time, the religion of the Brahmins can be held responsible for their depravity.[70]

Goel's confrontational statement indicates that the issue of St. Thomas's martyrdom is a central focus of his grievances pertaining to the Church's continued promotion of the St. Thomas story. More importantly, this statement reveals Goel's own investment in the Hindu nationalist cause, especially as it pertains to the primacy of Brahmin status and the role of caste distinctions within Hindu culture and religion.

One goal of many Hindu nationalists who subscribe to the ideology of Hindutva is to codify the Hindu religion into a single universal religious system based mainly on Brahmanical upper-caste traditions, and therefore do away with any low-caste religious deviations from this ideal.[71] Unsurprisingly, many Hindu nationalist thinkers, such as Vinayak Savarkar, were Brahmins, and the RSS and various other groups within the Sangh Parivar have had a long-standing tradition of upper-caste leadership and support.[72] As such, the Church's more recent progressions towards an official stand on Dalit rights and equality, as well as the development of a Dalit theology are perceived as challenges to the religious identity and authority of many high-level members of the Sangh Parivar, both political and spiritual.[73]

For the Church in Chennai, the political appeal for Dalit equality goes hand in hand with the recent set of revivals that have taken place at San Thome and St. Thomas Mount. Clearly, the continued pursuit of Dalit rights and the support of Dalit theology in Chennai are indicative of a revivalist strategy that hopes to connect the memory of St. Thomas as an egalitarian leader with the Church's current fight for social justice. After all, Dalits make up the largest portion of all Indian Christians, and as Fr. Lawrence noted to me, the Archdiocese of Madras-Mylapore is considered a primarily Dalit community by the Conference of Catholic Bishops of India.[74]

The then Archbishop of Madras-Mylapore, Rev. A. M. Chinnappa (2005–2012 ret.), is a very vocal advocate of Dalit rights. He has hosted seminars on Dalit liberation, sponsored books on the topic, and very recently inaugurated the release of the Dalit Bible Commentaries.[75] He is quoted in an Indian newspaper article as saying:

> Tamil Nadu is the State where casteism is most prevalent in India .... The attempt of the Dalit Bible Commentaries ... is to lead the people from darkness that casteism symbolises, into light ... the Dalits constitute the root of theology, and therefore, the task of liberation of Dalits should be taken up after integrating the different theologies. Any attempt at Dalit liberation should not only involve the oppressed people but also the oppressors, to have a holistic approach towards the goal of Dalit liberation.[76]

In 2010, the Archbishop was even arrested and briefly detained by police for participating in a march for Dalit Christian rights in Chennai.[77] In a sense, the Archbishop's continued political presence serves to maintain and raise the profile of the Church in Chennai, the Archdiocese, and his home cathedral, which is the site of St. Thomas's tomb.

High-profile condemnations of caste, like the ones made by Archbishop Chinnappa, have created cause for concern for Hindu right advocates like Sharan and Goel, who view stances like the Archbishop's as an attack on traditional Hindu culture. Undoubtedly, many in the Hindu right seem to view the Church's condemnation of the caste system as also being a condemnation of Brahmin religious and political authority. However, the roots of contemporary anti-Brahmanism, especially in South India, go far deeper than the Catholic Church's political and religious push for Dalit equality.

In fact, anti-Brahmin sentiment has been a staple of South Indian socio-religious and political discourses for a very long time. Although this particular discourse was rejuvenated during the colonial era by Catholic and Protestant missionaries, as well as Western scholars or Orientalists, and further solidified with the Dravidian or pro-Tamil movements of the twentieth century, its origins certainly pre-date the era of Western colonialism.[78]

It is easy to see how culturally ingrained discourses, such as South Indian anti-Brahmin sentiment, could be superimposed upon the story of St. Thomas, especially when the issue is so inexorably linked to contemporary political discourses such as Dalit rights. This was one of the many reasons why Ishwar Sharan was compelled to write his book on the St. Thomas tradition, which he saw as a manipulative tool used by the Church in order to add credence to their political views by asserting an ancient precedence. Oddly enough, it was not a Church publication that incited Sharan's response, but an English-language newspaper article published by *Indian Express* in late 1989. Other than the article's presentation of the St. Thomas story as near fact, Sharan took great offence to one particular paragraph.[79] The article's author, C. A. Simon, states:

> St. Thomas spent the last part of his life in Madras preaching the Gospel. A large number of people listened and embraced the way of life preached by him. The oppressed and downtrodden followed him and claimed equal status in society as it was denied them by the prevailing social norms. He condemned untouchability and attempted to restore equal status for women.[80]

The article does not link Brahmins to St. Thomas's death or even mentions them at all, but the above passage assigns an anti-caste position to St. Thomas, which can be viewed as a projection onto the St. Thomas story of the Church's contemporary stand on the issue at hand.[81]

As both Sharan and Goel related in their respective books, an interesting drama would unfold between Sharan and the editor of the *Indian Express* as Sharan attempted to lodge an immediate complaint and protest against the accuracy of C. A. Simon's article.[82] What followed would include a succession of correspondence between the two parties, as well as between Sharan and Simon, but in the end failed to adequately address or rectify Sharan's grievances. As we know, Sharan decided to write his own book, which was then quickly published by Goel's Voice of India.[83] In *The Myth of Saint Thomas*, Sharan addresses Simon's article quite thoroughly, and makes special mention of Simon's assertion that St. Thomas condemned untouchability. Sharan writes:

> Yet whatever efforts Hindu publishers have put into promoting the St. Thomas myth in Madras, it still belongs very much to the Roman

Catholic Church and is subject to her various conceits. When she wants to present herself as being socially conscious – which she is not and has never been – then St. Thomas too must be presented as having had a social conscience.[84]

Sharan's basic response is that the Church is willing and able to tailor the St. Thomas story in order to fit its own socio-political agendas, which it has been doing since the colonial era. Additionally, in the above quotation, Sharan also implicates India's secular media as being complicit in the perpetuation of the St. Thomas legend. Goel does this as well in his *History of Hindu Christian Encounters*. In a chapter entitled "Exploding a Mischievous Myth," Goel applauds Sharan's efforts at debunking the St. Thomas "myth," and ultimately concludes that this whole affair concerning Simon's controversial article proves that, "the major print media in India [are] owned by Hindu moneybags, they have handed it over to Hindu-baiters of all sorts," and that, "there is no law in the country which can deal with intellectual crimes committed by Christian scribes."[85] For Goel and Sharan the enemies of Hinduism are all around them, conducting activities that should be made illegal by the Indian government. This conspiratorial and unflinching attitude would undoubtedly extend to include Catholic renewal in India, especially at those sites associated with the death and burial of St. Thomas.

The Church in Chennai's handling of St. Thomas's martyrdom and responses to accusations of anti-Brahmanism

In Chapter 2 I noted that recent Church publications in Chennai on the historicity of St. Thomas did not focus heavily on what St. Thomas preached and practiced regarding Indian society and politics, or on details of St. Thomas's murder. However, it is with the strategic use of public forums, like masses and festivals, that priests and other clergy are able to interpret and glean some semblance of St. Thomas's teachings from local tradition and available historical narratives in order to put forward a St. Thomas that stands as a paramount role model, as missionary and martyr, for today's Indian Christians. The particulars of St. Thomas's death are ultimately not as significant for the Church as the simple fact that St. Thomas died a martyr on Indian soil. For instance, while S. J. Anthonysamy's *A Saga of Faith* does mention St. Thomas's death at the hand of Brahmins, it only does so as a brief summary of Malabar oral tradition, in which he also mentions the number of Brahmins who were converted by the Apostle.[86] Anthonysamy addresses many accounts of the St. Thomas narrative, but never with the intent to discern who killed St. Thomas. Rather, he demonstrates that the record of St. Thomas's martyrdom can be traced to early Christian sources.[87]

Today, Church administrators have become mindful of the issue surrounding who killed St. Thomas and the socio-political complications that could arise from such assertions, especially at high-profile shrines such as San Thome and St. Thomas Mount. Church administrators there have taken steps to gloss over those narratives that explicitly claim Brahmins as the Apostle's murderer. For instance, during the renovation of San Thome, Fr. Lawrence had the foresight to take extra care in the construction of a diorama depicting the last moments of St. Thomas's life, which he had placed in the foyer of the underground tomb chapel (Figure 3.1). The diorama depicts St. Thomas kneeling in prayer before the Bleeding Cross. Sneaking up behind the Apostle, his Indian assailant is positioned with his spear raised high ready to take the Saint's life.

I inquired as to whether the statue of St. Thomas's attacker was meant to specifically portray anyone. Fr. Lawrence commented, "No, no, nothing. That statue if you see, it is ... really, we don't show anything of that sort, neither a Brahman, nor a Hindu, nor a Muslim, nothing of the sort. So, that was the kind of dress they were using those days. Though, they say, only Hindu, but we don't want to say that. How do we know what happened in 72 AD?"[88] This same diorama was recently installed in the threshold of Our Lady of Expectation church on St. Thomas Mount, a more or less exact

Figure 3.1 Diorama of St. Thomas's last moments, which is located in the foyer of St. Thomas's underground tomb chapel at San Thome.
Photo: T. C. Nagy.

Figure 3.2 Similar diorama of St. Thomas's last moments more recently installed in the threshold of the Our Lady of Expectation church at St. Thomas Mount.

Photo: T. C. Nagy.

replica of Fr. Lawrence's project that demonstrates this same mindfulness (Figure 3.2). Overall, for such high-profile shrines as San Thome and St. Thomas Mount, St. Thomas's martyrdom on Indian soil is a far more significant detail than who ended his life.

Two years after the Cathedral's renovation, issues concerning the implicit anti-Brahmanism of the Catholic Church and its use of the St. Thomas story were implicated in the only two real instances of vandalism and violence against the St. Thomas sites in recent memory. Both instances took place at St. Thomas Mount and were supposedly perpetrated by men claiming to be a part of a Hindu nationalist organization that was contesting the religious ownership of the Mount, although this was never verified by the media.[89]

In the first instance, several statues that were situated around a larger statue of St. Thomas were knocked down and destroyed. The claim made by the perpetrators was that these statues represented Brahmins being converted by St. Thomas. According to Fr. Lawrence, these statues were never intended to depict Brahmins, but just generic Indian disciples.[90]

At the time, these statues were situated in a small park located near the entrance to the hilltop shrine. After this incident, Church administrators at St. Thomas Mount decided to play it safe and, after cleaning up the rubble, barred public access to the park. During the time of my first field trip to Chennai in 2009, the park was seemingly abandoned and unmaintained. Its entrance gate was locked, and while one could still see the statue of St. Thomas, the entire area around him was overgrown with vegetation (Figure 3.3). However, by December 2010, the site was refurbished, but instead of being restored to its original look, it was transformed into an outdoor auditorium that could be

Figure 3.3 The statue of St. Thomas preaching, but no longer with an audience.
Photo: T. C. Nagy.

used for special events. Obviously, the Mount's administrators decided that is was best to leave this site alone until something less controversial and more practical could be put in its place. In a sense, the Church had to cut its losses regarding this incident, given the volatile nature of the situation.

Sadly, the second incident was far more violent. On November 26, 2006, a "fanatic" came to the mount to protest. An altercation ensued where he proceeded to attack and kill the manager of the St. Thomas Mount Hill Shrine, a Christian man by the name of Mr. Jacob. The murderer was arrested and supposedly imprisoned.[91] Nobody I spoke with was able to provide any more information, only that the incident was never publicized. However, sometime after Mr. Jacob's death, a bell tower memorial was erected on St. Thomas Mount. Inside the central base of the tower is a plaque bearing an image of the deceased and the following inscription:

> This historical monument commemorates with gratitude the heroic martyrdom of Mr. Jacob the Manager of this Shrine. He was killed by a fanatic while defending the Christian ownership of this holy hill on the 26th November 2006 the Solemnity of Christ the King shedding blood on this very spot for his Lord and God after the model of St. Thomas, the Apostle Martyr of this Shrine (Figure 3.4).

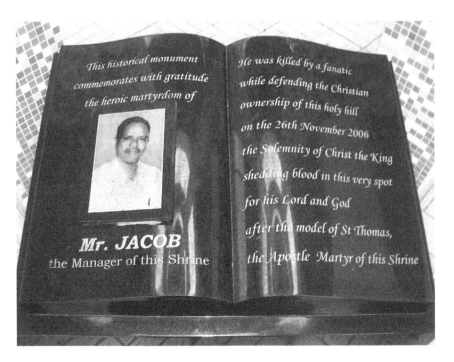

Figure 3.4 Memorial plaque to Mr. Jacob at St. Thomas Mount.
Photo: T. C. Nagy.

As it stands, this incident and subsequent memorial serves to reinforce St. Thomas Mount's significance as the site of the Apostle's martyrdom and how Indian Christians today may be called upon to follow in St. Thomas's footsteps. But in a broader sense, this memorial also attests to Christian claims of indigeneity, which are validated by the belief that St. Thomas shed his blood on Indian soil, a "heroic" legacy that lives on in the sacrifices made by today's Indian Christians, such as Mr. Jacob.

Regardless of certain Hindu right criticisms of the St. Thomas tradition, the Church in Chennai is unlikely to relinquish the belief that St. Thomas was martyred on St. Thomas Mount and buried on Mylapore beach. Even though the Church is making an effort to play down the idea of a Brahmin murderer, Hindu nationalists like Goel and Sharan still take offence at the martyrdom story in general, since it still implies a Hindu killer. More importantly, they object to the notion that St. Thomas's martyrdom somehow allows Indian Christians to claim an indigenous pre-colonial heritage. Goel is especially distrustful of this idea, since he is convinced that Christianity was founded in India during the colonial era. In his list of concerns regarding the Church's manipulation of the St. Thomas legend he returns to the subject of Christianity's fabricated indigeneity several times. He writes:

> If it can be established that Christianity is as ancient in India as the prevailing forms of Hinduism, no one can nail it as an imported creed brought in by Western imperialism .... The commencement of the Church can be disentangled from the advent of the Portuguese by dating the Church to a distant past. The Church was here long before the Portuguese arrived. It was a mere coincidence that the Portuguese also called themselves Catholics. Guilt by association is groundless. Lastly, it is quite within the ken of Catholic theology to claim that a land which has been honoured by the visit of an apostle has become the patrimony of the Catholic Church. India might have been a Hindu homeland from times immemorial. But since that auspicious moment when St. Thomas stepped on her soil, the Hindu claim stands cancelled. The country has belonged to the Catholic Church from the first century onwards, no matter how long the Church takes to conquer it completely for Christ.[92]

Once again, Goel's objections stem from his Hindu nationalist concerns. He asserts that the Church's attempts to claim indigeneity are really designed to hide or cover up its close connection to Portuguese and European colonialism. Goel argues that the modern-day Church is still engaged in colonial and imperialistic endeavors, and that St. Thomas and the claim to indigeneity serves to justify the Church's missionary agendas, as well as its goals to subvert Hindu culture and religion. The Church in Chennai clearly is attempting to utilize St. Thomas's legacy as a way to claim an indigenous faith, which is highlighted by Mr. Jacob's memorial and the link it creates between St. Thomas's spilled blood and the soil of India. Nevertheless, it is difficult to find evidence for Goel's conspiratorial assertions.

Of course, the Church is well aware of the many criticisms levelled by Hindu nationalists, and clearly recognizes Hindutva and its ideologues as the primary source for this kind of anti-Christian rhetoric in India. A recent issue of the Archdiocese of Madras-Mylapore's weekly magazine *The New Leader* featured an article written by Archbishop of Delhi Vincent M. Concessao entitled, "In the Face of Communal Violence what can the Church do?" In this article, Archbishop Concessao carefully argues that the recent outbreak of anti-Christian violence is due to Hindutva and its "evil designs," and that Christians must stand united against it. He states:

> By the same token we need to expose Hindutva and the designs of the Sangh Parivar. Though we need to be worried about what has happened, what must concern us really is the larger plan contained in Hindutva ideology and its strategy .... It is very important that we challenge Hindutva – not as Christians but as citizens of India – a secular democracy.[93]

The most interesting facets of the Archbishop's words is that he emphasizes Indian identity over Christian identity and that in order for Indian Christians to properly combat the ideology of Hindutva they should, first and foremost, stand as citizens of India and not only as Christians. In that sense, the Archbishop is also emphasizing Indian indigeneity as an integral part of modern-day Indian Christian identity. This same line of thinking is also apparent in the recent St. Thomas revivals in Chennai. As the progenitor of Christianity in India, St. Thomas is the central figure in any Christian claim for indigeneity; any revival done in his name is fundamentally a reinforcement of this claim.

Fr. Lawrence was well aware of Ishwar Sharan and his criticisms. During one of our interviews, he even broached the subject of Sharan's book before I had a chance to inquire about it. Fr. Lawrence has implied that for him and other Church administrators in Chennai, the active preservation of St. Thomas's missionary legacy represents a strategic response to Hindutva criticisms of Indian Christianity's imperial origins. At the same time, by generating more positive exposure for the St. Thomas sites, Church administrators hope to further solidify the idea of an ancient Christian origin in the hearts and minds of Christians locally and abroad. It is probably no coincidence that Fr. Lawrence named San Thome's quarterly magazine *Voice of St. Thomas*, which is strikingly similar to Sita Ram Goel's publishing house "Voice of India." Goel's use of naming convention for his publishing house is certainly meant to elicit the notion that his socio-religious and political views, as well as the views presented in his many publications, are indicative of what most Indians believe. Thus, his publications claim to act as the true "voice of India," which speaks on behalf of the majority of Indians. In opposition to Goel's assumption is Fr. Lawrence's use of St. Thomas's "voice" as a device that offers an alternative voice or perspective to the one offered by Goel or Sharan. Seeing as Fr. Lawrence promoted St. Thomas as the founder of Christianity in India, it makes sense that St. Thomas would represent the voice of Indian Christianity, a voice that does not seem to be a part of Goel's India, but that certainly has something left to say.

As discussed in the previous chapter, many of the recent publications to come out of San Thome and St. Thomas Mount have served to create a valid historical narrative of the St. Thomas tradition, establishing the physical link between St. Thomas, his shrines in Chennai, and the soil of India. This blood and soil narrative is more prevalent at St. Thomas Mount than anywhere else, because it is the purported site where St. Thomas died and literally bled on Indian soil. In the inaugural issue of St. Thomas Mount's monthly magazine *The Voice from the Hill*, the Hill Shrine's rector writes:

> St. Thomas proclaimed the truth from this hill-top, he embraced all the sufferings and pain with great joy and even shed his blood for the love of his Master on this Mount and it can be rightly called "the Calvary of India". Since his blood was shed on this mount, it can be called the "Mountain of Blood", overflowing with God's Mercy.[94]

When coupled with the tradition of the Bleeding Cross, the Mount's most holy relic, St. Thomas's link to the Indian soil becomes a physical and spiritual reality that also binds the Christian community to the Indian land.

The Church and colonialism: temple destruction in Mylapore

Paramount in the current debate surrounding the place of Christianity in modern-day India is the issue of its past ties to European colonialism. During the Portuguese era the Catholic Church made extensive use of the Jesuit Order and Inquisition; entities which were fueled by the zeal of the Counter-Reformation. During the height of British rule was the seemingly unrestricted inundation by Protestant missionaries into India. Signs of Chennai's British heritage and Mylapore's Portuguese occupation are still prevalent to this day. Many of the old British administration buildings still stand, as well as statues to various British monarchs. Mylapore and the surrounding areas are home to a number of historic Portuguese churches.

From Sharan's perspective, San Thome and other such sites represent living monuments to the legacy of British and Portuguese colonialism. For Sharan, the existence of such monuments is problematic because they serve to memorialize colonialism's long-standing legacy in India. Furthermore, it is not only the physical structures that have endured, but also traditions such as the legend of St. Thomas. Sharan explains:

> The Portuguese had come to India to spread their religion and to trade .... In the process they acquired the raw materials for a new cult,

the St. Thomas legend, which would prove to be their most enduring 'gift' to Mylapore – along with a large number of churches that have been built on temple sites around the southern coast. The cult would also give imported Christianity the veneer of being an indigenous Indian religion, a political gift to the Catholic Church more valuable than all the pearls and pepper that went to Lisbon.[95]

Sharan's basic argument is that the St. Thomas tradition was ultimately a Portuguese fabrication and that it is still being politically utilized by the Church today. According to Sharan, the Church's claim for an indigenous Indian Christianity is a prime example of the Church's political machinations, which Sharan equates with modern-day colonialism.

For Hindu right advocates like Goel and Sharan, Catholicism's colonial-era heritage is not so very far removed from its contemporary missionary endeavors, which serve as an unwelcome reminder of India's long history of subjugation by foreign powers. Sharan writes, "Christianity, and especially Roman Christianity, has very little to do with religious faith. It is and has always been a system of imperialist politics and financial racketeering practiced under the guise of religion."[96] To that extent, modern-day Catholicism is now synonymous with the imperialistic and colonial regimes of the past. Again, Sharan explicitly states, "The Indian church today is not so much different from the original 17th century Portuguese church that created it. It is very wealthy and corrupt and politically ambitious. But it has learned the propaganda value of social service and is making a great effort to disassociate itself from its colonial origins. This involves a lot of deceit, of course, and a massive cover-up of past evil deeds."[97] Or as Goel succinctly states, "Christianity has never been a religion; it has always been a predatory imperialism par excellence."[98] The real issue at hand is not Christianity's presence in India, but how Christianity's proselytizing efforts ultimately contradict and challenge key Hindutva goals.

Returning to Jyotirmaya Sharma's ideals of Hindutva, we see that the issue of the Church's colonial past is something that many Hindu nationalists can never overlook. For them, the presence of foreign religious ideologies and institutions serve as a continual reminder of what India, Hinduism, and the Hindu people have lost. In terms of religious and political heritage, they posit the loss of a Hindu golden age, something that cannot be reclaimed until all foreign elements have been driven out. Socially, and possibly psychologically, they lament the loss of Hinduism's masculinity and warrior pride, things lost due to the onset of foreign colonialism and missionization. It is not surprising that many Hindu nationalists maintain a line of rhetoric that insinuates far-reaching conspiracies from disruptive elements at home and abroad.[99]

One prevalent line of Hindu nationalist rhetoric posits the idea of a Christian conspiracy that means to destroy Hindu culture through the proselytization and conversion of its people. What makes it worse is the view that such ventures are backed and funded by foreign entities with vast monetary resources, and that the Indian government and media are complicit. Sharan writes, "The myth of St. Thomas in Malabar and Mylapore, which we have reviewed in this essay, is one such fairy tale and communal virus. That it is promoted by the Roman Catholic Church through her various institutions and media is one thing, that it is cultivated by the government of India and willfully spread among the people by responsible Hindu citizens and their prestigious business houses is quite another."[100] For Sharan, the St. Thomas tradition in Chennai truly exemplifies the lengths to which the Catholic Church will go in order to sabotage Hindu culture for their own agendas, and is a perfect case study for modern-day imperialism in action.

According to Sharan, the St. Thomas myth begins with the Portuguese, whom he describes as "pious forgers and pirates," and any pre-colonial evidence that favors St. Thomas he also considers unreliable.[101] The majority of Sharan's book is a critical analysis and evaluation of many of the same primary sources utilized by Church historians like Medleycott and Anthonysamy. For example, Sharan writes, "The Portuguese preferred the Pagan-priest-with-a-lance story found in *De Miraculis Thomae*. They added Marco Polo's seaside tomb to it, and elements from Syrian Christian traditions they had gathered in Malabar, and concocted a legend, largely European in character, that they identified with various Hindu sites in Malabar and Mylapore."[102] Sharan's mistrust of these common sources provide him with the evidence needed to disprove St. Thomas, while Church scholars like Anthonysamy can gleam positive evidence from Portuguese and older sources in favor of the historical St. Thomas.

Anthonysamy is aware of Sharan's writings and thus notes in his own book, "There have been some authors who tried to dismiss the entire truth of the tomb at Mylapore as a Portuguese fraud, possibly in their hatred for their overzealous colonizing spirit. Among them there could have certainly been some well-meaning extremists. But the Portuguese did not definitely invent the tomb, rather they discovered it with great enthusiasm and set about to make it popular thanks to their religious zeal."[103] It is impossible to deny that the Portuguese were responsible for various acts of religious violence and desecration, especially in Goa. However, there is evidence, or lack thereof, to suggest that Mylapore may have been an exception.

Sharan's personal investment in this debate is most blatant with regard to the issue of the Portuguese's supposedly violent occupation of Mylapore. His major claim is that San Thome was built over the site of the original Kapaleeswara temple dedicated to Lord Shiva. He also claims that St. Thomas Mount was once the site of a temple to Lord Vishnu, and that Little Mount was initially a temple dedicated to the god Murugan.[104] As mentioned before, Mr. Jacob's murder at St. Thomas Mount was speculated as having been instigated by a protest against Catholic ownership of the site.

The assertion that San Thome was built over the demolished Kapaleeswara is not taken lightly by the Church in Chennai, especially since it places doubt on the authenticity of St. Thomas's tomb. Joanne Waghorne, whose own research focuses on Hindu temple building in Chennai, notes the contentious nature of this issue, which she describes as "a touchy subject for many Roman Catholics."[105] Of course, there are several different explanations as to what actually happened to the original temple, which vary from source to source. Besides Sharan's version, most Church historians like Anthonysamy favor the explanation that the original Shiva temple was simply eroded away by the sea, which instigated the construction of the current one.[106]

Local historian Subbiah Muthiah offers a more neutral explanation, noting that the temple could have been eroded by the sea and that it was certainly gone by the time the Portuguese arrived, but he never states that the Portuguese destroyed it.[107] This same kind of neutral explanation is employed by the administrators of the Kapaleeswara temple. Upon entering the temple structure, to the visitor's immediate left, is a large plaque that offers a brief historical survey of the temple in both English and Tamil. It states, "Mylapore fell into the hands of the Portuguese in 1566, when the temple suffered demolition. The present temple was rebuilt about 300 years ago. There are some fragmentary inscriptions from the old temple, still found in the present shrine and in St. Thomas Cathedral." Interestingly, Sharan has written the temple in protest of the plaque's seemingly vague explanation, as well as the fact that it also mentions St. Thomas as having possibly visited Mylapore.[108]

Waghorne suggests the most probable explanation for the demise of the original temple. She writes, "In an interview, the chairman of the board of trustees suggested that the Portuguese took permission to tear down the temple and extended compensation for its reconstruction .... The Kapaleeswara stands as a very early case of new urban dwellers renovating, in this case recreating, older temples."[109] Speaking with Fr. Lawrence on the matter, he made it clear that there is no antagonism between San Thome and Kapaleeswara. He stated to me, "In fact we ... send our children and so on to that place [Kapaleeswara], they come here, and the trustees of the temple, also they are very friendly. So, we don't have any problem." Fr. Lawrence also added that, "Nobody bothers about those kinds of things. Only these one or two persons are writing about all that."[110] This comment was an obvious reference to Sharan, who, according to Fr. Lawrence seems to be one of the few people who keep returning to this debate.

Clearly, the issue of Portuguese colonialism can easily become a sensitive subject for the Church, which is why it is often sidestepped in favor of focusing on the Church's more recent contributions to Indian society, such as its schools and medical facilities. With this in mind, St. Thomas's mission in India becomes the historical and socio-religious context from which the modern-day Roman Catholic Church undertakes its renewal efforts in

India. On the other hand, this is exactly what Ishwar Sharan is accusing the Church of doing and he is generally correct. However, his treatment of this issue stems from his assertion that the St. Thomas story was a colonial-era fabrication, which speaks to the larger Hindu right concern that Christian missionization has the potential to destroy Hindu culture.

Post-colonial theory and the Hindu right

After having gone through several examples of the kind of rhetoric typically used by Hindu right advocates such as Goel and Sharan, it is increasingly apparent that much of this rhetoric utilizes the language of post-colonial theory. To be fair, the discourse of post-colonialism has been very important in the struggle for formerly subjugated communities to express and come to terms with their new identities as post-colonial peoples looking toward the uncertain future of a new or recent nationalist identity. Also, post-colonial theory has provided scholars with a workable starting point in being able to analyze, study, and give voice to formerly subjugated communities within the social sciences. However, as the influential literary theoretician Edward Said warns:

> To become aware of one's self as belonging to a subject people is the founding insight of anti-imperialist nationalism. From that insight came literatures, innumerable political parties, a host of other struggles for minority and women's rights, and, much of the time, newly independent states. Yet, as Fanon rightly observes, nationalist consciousness can very easily lead to frozen rigidity; merely to replace white officers and bureaucrats with colored equivalents, he says, is no guarantee that the nationalist functionaries will not replicate the old dispensation.[111]

What then, are post-colonial theorists supposed to do when formerly subjugated peoples start acting like their one-time oppressors?

Arun Mukherjee, a scholar of post-colonial literature, goes further by implying that post-colonial theory can be used as a nationalist discourse that can be implemented as a justification for violence against minority religions within a post-colonial context. Mukherjee states:

> One of these pressing concerns is the rising tide of Hindu fundamentalism in India. Since December 1992, thousands of people have paid a heavy price for their religious identity. The Hindu fundamentalists spout a rhetoric that has some uncanny resemblances to the language of postcolonial theory. They speak about Muslim "colonizers" that subjugated India and "colonized" the Hindus. They speak about the need for the Hindu "colonized" to regain their identity. So, I ask, how are the postcolonial theorists going to distinguish between their colonizer and the colonized that the Indian fundamentalists are talking about?[112]

She continues, "If I were to use the language of postcolonial theory, I would describe the efforts of VHP/ BJP intelligentsia as 'resisting' the discourses of the so-called Muslim colonizers of India. Their determination to demolish Muslim mosques would amount to getting rid of the symbols of colonial domination."[113] Doniger also returns to this issue in her validation of post-post-colonialism when she writes, "As a more political and less scholarly movement, this resistance [postcolonialism] has taken on a new face in our day, in the form of violence directed by Hindus (largely incited by right-wing Hindu fundamentalists) against Indian Christians, violence that has been luridly documented in the Western press. Who, now, are the victims and who the resistors?"[114] With regard to the above criticisms, perhaps it is time to move beyond post-colonialism, or at least reconsider post-colonialism's usefulness and identify its inadequacies when applied to the socio-religious and political matters of globally-minded communities such as the Indian Christians.

Chapter summary

Ishwar Sharan's book was written in the mid 1990s, but he has certainly kept tabs on the Church in Chennai's recent revival of the St. Thomas tradition. Within the last decade he has upgraded his website and has updated it more frequently than ever. No doubt, the immediate successes of San Thome and St. Thomas Mount's renovations were the impetus for the release of his book's third edition in 2010, where in the preface he adds:

> We observe that this pretended burial place of St. Thomas – an empty tomb that has been refurbished at the cost of lakhs of rupees since the publication of this book in 1991 – must now become a center of pilgrimage for archaeologists, historians and philosophers who do not have a theological axe to grind like the pilgrims of old and the priests of today, but who would know the plain truth about old Mylapore and record it for our children.[115]

Sharan's words evoke the same kind of Hindu nationalist rhetoric utilized in the wake of the Babri Mosque incident, which to this day is still an unresolved and polarizing socio-political issue in India.

It is clear by now that the specific criticisms leveled at the St. Thomas tradition in Chennai by Sharan and Goel are mainly informed by the larger political ideology and discourse of Hindutva. Due to the Catholic Church's high-profile stand against caste, and its promotion of Dalit rights, the Church is seen by many Hindutva ideologues as touting characteristically Orientalist and Tamil traditionalist ideals that have been typically anti-Brahmin in ages past. The Church's use of the St. Thomas story as a validation of both an indigenous Indian origin and pre-colonial history contradicts Savarkar's assertion that Christianity is a foreign religion not of India's soil. For many Tamil Catholics, the St. Thomas tradition depicts the historic life and death endeavors of India's most important Christian saint. On the other hand, for Hindutva advocates like Sharan and Goel, the St. Thomas legend is a colonial era fabrication that was started by the Portuguese, and is being perpetuated by the Church in India for its modern-day colonial agendas. Clearly, Catholicism's Portuguese colonial heritage is a constant reminder to many Hindu nationalists of what Hinduism has lost due to Western imperialism. Finally, the influx of missionaries, local and foreign, also casts the shadow of present-day colonialism.

The recent revivals in Chennai have dealt with these issues in kind, but ultimately it is business as usual for the Church. Fr. Lawrence made this final comment with regard to Sharan's research,

> If you ask about this issue ... none of our Catholics or priests will ... know anything. Oh, definitely, I came to know because I was there, and he [Sharan] was still sending letters to me and so on. I never thought more about it and never replied, also ... because if we begin to have correspondence and so on, it becomes serious, as we are bothered about it and read about it, and so on, well, yeah, that's it, I made that point, no?[116]

In other words, according to Fr. Lawrence, the best strategy that the Church can undertake in dealing with individuals like Sharan is to not enter into a discourse with them in the first place.

Finally, this chapter has been more focused on the socio-religious and political context of India's political landscape than on the revivalist strategies undertaken at San Thome and St. Thomas Mount. India's current political landscape is the primary context from which San Thome and St. Thomas Mount's recent revivals initiated, which in turn has had a great influence on the kinds of marketing strategies utilized by the Church in Chennai.

Thus, in the following chapter, we will be able to analyze in greater depth the 2004 renovation of San Thome, in which Fr. Lawrence utilized the actual physical refurbishment of the Cathedral and tomb chapel as a way to combine several key marketing strategies under the auspices of a fully-realized St. Thomas brand.

Notes

1 Jyotirmaya Sharma, *Hindutva: Exploring the Idea of Hindu Nationalism* (New Delhi: Viking, 2003), 7.
2 Christophe Jaffrelot, "Introduction: The Invention of an Ethnic Nationalism," in *Hindu Nationalism: A Reader*, ed. Christophe Jaffrelot (Princeton, NJ: Princeton University Press, 2007), 17.
3 Ibid, 19–20.
4 Ibid, 17–19.
5 Christophe Jaffrelot, "The RSS: A Hindu Nationalist Sect," in *The Sangh Parivar: A Reader*, ed. Christophe Jaffrelot (New Delhi: Oxford University Press, 2005), 57.

6 Sharma, *Hindutva*, 4. See also: Jaffrelot, "Introduction: The Invention of an Ethnic Nationalism," 86.
7 Jaffrelot, "Introduction: The Invention of an Ethnic Nationalism," 85.
8 Sharma, *Hindutva*, 8–12.
9 Jaffrelot, "Introduction: The Invention of an Ethnic Nationalism," 5.
10 Vinayak Damodar Savarkar, "Extract from *Hindutva: Who is a Hindu?*" in *Hindu Nationalism: A Reader*, ed. Christophe Jaffrelot (Princeton, NJ: Princeton University Press, 2007), 95.
11 Ibid, 23.
12 See: Chetan Bhatt, *Hindu Nationalism: Origins, Ideologies and Modern Myths* (Oxford and New York: Berg, 2001), 198–202.
13 Walter K. Andersen and Shridhar D. Damle, "RSS: Ideology, Organization, and Training," in *The Sangh Parivar: A Reader*, ed. Christophe Jaffrelot (New Delhi: Oxford University Press, 2005), 25.
14 Rajeev Srinivasan, *Ishwar Sharan Interview*, http://bharatabharati.wordpress.com/ishwar-sharan-interview (accessed June 22, 2011).
15 Christophe Jaffrelot, "The BJP at the Centre: A Central and Centrist Party?" in *The BJP and the Compulsions of Politics in India*, eds Thomas Blom Hansen and Christophe Jaffrelot (New Delhi: Oxford University Press, 2001), 365.
16 Bhatt, *Hindu Nationalism*, 198.
17 V. Sridhar, *Communalism: A Numbers Game*, http://www.frontlineonnet.com/fl1625/16250930.htm (Accessed March 13, 2012).
18 Christophe Jaffrelot, "Conversion and the Arithmetic of Religious Communities," *Hindu Nationalism: A Reader*, ed. Christophe Jaffrelot (Princeton, NJ: Princeton University Press, 2007), 235.
19 Jaffrelot, "The BJP at the Centre: A Central and Centrist Party?" 365.
20 Bhatt, *Hindu Nationalism*, 198.
21 Ibid, 198–200. For a more in-depth study on the Hindu right's "reconversion" campaigns see Chapter 7 of Jaffrelot's recently published compilation of past articles: Christophe Jaffrelot, *Religion, Caste and Politics in India* (New York: Columbia University Press, 2011), 144–169.
22 Laura Dudley Jenkins, "Legal Limits on Religious Conversion in India," *Law and Contemporary Problems* 71, 109 (Spring 2008): 109, and 120–121.
23 Ibid, 119.
24 S. Viswanathan, "A Decree on Animal Sacrifice," http://www.frontlineonnet.com/fl2020/stories/20031010001205000.htm (Accessed December 1, 2012).
25 Laura Dudley Jenkins, "Legal Limits on Religious Conversion in India," 109, and 119–121.
26 See: C. J. Fuller, *The Renewal of the Priesthood: Modernity and Traditionalism in a South Indian Temple* (Princeton and Oxford: Princeton University Press, 2003), 130–137. See also: C. J. Fuller, "The 'Vinayaka Chaturthi' Festival and Hindutva in Tamil Nadu," *Economic and Political Weekly* 36, 19 (May 12–18, 2001): 1614–1615.
27 M. S. S. Pandian, "Tamil-Friendly Hindutva," *Economics and Political Weekly* 35, 21/22 (May 27–June 2, 2000), 1805–1806.
28 Fuller, *The Renewal of the Priesthood*, 142.
29 Fuller, "The 'Vinayaka Chaturthi' Festival and Hindutva in Tamil Nadu," 1615.
30 Bhatt, *Hindu Nationalism*, 198–199.
31 Ibid, 199.
32 Jaffrelot, "The BJP at the Centre: A Central and Centrist Party?" 366.
33 Ibid, 366.
34 Bhatt, *Hindu Nationalism*, 202.

35 Dan Isaacs, "What is Behind Hindu-Christian Violence," http://news.bbc.co.uk/2/hi/south_asia/7214053.stm (Accessed March 18, 2012). See also: BBC News, "India Christians Shelter in Camps," http://news.bbc.co.uk/2/hi/7591217.stm (Accessed March 18, 2012). See also: One News Now, "India Braces for More Violence against Christians," http://www.onenewsnow.com/Persecution/Default.aspx?id=312620 (Accessed March 18, 2012). See also: BBC News, "Orissa Mob Attacks Police Station," http://news.bbc.co.uk/2/hi/south_asia/7618031.stm (Accessed March 18, 2012). See also: Sandeep Sahu, "Riots Grip India's Orissa Region," http://news.bbc.co.uk/2/hi/south_asia/7582887.stm (Accessed March 18, 2012). See also: John Malhotra, "Indian Christians seek protection from Hindu nationalist government," http://www.christiantoday.com/article/indian.christians.seek.protection.from.hindu.nationalist.government/25760.htm (Accessed March 18, 2012).
36 P. V. Thomas, "Church Watches Anxiously as General Election Begins," http://www.ucanews.com/story-archive/?post_name=/2009/04/16/church-watches-anxiously-as-general-election-begins&post_id=713 (Accessed March 23, 2012).
37 Loreto A. Xavier, "Rally-cum-Demonstration: To Condemn Orissa Violence," *Voice of St. Thomas* 1, 11 (January–March 2009): 21. See also: Julio Ribeiro, "The Testimony of One Christian: Religion was in the Private Domain. No One made Me Feel 'Different.' Until Now," *Voice of St. Thomas* 1, 12 (April–June 2009): 19. *VoST* also published an additional article on the violence in Orissa in 2011, see: Mukti Clarence, "My Experience of the First 48 hours of Kandhamal Violence," *Voice of St. Thomas* 2, 7 (January–March 2011): 6–8.
38 Xavier, "Rally-cum-Demonstration: To Condemn Orissa Violence," 21.
39 Ibid.
40 Ribeiro, "The Testimony of One Christian," 19.
41 Ibid.
42 Ibid.
43 Interview with Mr. Mark, Chennai, July 23, 2009.
44 Interview with Brother Joe, Chennai, June 11, 2009.
45 Interview with Sr. Merrill, Chennai, June 13, 2009.
46 *Frontline: India's National Magazine* 26, 11 (May 23–June 5, 2009): cover page.
47 Interview with Mr. Mark, Chennai, July 23, 2009.
48 Not too long ago, Ishwar Sharan's main website was www.hamsa.org, but recently it has been updated and/or replaced with a more professional looking site: ActaIndica: The St. Thomas in India Swindle, "Articles on the Dubious Saint Thomas in India Legend by Noted Historians, Researchers, and Journalists," http://apostlethomasindia.wordpress.com (accessed June 22, 2011). As previously cited, for an interview with Ishwar Sharan see: Srinivasan, *Ishwar Sharan Interview*.
49 Srinivasan, *Ishwar Sharan Interview*. See also: The Ishwar Sharan Archive, "About Us," http://ishwarsharan.wordpress.com/about-us/ (Accessed March 13, 2013).
50 Ishwar Sharan, *The Myth of Saint Thomas and the Mylapore Shiva Temple* (New Delhi: Voice of India, 1995), 125.
51 My physical copy of Ishwar Sharan's book *The Myth of Saint Thomas and the Mylapore Shiva Temple* is the second revised edition dated 1995, and which will be used for the purposes of citation. The first edition can be accessed on Sharan's website: http://apostlethomasindia.wordpress.com/the-myth-of-saint-thomas-and-the-mylapore-shiva-temple-2010-ishwar-sharan/posts/ (Accessed March 27, 2012). Sharan updated and added new articles to his book, releasing its third revised edition in 2010, this can be found on its own website: The New Ishwar Sharan Archive, *The Myth of Saint Thomas and the Mylapore Shiva Temple* (New Delhi: Voice of India, 2010), http://ishwarsharan.wordpress.com (accessed March 27, 2012).

52 David Mosse, *The Saint in the Banyan Tree: Christianity and Caste Society in India* (Berkeley and Los Angeles, CA: University of California Press, 2012), 1.

53 Sharan, *The Myth of Saint Thomas and the Mylapore Shiva Temple*, 77.

54 Hinduism Today, "Interview with Voice of India," http://www.scribd.com/doc/42222793/14/Interview-with-Voice-of-India (Accessed March 25, 2012). This particular article is cited by Michael Bergunder (2004), but the link to the article he provides no longer exists.

55 Sebastian C. H. Kim, *In Search of Identity: Debates on Religious Conversion in India* (New Delhi: Oxford University Press, 2005), 141.

56 Ibid, 141–142.

57 Michael Bergunder, "Contested Past: Anti-brahmanical and Hindu nationalist reconstructions of early Indian history," *Historiographia Linguistica* 31, 1 (2004): 91.

58 Prabha Bhardwaj, "Book Barons of Delhi: Decades-old Publishing Dynasties Protect, Promote and Preserve Dharma," http://www.hinduismtoday.com/modules/smartsection/item.php?itemid=4583 (Accessed March 25, 2012).

59 Bergunder, "Contested Past," 91–93.

60 Kim, *In Search of Identity*, 141.

61 Meera Nanda, *The God Market: How Globalization is Making India more Hindu* (Noida, Uttar Pradesh: Random House India, 2009), 160.

62 Sita Ram Goel, *Papacy: Its Doctrine and History* (New Delhi: Voice of India, 1986), 56–57.

63 Sharan, *The Myth of Saint Thomas and the Mylapore Shiva Temple*, 7–9.

64 Goel, *Papacy*, 56–57. See also: Sharan, *The Myth of Saint Thomas and the Mylapore Shiva Temple*, 7–9.

65 Sharma, *Hindutva*, 8–12.

66 Ibid, 12.

67 Sita Ram Goel, *History of Hindu-Christian Encounters: AD 304 to 1996* (New Delhi: Voice of India, 2010), 420.

68 Ibid, 434.

69 Srinivasan, *Ishwar Sharan Interview*.

70 Goel, *History of Hindu Christian Encounters*, 422–423.

71 Sharma, *Hindutva*, 8–9.

72 Christophe Jaffrelot, "The Sangh Parivar Between Sankritization and Social Engineering," in *The BJP and the Compulsions of Politics in India*, eds Thomas Blom Hansen and Christophe Jaffrelot (New Delhi: Oxford University Press, 2001), 22–40.

73 For a highly researched examination of the history and development of the Dalit Christian movement in South India, as well as a detailed analysis of how Dalit theology has become a significant force in the shaping of Dalit Christian identity and political activism, see David Mosse's recent book as cited previously: Mosse, *The Saint in the Banyan Tree*. For further readings on the topic of Dalit Christianity and theology, there have been several recent scholarly publications detailing this socio-political struggle for caste equality in India. See: Sebastian C. H. Kim (ed.), *Christian Theology in Asia* (Cambridge: Cambridge University Press, 2008). See also: Sathianathan Clarke, Deenabandhu Manchala, and Philip Vinod Peacock (eds), *Dalit Theology in the Twenty-first Century: Discordant Voices, Discerning Pathways* (Oxford: Oxford University Press, 2010). See also: Peniel J. R. Rajkumar, *Dalit Theology and Dalit Liberation: Problems, Paradigms and Possibilities* (Farnham: Ashgate, 2010). See also: Keith Hebden, *Dalit Theology and Christian Anarchism* (Farnham: Ashgate, 2011). See also: Anderson H.M. Jeremiah, *Community and Worldview among Paraiyars of South India: 'Lived' Religion* (London: Bloomsbury Academic, 2013).

74 Field Notes, Chennai, December 20, 2010. See also: Robert Eric Frykenberg, *Christianity in India: From Beginning to the Present* (New York: Oxford University Press, 2008), 463–4.

75 Special Correspondent, *Archbishop Chinnappa puts Onus of Dalit Liberation on Christian Leaders*, http://www.thehindu.com/todays-paper/tp-national/tp-tamilnadu/article626427.ece (Accessed July 26, 2011).

76 Special Correspondent, *Stress on Holistic Approach to Dalit Liberation*, http://www.hindu.com/2011/05/02/stories/2011050253160300.htm (Accessed July 26, 2011).

77 Nirmala Carvalho, *Tamil Nadu: Police Arrests then Releases Bishops and Faithful Marching for Christian Dalit Rights*, http://www.asianews.it/news-en/Tamil-Nadu:-police-arrests-then-releases-bishops-and-faithful-marching-for-Christian-Dalit-rights-17808.html (Accessed July 26, 2011).

78 Stuart Blackburn, "The Legend of Valluvar and Tamil Literary History," *Modern Asian Studies* 34, 2 (May, 2000): 459. See also: Richard M. Eaton, "(Re)imag(in)ing Otherness: A Postmortem for the Postmodern in India," *Journal of World History* 11, 1 (Spring 2000): 77–78. For an article that offers the Hindu nationalist perspective on Christian anti-Brahmanism see: Koenraad Elst, *St. Thomas and Anti-Brahmanism*, http://apostlethomasindia.wordpress.com/2010/08/17/st-thomas-and-anti-brahminism-koenraad-elst/ (Accessed April 9, 2012).

79 Sharan, *The Myth of Saint Thomas and the Mylapore Shiva Temple*, 75–76.

80 Originally published in the *Express Weekend* dated December 30, 1989, this article is reprinted in its entirety in Ishwar Sharan's book: C. A. Simon, "In Memory of a Slain Saint," *The Myth of Saint Thomas and the Mylapore Shiva Temple*, ed. Ishwar Sharan (New Delhi: Voice of India, 1995), 152.

81 It is worth noting that the Catholic Church in India's overt position on caste equality is a fairly recent development. For centuries the Church has been known to support, encourage, and even integrate the ancient system of caste privileges and honours within the auspices of Catholic worship and ritual throughout India. See: David Mosse, "Honour, Caste and Conflict: The Ethnohistory of a Catholic Festival in Rural Tamil Nadu (1730–1990)," 71–120. Additionally, as discussed by Selva Raj, the Catholic Church in India still allows the integrated practice of *mandakapadi* in certain villages in South India. This tradition is a "system of leasing honour to select individuals or families" during the festival season. While this practice is not specifically geared towards caste, the social implications of status and wealth are still apparent and most likely intrinsically tied to local caste distinctions. See: Selva J. Raj, "Public Display, Communal Devotion: Procession at a South Indian Catholic Festival," in *South Asian Religions on Display: Religious Processions in South Asia and in the Diaspora*, ed. Knut A. Jacobson (London and New York: Routledge, 2008), 86.

82 See: Sharan, *The Myth of Saint Thomas and the Mylapore Shiva Temple*, 74–76, and 151–159. See also: Goel, *History of Hindu Christian Encounters*, 420–433.

83 Goel, *History of Hindu Christian Encounters*, 424–431.

84 Sharan, *The Myth of Saint Thomas and the Mylapore Shiva Temple*, 75–76.

85 Goel, *History of Hindu Christian Encounters*, 433.

86 S. J. Anthonysamy, *A Saga of Faith: St. Thomas the Apostle of India* (Chennai: National Shrine of St. Thomas Basilica, 2009), 91–92.

87 Sharan, *The Myth of Saint Thomas and the Mylapore Shiva Temple*, 57–64.

88 Interview with Fr. Lawrence Raj, Chennai, June 30, 2009.

89 Interview with Mr. Franks, Chennai, July 16, 2009.

90 Interview with Fr. Lawrence Raj, Chennai, June 30, 2009.

91 Interview with Mr. Franks, Chennai, July 16, 2009.

92 Goel, *History of Hindu Christian Encounters*, 422–423.
93 Vincent M. Concessao, "In the Face of Communal Violence what can the Church do?" *The New Leader* 121, 20 (October 16–31, 2008): 10–11.
94 G. Backiya Regis, "From the Editor's pen," *The Voice from the Hill* 1, 1 (July 2010): 3.
95 Sharan, *The Myth of Saint Thomas and the Mylapore Shiva Temple*, 66.
96 Ibid, 121–122.
97 Srinivasan, *Ishwar Sharan Interview*. See also: Kim, *In Search of Identity*, 141–142, and 155–179.
98 Goel, *History of Hindu-Christian Encounters*, v.
99 Sharma, *Hindutva*, 8–12.
100 Sharan, *The Myth of Saint Thomas and the Mylapore Shiva Temple*, 125.
101 Ibid, 40.
102 Sharan, *The Myth of Saint Thomas and the Mylapore Shiva Temple*, 67.
103 Anthonysamy, *A Saga of Faith*, 97.
104 Sharan, *The Myth of Saint Thomas and the Mylapore Shiva Temple*, 103–107.
105 Joanne Punzo Waghorne, *Diaspora of the Gods: Modern Hindu Temple in an Urban Middle-Class World* (New York: Oxford University Press, 2004), 85.
106 Anthonysamy, *A Saga of Faith*, 91.
107 S. Muthiah, *Madras Rediscovered* (Chennai: East West, an imprint of Westland Limited, 2008), 215–216.
108 Ishwar Sharan, *Kapaleeswara Temple Memorial Plaque*, http://apostlethomasindia.wordpress.com/2010/04/17/kapaleeswara-temple-plaque-ishwar-sharan/ (Accessed April 12, 2012).
109 Waghorne, *Diaspora of the Gods*, 85.
110 Interview with Fr. Lawrence Raj, Chennai, June 15, 2009.
111 Edward W. Said, *Culture and Imperialism* (New York: Alfred A. Knopf, Inc., 1993), 214.
112 Arun Mukherjee, *Postcolonialism: My Living* (Toronto: TSAR Publications, 1998), 21–22.
113 Ibid, 22.
114 Wendy Doniger, "Foreword: The View from the Other Side: Postpostcolonialism, Religious Syncretism, and Class Conflict," in *Popular Christianity in India. Riting Between the Lines*, eds Selva J. Raj and Corinne G. Dempsey (Albany, NY: State University of New York Press, 2002), xii.
115 The New Ishwar Sharan Archive, *The Myth of Saint Thomas and the Mylapore Shiva Temple* (New Delhi: Voice of India, 2010), http://ishwarsharan.wordpress.com/introduction-ishwar-sharan/ (Accessed April 12, 2012).
116 Interview with Fr. Lawrence Raj, Chennai, June 15, 2009.

4 The physical renovation of San Thome Cathedral

Revival through tourism, branding, and heritage preservation

Introduction

The revival of St. Thomas in Chennai represents a uniquely modern evangelization venture within the greater Catholic mission in India. In 1999, Pope John Paul II delivered his exhortation *Ecclesia in Asia* in New Delhi, India, in order to publically re-affirm the Catholic Church's goal to missionize Asia. He stated:

> With the Church throughout the world, the Church in Asia will cross the threshold of the Third Christian Millennium marveling at all that God has worked from those beginnings until now, and strong in the knowledge that "just as in the first millennium the Cross was planted on the soil of Europe, and in the second on that of the Americas and Africa, we can pray that in the Third Christian Millennium *a great harvest of faith* [emphasis in original] will be reaped in this vast and vital continent."[1]

In many ways, Fr. Lawrence's revival of St. Thomas in Chennai can be viewed as an extension of the *Ecclesia in Asia*. With this in mind, this chapter argues that the Church in Chennai's current missionary efforts can be understood as a simultaneous two-step evangelical strategy that entails both the seeking out of new converts and the active maintenance of established Catholic communities that will locally serve as the foundation for current and future evangelization efforts. As this chapter will demonstrate, the Church's current renewal activities serve to cultivate potential Catholic converts through the use of various rural and urban development projects, of which the fostering of saint cults and shrinal-based veneration play an important part. This is especially true for shrines like San Thome and St. Thomas Mount, whose significant historical, cultural, and religious value lends credence to the Church's renewal and development projects.

During Fr. Lawrence's short tenure at St. Thomas Mount, several years before his time at San Thome, he witnessed what was, in his opinion, a missed opportunity on the part of the Church to market and preserve the historical integrity of St. Thomas and those sites directly connected with him in Chennai. After many years of serious thought and a number of successful building projects behind him, Fr. Lawrence formulated a driving ethos for the preservation of the Catholic faith in India. Fr. Lawrence explains:

> So, today, evangelization … I have written that by building churches, we are building God's kingdom. So, that is one of the reasons why I wanted to develop these places. By developing, you attract more people; you are bringing more faith into the people. And these are now monuments where, whether you like it or not, everyone will come to visit.[2]

Many of the physical renovations and new building projects that have taken place at San Thome and St. Thomas Mount in the last decade are expressions of a premeditated marketing strategy on the part of Fr. Lawrence and other Church administrators in Chennai. This marketing strategy has taken into consideration Chennai's growing tourism industry and local heritage preservation. Thus, many of these new building projects were initiated out of the desire to make these sites more accessible to both pilgrims and tourists.

The mainstay of Fr. Lawrence's marketing vision was his "branding" of St. Thomas, from which he could successfully promote the Apostle's historical and religious Indian legacy in Chennai and abroad. I argue that Fr. Lawrence and other Church administrators at San Thome have utilized the physical renovations and additional building projects in order to reinforce and maintain a St. Thomas "faith brand," and that the establishment of this faith brand through the revivals at San Thome and St. Thomas Mount is another clear example of a renewal and revivalist strategy developed and implemented by the Church hierarchy in Chennai.

Religious tourism

We might assume that Fr. Lawrence's principal religious objective in renovating and promoting San Thome was to attract the attention of more Christian pilgrims. However, he has made it clear to me that his intended audience was never limited to just pilgrims, let alone to just Christians. In addition to the great number of Hindus that visit Christian sacred sites, he also wanted to attract tourists from all over the world to San Thome so as to better promote St. Thomas's tomb and the Cathedral as authentic Indian cultural heritage sites. He stated:

> See, anybody who comes from abroad now, one of the main places for them to see is San Thome, irrespective of their religion or anything of that sort, and many people when they come to see the Cathedral they are surprised because they have different ideas about India. And when they see such big churches and so on, they are surprised, and they are

so happy to see such big churches here. So therefore, they should be well maintained and protected, so that is my idea, and by doing that, a lot of people will start coming.[3]

With a broad target audience, Fr. Lawrence's marketing strategy for San Thome aimed to be multi-faceted in order to cater to both pilgrims and tourists of various backgrounds and motivations. We can also see in Fr. Lawrence's words a desire to raise greater international awareness about Christianity in India. He notes that many visitors are "surprised" to see Christian churches in India, which seems to suggest that it is a preconceived notion on the part of many foreigners that Christianity is non-existent there. This too is a misconception that Fr. Lawrence hoped to remedy with his new marketing strategy. Fr. Lawrence's marketing ethos is intriguing both because the concept of religious tourism was so readily factored into his general marketing strategy, and because he does not deny the touristic aspirations he held for San Thome. Fr. Lawrence hoped to make the Cathedral and the tomb of St. Thomas a better pilgrimage site, as well as a better tourist attraction.

Another interesting aspect of Fr. Lawrence's marketing vision is that it seemingly contradicted the Catholic Church's traditional position on tourism, which is to "renounce the touristic nature of religiously motivated travel."[4] However, with modern developments in transportation technology precipitating the rapid growth of the tourism industry, especially in Europe, even the Catholic Church has had to take notice and re-evaluate its traditional position.[5] This re-evaluation has resulted in the concept of "religious tourism," a phrase used by both the Catholic Church and tourism theorists and scholars. According to tourism scholars Mary Lee and Sidney Nolan, the Church in Europe has come to understand religious tourism as "the system that encompass a range of holy places, from the grandest cathedral to the smallest rural chapel, the service facilities associated with them, and the spectrum of visitors from the devout to the secular."[6] Thus, the Church's acceptance of religious tourism can be seen as a practical compromise from its traditional stance in the face of modernity.[7]

Faith brands

Recent theories regarding the marketing of religion can shed some light on the recent revivals at San Thome and St. Thomas Mount. The theories of Mara Einstein, a media studies researcher whose work focuses on the marketing of religion in America, are especially useful. In order to better qualify the use of certain marketing ideas in this chapter, I will draw upon Einstein's book *Brands of Faith: Marketing Religion in a Commercial Age*, which analyzes the creation and marketing of "faith brands" by various religious institutions, mainly Evangelical Christians, as a way to evangelize and preserve religion's relevance in today's competitive secular and spiritual markets. I will use the idea of religious marketing as a starting point in understanding Fr. Lawrence's marketing vision for St. Thomas's tomb. Einstein states, "It [religion] is at its base a product, competing against an overwhelming number of other products in the consumer marketplace."[8] Although Einstein is writing about American culture, her assertions and theories regarding religious marketing can be easily applied to certain case studies in India, especially now with its booming IT industry, steady economic growth, and subsequent mass consumerism.

Behind the concept of a "faith brand" is the basic understanding of branding as a contemporary marketing strategy. Einstein begins her discussion on branding with a quote by David Ogilvy, an influential marketing pioneer in the advertisement industry. According to Ogilvy, a brand can be defined as "the intangible sum of a product's attributes: its name, packaging, and price, its history, its reputation and the way it is advertised."[9] Einstein adds to this definition:

> Branding is about making meaning – taking the individual aspects of a product and turning them into more than the sum of their parts. It is about giving consumers something to think and feel about a product or service beyond its physical attributes. It's about fulfilling a need; providing what marketers call the benefit.[10]

In terms of branding's financial aims, marketing researchers Don Schultz and Heidi Schultz, have laid out several key things that brands are meant to accomplish. Most significantly, brands should create monetary value for the owner and provide tangible value for customers that will draw them towards the brand. Additionally, the brand should nurture strong relationships between the owner, employees, and customers. Lastly, branding helps to foster a product's longevity within the market place, and with luck, "become a part of culture. Cultural icons have great value."[11]

Much of what Fr. Lawrence and other Church administrators wanted to accomplish can be translated to and from the language of brand marketing. The "owner" is the Church, but more specifically the self-sufficient parish, which is the immediate community of both clergy and laymen who stand to gain prestige or better finances from their parish's rise in popularity. The "customer" can be any local or foreign visitor to the shrine, either pilgrim or tourist, who can potentially contribute to the site's preservation and spread the word about the shrine's existence and general importance. Finally, "employees and other interested stakeholders" denote the parish community more directly, since it is ultimately on their shoulders whether or not to maintain the standards of quality set by the project leader.

Einstein adds her own insights to Schultz and Schultz's list. For example, many brands utilize specialized logos, usually a simple symbol that easily distinguishes the brand from its competitors whose uniqueness serves to generate automatic recognition.[12] She also asserts that brands can create for themselves myths, or narratives that serve to frame the product's history and reliability, something that is already inherent to the historical narratives surrounding the life and death of St. Thomas.[13] Brands also help in the creation of personalized identities, especially among their most loyal customers, who become, to some extent, the embodiment of the product's mythos.[14] San Thome's newly designed logo is a good example that encompasses many of the above points. Underscoring a stylized outline of San Thome's unique neo-Gothic facing and spires are the words declaring, "San Thome Church: Source and Summit of Indian Christianity."[15] Here the legacy of San Thome and St. Thomas's tomb are touted as being the place of origin for Christianity in India. This emphasis on St. Thomas's role as spiritual progenitor re-affirms local parish identity and links it to the wider global Catholic community, thus legitimizing the indigeneity and communal longevity of those Indian Christians who link themselves to the person of St. Thomas. As we can see, such instances demonstrate that religion and branding can go hand in hand, or as economics educator Boris Vukonic asserts, maintain "a convenient symbiosis."[16]

When religion becomes a branded product, potential converts become consumers. In much the same way as marketers hope to create a community of brand loyal customers, a religion will hope to convert loyal new members in order to expand its congregation. In this way, a religious commodity marketed by a religious institution becomes what Einstein calls a "faith brand," or "spiritual products that have been given popular meaning and awareness through marketing."[17] She explains that both religious faiths and branded products are central to a consumer's sense of identity. Therefore, the world of religion can be combined into the world of brand marketing in order to create branded religious products that seemingly enhance and speak directly to the consumer's spiritual identity. As Einstein notes, faith brands can come in many different shapes and forms, such as books, courses, Evangelical seeker churches or megachurches, and other such institutions.[18] According to Einstein, whether it is a faith brand or any branded product, the primary goal is the same, to foster growth and expansion.[19]

Many of the essential characteristics of a faith brand, as discussed by Einstein, are readily exemplified in the marketing strategies employed by Church administrators at San Thome and St. Thomas Mount. It is clear that the "spiritual products" being offered are the spiritual power and grace one could receive from visiting these sites. Pilgrims and other believers who visit and pray here could potentially benefit from St. Thomas's intercessions by way of answered petitions. For a non-pilgrim or tourist, the product being offered could include the site's religious and historical significance or novelty, which one could derive from the basic fact of seeing such a large and interesting Catholic cathedral in India. The marketing strategies used by Fr. Lawrence and other Church administrators possess an ambition and visionary scope that look to see St. Thomas's Indian legacy transformed into a faith brand much like the American examples discussed by Einstein. While much of what I have asserted could be applied to a spectrum of various institutions, what makes the St. Thomas presented at San Thome and St. Thomas Mount a veritable faith brand is the local Church's overt agenda of evangelization and missionization and its sophisticated marketing thereof.

St. Thomas the movie and Mel Gibson's "The Passion of the Christ"

A good example of San Thome's transformation into a faith brand can be seen in its poorly planned bid for a St. Thomas movie. The bid was first made official through a joint announcement held at the Cathedral by representatives of the Tamil Nadu government and the Catholic Church. The plan was to produce a big budget blockbuster motion picture about the life of St. Thomas, mainly focused on his time in India. This elaborate and nationally publicized function was held during the Feast of St. Thomas on July 3, 2008. The guest of honor was Tamil Nadu's Chief Minister M. Karunanidhi, who triggered a ceremonial switch to inaugurate the commencement of this film project. Karunanidhi also gave a speech at this event that highlighted the accomplishments of Indian minorities and related his excitement over the possibility of spreading the knowledge of St. Thomas's life in India to an international audience through this film.[20]

According to a couple of Indian English-language news sites, the film's budget was estimated at 50 crore INR (approximately 11 million USD) or more, and would feature songs in both Tamil and Malayalam. In addition, the film's screenwriter and researcher, Rev. Fr. Paulraj Lourdusamy, painted a very ambitious portrait of the film's potential with regard to its casting. In an effort to produce the film in Tamil, Malayalam, and English, negotiations were supposedly underway to hire well-known actors from Kerala and Tamil Nadu to play various roles, as well as securing Hollywood actors to play St. Thomas and Jesus. Names dropped included the famous Tamil superstar Rajinikanth as Thiruvalluvar, and James Caviezel to reprise his role as Jesus from Mel Gibson's *The Passion of the Christ* (2004).[21]

It is significant that the Church's spokesperson would mention Mel Gibson's controversial film about the last days of Jesus. As Einstein points out, this film was an unexpected box office hit in 2004, earning more than 600 million dollars (USD) worldwide, making it the highest grossing non-English language film ever produced.[22] Einstein concludes that the film's success was not due to the movie's overall production quality, nor was it due to the devotion of American Christian fans, but instead it owed its major success to marketing.

The Passion was undoubtedly a hit with the Church in Chennai, since they so readily associated it with their own motion picture venture about St. Thomas. By hinting at the idea that they could get James Caviezel to reprise his role as Jesus, they were implying that this new St. Thomas movie would be something of a sequel to Mel Gibson's *The Passion*. Obviously, the Church saw *The Passion's* marketing success as a model to emulate, since it proved that a non-English multilingual production could be internationally well-received and profitable. For Einstein, *The Passion* clearly demonstrates the promotion of religion through its commodification. She explains, "*The Passion* started with a defined target audience, created secondary targets through promotion and publicity, and perpetuated the product's relevance through creating ancillary businesses".[23] Most likely, Church officials and advertising executives in charge of the St. Thomas film would have copied many of the marketing strategies that led *The Passion* to its unprecedented success and status as a successful faith brand. Unfortunately, the production of this movie seems to have been placed on permanent hiatus.

I first learned about this movie project during my initial stay in Chennai in 2009, which would have been about a year after the film's inauguration. According to previously cited materials, the film was said to be two years in the making.[24] As of my December 2010 trip to Chennai, nothing new had transpired regarding the film's production. I inquired about the film's status at San Thome, and it appeared the project had stalled. I asked Fr. Lawrence, who had no part in the movie's development, about it, and in his opinion it was all just "a very big show."[25] According to an online article by Ishwar Sharan, the movie was shelved due to protest from Tamil scholars about the film's possibly inauthentic script.[26] Whatever the reasons were for the film's current pre-production limbo or possible termination, the initial inaugural ceremony and the publicity it garnered demonstrates the Church's ambition in hoping to transform St. Thomas's Indian legacy into a marketable commodity that could promote both St. Thomas and the Catholic Church in India. The failed movie project provides an indication of the Cathedral's limitations. Regardless, this whole incident shares many characteristics with how faith brands in America have been marketed and branded.

Initial steps towards San Thome's renovation

Ultimately, it is the Cathedral's renovation and new underground tomb shrine that best exemplify the Church in Chennai's utilization of a St. Thomas faith brand. This next section will highlight how the Cathedral's renovation has acted as a primer for Fr. Lawrence's religious marketing of St. Thomas, as well as give a sense of what pre-existing tourism and marketing models served to inspire Fr. Lawrence in his bid to rejuvenate San Thome. It is clear that Fr. Lawrence wanted to draw both pilgrims and tourists to San Thome, which is why it was necessary for him to raise the standards of quality to which the Cathedral had previously been maintained. He set out to renovate the Cathedral proper, as well as its grounds and attached primary school, and also to improve the standards by which the parish was managed. Among other things, he enacted several new policies with the explicit purpose of making the Cathedral and parish a more welcoming place for both visitors and parishioners. These initial steps served a dual purpose: to spark interest in San Thome's religious legacy internationally; and to instil pride in the local Catholic population. In an interview given for a special booklet published in honor of Fr. Lawrence's priestly silver jubilee, he states, "The only dream that I have for this parish is that the fame of St. Thomas should spread to distant lands and that our unity as a parish community must be a source of inspiration for the entire Archdiocese."[27] Clearly, before Fr. Lawrence could market San Thome to outsiders, he needed to unify and convince San Thome's parishioners that this undertaking would be worth the effort and risk.

According to Mr. Zander, a parishioner at San Thome who has seen many parish priests come and go, Fr. Lawrence's greatest asset as parish priest was his ability to "communicate."[28] Fr. Lawrence was able to talk to people, and more importantly, he was able to motivate them. As Mr. Zander states, "Father [Lawrence] came; he made me involved in the church activities ... see, he'll be knowing each and every person by name ... and he should make them get [involved] in all of the church activities."[29] For instance, after every mass, he would go out and mingle with the community. He talked, listened, and joked with his parishioners, more so than previous parish priests. But, most importantly, he made himself accessible, both in-person and on the phone.[30] In short, Fr. Lawrence dedicated himself fully to the parish and to San Thome's renovation, something that the whole community could see and draw motivation from. As stated before, branding aims to "create relationships with employees and other interested stakeholders so they want to continue to be associated with and support the brand."[31] By demonstrating his willingness and aptitude for supporting and improving the parish, Fr. Lawrence demonstrated to the parish community that he was up to the task of renovating San Thome and reviving the legacy of St. Thomas. Clearly, his initial endeavors were about creating positive "relationships" with the people who stood to either gain or lose the most from his grand scheme, and who would be entrusted to carrying on what he started after his inevitable re-assignment.

The 2004 renovation of San Thome

In the souvenir booklet published in honor of San Thome's 2004 renovation, Fr. Lawrence wrote, "The singular motive for the renovation of Santhome Cathedral Basilica was to restore the pristine beauty of this heritage monument and to bring glory and honor to St. Thomas, the Apostle of India."[32] In early 2002, Fr. Lawrence began his initial investigation into the work required to safely and properly restore the old Cathedral, and what he discovered was a daunting task that would require a great deal of specialization and money. While it is difficult to find pictures of San Thome from before its 2004 renovation, various sources indicate that the Cathedral's prior visage was not up to the standards expected of a world-class attraction.

Writing in the 1960s, journalist and travel writer Duncan Forbes remarked on its rundown condition: "So the legend [of St. Thomas] survives in the hot air of the new cathedral, which in that steamy climate already looks shabby after only seventy years."[33] Charlie Pye-Smith visited the Cathedral much more recently, in 1996, but was equally unimpressed:

> Like many Catholic churches built during the past century – it [San Thome] was exactly a hundred years old – it was marginally more attractive when seen from a distance than it was close up. Spikey Gothic, with a profusion of pinnacles and spires, it looked like a Cubist porcupine that had clambered through a tin of white paint. The monsoon rains had streaked the walls grey and black, and in places below the guttering the paint had begun to peel away.[34]

Pye-Smith noted that the Cathedral's interior was "immaculate," however, which implies that priority was given to maintaining those parts of the Cathedral that were in daily use.[35] Fr. Lawrence himself had this to say about the Cathedral's state, "Now when I took over, the whole church was in a very, very dilapidated condition and looking very miserable, like a god-forsaken place, so God's pleased to declare it a god-forsaken place!"[36] Long-time parishioner Mr. Zander described it as "a dungeon," adding that "nobody used to come inside."[37]

In our interviews, Fr. Lawrence laid out for me the various options he considered in order to transform San Thome into a world-class pilgrimage shine and tourist attraction. He mentioned a number of notably successful tourist and pilgrimage sites from which he drew inspiration. In particular he noted the success and local popularity of the Shrine Basilica of Our Lady of Vailankanni. He also displayed a particular fascination with The Sacré-Cœur Basilica, on the summit of Montmartre hill in Paris, France. According to Fr. Lawrence, The Sacré-Cœur Basilica exemplifies the touristic potential a Catholic shrine can achieve with just the right amount of novelty.[38] Sacré-Cœur Basilica is an incredibly popular tourist attraction that also entertains its fair share of pilgrims. It is a prime example of the religious tourism phenomenon that Fr. Lawrence wanted to attract to the St. Thomas sites in Chennai.

In terms of world-class standards for heritage preservation and maintenance, Fr. Lawrence desired to emulate the quality of work demonstrated by The Archaeological Survey of India (ASI), which is a branch of India's Ministry of Culture. Some of its most notable projects include the famous Taj Mahal, and the tomb of St. Francis Xavier in Goa. According to Fr. Lawrence, if the Cathedral continued to languish as it did, it would have probably been given over to the ASI.[39] In fact, some members of the San Thome parish believed that turning over the Cathedral to the ASI was the best course of action for its preservation. However, Fr. Lawrence and many other parish members were very much against this idea because under ASI jurisdiction, he and the parish would lose all control over the management of the Cathedral. Also, as a government agency, the ASI would only just protect and maintain the physical structure, and would, therefore, have nothing to do with the promotion of Catholicism and religious renewal. Using the tomb of Francis Xavier as an example, he explains:

> For anything and everything they [local priests in Goa] are to get permission from these people, from the government. So, individually, independently, they cannot act. So, there in San Thome, that problem is not there at all. It is 100 percent under our control, so we can do whatever we want. See, if [it had come] under their [ASI] control, even to remove a brick, we have to get their permission, even the whitewash; we have to get their permission.[40]

In Fr. Lawrence's mind, handing over the Cathedral to the ASI was a last resort, only justifiable if the condition of the structure was well beyond anything the parish could manage.[41]

Fr. Lawrence believed it was manageable, and thus orchestrated the full restoration and renovation of the Cathedral. Clearly, Fr. Lawrence's endeavor needed to be equal in quality to what the ASI could have accomplished, especially if he wanted San Thome to be widely seen as a properly preserved heritage site that was simultaneously a well-managed canonically recognized shrine. Thus, Fr. Lawrence hired various specialists in the fields of heritage preservation, architecture, and building construction in order to return San Thome to its original state and beyond. As S. J. Anthonysamy writes:

> Considering the nature of this magnificent structure as ancient as well as sacred and bearing in mind the hallowed nature of the tomb enshrined in it, the restoration had to be done on a serious scale. Experts had to be involved in the entire operation. Scientific precision had to be kept in mind restoring such pristine monuments. Above all there were also the financial considerations.[42]

The full cost of the complete renovation project, including the new tomb shrine, was understandably never made known to me, nor was it published in any of the sources at my disposal. Undoubtedly, the cost was very high, and Fr. Lawrence had to work hard to collect the entire amount. Mr. Zander estimated that the cost was somewhere between 30–50 million INR, or possibly more.[43]

Inspired by the layout of Vailankanni shrine, Fr. Lawrence's renovation plans for San Thome included a restructuring of the Cathedral's courtyard. Vailankanni's large basilica was surrounded by a spacious courtyard that helped accommodate its massive visitor traffic during the festival season. As Fr. Lawrence explained, "And there was no space around. Now, the space that you see around the church was cleared upwards ... so, a lot of work we did like that and then made space first of all around the Church [San Thome]."[44] The work that Father Lawrence was speaking about involved the demolition of several courtyard facilities, including a common building, the old primary school, servant's quarters, and a Lourdes grotto, from alongside the Cathedral. These structures were all either moved or re-built in different locations as the renovations progressed.[45] At the far end of the Cathedral's grounds, near where the servant's quarters and Lourdes grotto used to be, a large stage was eventually erected in order to better facilitate large outdoor services for festivals and other such occasions (Figures 4.1 and 4.2). All later additions to the grounds would be built along the sides of the courtyard, in order to maintain the wide open area just left of the Cathedral, as well as the space that runs completely around it.

With the Cathedral's grounds now more spacious, Fr. Lawrence could begin work on the Cathedral itself. In his overall project itinerary, the renovation of San Thome would be the first of three main phases. The second phase involved the construction of the underground tomb chapel, while the third phase included the construction of a new museum and auditorium over the tomb chapel's entrance.[46] The first thing Fr. Lawrence needed to do was get an official assessment on the Cathedral's condition, as well as an estimate on the cost to restore it. As Fr. Lawrence tells it:

Figure 4.1 The courtyard stage on the occasion of the Feast of St. Thomas July 4, 2009.

Photo: T. C. Nagy.

Figure 4.2 The courtyard filled to capacity for outdoor mass July 4, 2009.
Photo: T. C. Nagy.

Then, I was very serious to bring aboard the restoration, because it was high time we thought that something should be done to preserve the antiquity of this great Basilica. So, with the conference of the Archbishop and the Council ... I started the work and I entrusted the work to one restoration company, they are already popular in India, Ravi Gundu Rao [&] Associates. So, they started the work, the restoration work. And we wanted to see that everything is preserved as it is. We did not want to unnecessarily add anything with modern materials and so on. So that was the idea.[47]

Ravi Gundu Rao & Associates is a nationally respected architectural firm based out of Mysore that specializes in the conservation of heritage buildings. The old Portuguese-built San Thome Cathedral was demolished in 1893 after being deemed too small for the parish's growing community, as well as too simplistic given its prestigious connection to St. Thomas. Construction on the current Cathedral, an elaborate nineteenth-century neo-Gothic structure, began immediately after the demolition and was completed in 1896. Now, well over a century old, SanThome is deserving of its status as a protected heritage building.[48]

The Cathedral's poor state prior to renovation was due to many factors, primarily concerning its location. Having been built right on the coast of the Bay of Bengal, it has always been at the mercy of the elements. It is also situated on a busy thoroughfare, and has suffered due to pollution.[49] In a report submitted to Fr. Lawrence and the parish, Ravi Gundu Rao & Associates identified several key issues concerning the integrity of the Cathedral structure, along with recommendations as to how these problems should be addressed. Due to prolonged leakage caused by the elements, much of the wood, stained glass, and plaster were in need of immediate repair, especially the Cathedral's wooden roof, which had rotted over the years. The architectural firm also uncovered evidence of past attempts at repairing the Cathedral, most notably from 1972.[50] These were deemed "incorrect past interventions using incompatible modern materials for repairs," which clearly demonstrated a "lack of technical knowledge in handling heritage buildings" to the ultimate detriment of San Thome.[51] With the basic assessment completed, it was deemed imperative that the Cathedral's conservation process commence immediately.

The bulk of the work involved the restoration of the roof and ceiling, all stained glass, louvered windows, doors, ventilators, and all art work including the original Stations of the Cross murals, as well as structural repairs to all external masonry work and internal lime plaster and mortar work. They also designed a new electrical system for the Cathedral in order to facilitate modern-day use. Overall, great care was made by Ravi Gundu Rao & Associates to use all the correct materials in line with the Cathedral's original specifications, as well as in following the highest standards of conservation practice (Figure 4.3 and 4.4). Additional work to San Thome undertaken by different companies included the laying of new marble tiles for the Cathedral's floor, a specially designed and highly ornate carved wooden altar to hold the venerable Our Lady of Mylapore statue, as well as additional lightning and other such amenities for contemporary use. Outside, a brand new Lourdes grotto (Figure 4.5) and a large golden signpost were installed next to the main gate of the courtyard, and nearby a new multi-purpose center was erected, and finally, an outdoor side chapel to Our Lady of Mylapore was built to the right of the Cathedral. The restoration work officially began in June of 2003, and was completed by the first week of December of 2004.[52]

The (Inter)National Shrine of San Thome Cathedral Basilica

With San Thome's renovation finally completed, Fr. Lawrence was able to obtain for the Cathedral an important accolade: National Shrine status. During the Cathedral's renovation process, Fr. Lawrence decided to submit an application to the Conference of Catholic Bishops of India in order to get San Thome canonically recognized as a National Shrine. The last time the Cathedral was recognized in any significant way was when it was elevated to the status of a minor Basilica in 1956. According to the Catholic Church's *Code of Canon Law*, a "shrine is understood to be a church or

Figure 4.3 Interior of San Thome today. Note the original wood finish of the ceiling.
Photo: T. C. Nagy.

Figure 4.4 Exterior shot of San Thome's side facing the courtyard.
Photo: T. C. Nagy.

Figure 4.5 San Thome's new and strikingly lush (for Chennai) Lourdes grotto.
Photo: T. C. Nagy.

other sacred place to which numerous members of the faithful make pilgrimage for a special reason of piety, with the approval of the local ordinary."[53] As such, any designated sacred place can be elevated to one of three canonically recognized shrinal statuses befitting its prestige. The lowest status is that of Diocesan Shrine, which only requires the recognition of the local ordinary to confer. Next is National Shrine status, which requires the approval of the country's Conference of Bishops, as per the case of San Thome. The most prestigious status is that of International Shrine, which requires the approval of The Holy See in the Vatican.[54]

According to Fr. Lawrence, once the renovations were completed and San Thome's local and international visitor traffic visibly increased, the Conference of Catholic Bishops of India was quick to confer on San Thome the title of National Shrine. Taking it one step further, Fr. Lawrence immediately applied directly to the Vatican to get San Thome recognized as an International Shrine. However, the Vatican decided that because San Thome had only just been recognized as a National Shrine that it should wait several years before being granted the title of International Shrine.[55] Fr. Lawrence was so certain that San Thome would receive this status immediately that he had the Cathedral's main entrance sign constructed to read "International Shrine of St. Thomas Basilica" (Figure 4.6). As of my last visit to Chennai in 2010 San Thome had yet to be conferred with this title, but Fr. Lawrence was certain that it would happen very soon.[56]

The main point to note in this entire process was how easily San Thome was given the status of National Shrine, which begs the question: why did this not happen earlier? The answer is much the same as why the act of renewal did not happen years ago: previous parish priests either did not see the merits of such an undertaking or were uninterested in taking on such a significant and work-intensive endeavor. But clearly, this particular status means a great deal, and represents official Church approval and recognition, which helps to market the site to pilgrims and tourists alike. The approval of the Conference of Bishops, and to a greater extent The Holy See, demonstrates the significance of having a spokesperson or a clearly recognizable authority endorse one's product. Fr. Lawrence certainly saw these titles as worthwhile steps towards raising San Thome's profile. Finally, National Shrine status also serves to

Figure 4.6 Cathedral welcome sign at main gate.
Photo: T. C. Nagy.

improve the St. Thomas brand by further legitimizing San Thome's local and national significance as an Indian heritage site, which also highlights the unity of the Church in India. If and when San Thome obtains International Shrine Status, this too will serve to better the St. Thomas brand by highlighting San Thome's illustrious place within the greater global Roman Catholic Church.

San Thome as an aspect of the St. Thomas brand

In marketing St. Thomas's legacy, how exactly does this hundred-year-old structure contribute to the St. Thomas brand? Indeed, it marks the site of St. Thomas's tomb, but there is clearly more to it than that if we look at the Cathedral as a separate entity from the tomb. As defined by Einstein, "Branding is about making meaning – taking the individual aspects of a product and turning them into more than the sum of their parts."[57] San Thome Cathedral is definitely a prime "aspect" of the St. Thomas brand, as is the local and more immediate history it represents. What kind of "meaning" then can be made from highlighting and preserving the historical and religious value of this structure? The answer is simply identity, but more specifically, an Indian Roman Catholic identity that was instigated and nurtured by Portuguese missionaries, and later a Portuguese hierarchy, all in the name of preserving St. Thomas's legacy. In other words, the Church in Chennai is currently promoting a Catholic/ Christian identity and heritage that is both local and global, and that meaningfully originated out of Western colonialism.

However, when the Church presents anything that happens to highlight its historical and socio-political connection to India's colonial era, it will often distil this knowledge to its most meaningful parts as a precaution against the negative political rhetoric that is often applied to anything associated with this era of Indian history. The Portuguese are not forgotten by the Church, but their less scrupulous acts are downplayed in favor of their most significant contributions to contemporary Indian Catholicism, such as their historic buildings and architecture. As Anthonysamy writes:

> The Portuguese efforts in making the memory of the saint alive with a focus of faith on the tomb had borne excellent benefits. The *Padroado* jurisdiction lasting for nearly three centuries and a half had done much for the missionary expansion of the Church. The construction of the majestic gothic Cathedral over the tomb of St. Thomas was a sign of a glorious faith on the martyred saint.[58]

Clearly, Anthonysamy includes to the list of Portuguese accomplishments the caretakership and promotion of St. Thomas and his tomb, as well as their overall missionary success in India, two things that the current Indian Church hopes to emulate.

Another indication of this sentiment is visible in the esteem in which these colonial era missionaries are held, most notably St. Francis Xavier (b. 1506 –

d. 1552) and St. John de Britto (b. 1647 – d. 1693). Both of these saints are highly regarded by the Church and the local Christian community for their missionary accomplishments in Tamil Nadu. Statues of both saints are afforded a prominent place on either side of San Thome's main altar, and actively display the modern-day Church's direct link to the spirit of colonial era missionization. Thus, even with the pervasiveness of Hindutva rhetoric, the Church in India is still not willing to sever all of its ties to its colonial past.

Regardless, due to the disparaging rhetoric of Hindutva advocates, Indian Christians may ultimately feel a sense of "rootlessness" within their own country. If this is indeed the case, it would certainly explain why a portion of the St. Thomas brand is so focused on the re-affirmation of an indigenous Indian Christian identity. As discussed in the previous chapter, some Hindu nationalists still associate contemporary Catholicism with the Western colonialism of the past, to the dismay of the Church in India. However, the pluralistic nature of the Tamil Nadu region affords the Indian Christian community a great deal of protection from the worst machinations of the Hindu fundamentalist movement.

For the Church in India, its colonial era heritage is not necessarily something they want its members to completely forget, especially since it reinforces Indian Catholic identity in relation to Catholicism's global character. The Portuguese, as an ecclesiastical and political body, are no longer here. Instead, the caretakership of San Thome and other such shrines fall to the Tamil Indian Christian clergy and laity who still remain to this day. In this way, through the preservation of such edifices and the religious and indigenous traditions and history so closely linked to them, they are preserving their own legacy and unique identity as Tamil Indian Christians/Catholics.

Fr. Lawrence clearly recognized the significance behind restoring the Cathedral to its original specifications. By declaring the current Cathedral a local and national heritage site, the Church in Chennai was explicitly promoting its place in India, as well as re-affirming an Indian Catholic identity that has its roots in Western colonialism. In my interview with Mr. Zander, he noted this fact with pride, stating:

> They [European missionaries] gave the Indians awareness! .... Because [of] that awareness, I think, willingly people became Christians out of the service done by the first Portuguese ... they gave education, they gave medical facilities, they gave awareness. Because of these [things], willingly people became Christians ... because my forefathers ... some ... one or two generations back they became Christians. I'm a Christian because of my forefathers.[59]

While Mr. Zander's words do not directly connect San Thome's renovation to the promotion of a colonial heritage, they demonstrate the positive light that is generally shown to the heritage of Portuguese missionization. By fully restoring the Cathedral, Fr. Lawrence was, in a way, restoring the community's pride in what this structure stood for in terms of local identity and heritage, a heritage that has recently been under attack by individuals associated with the Hindu right. By re-enforcing this aspect of St. Thomas's local legacy, or the St. Thomas brand, special meaning is derived that not only emphasizes the community's past, but also validates and rejuvenates the community's place in the present day. After all, it was due to the commitment of the Portuguese that St. Thomas's tomb was preserved and revived in the first place, and thus, the legacy of both St. Thomas and the early Portuguese missionaries are inexorably tied to San Thome parish's Indian Christian identity.

Designing the new tomb of St. Thomas

Fr. Lawrence's decision to construct a new underground chapel or crypt to display the tomb of St. Thomas was both innovative and risky. Prior to the 2004 remodeling, the tomb of St. Thomas was a far simpler and less conspicuous monument. The tomb was originally constructed in 1903 and remained virtually unchanged until 2004. It was located at the end of the Cathedral's nave, situated in front of the altar, or directly in the center of the Cathedral's crossing, between the transepts. Anthonysamy refers to the old tomb as an "open crypt," that was built into the Cathedral's floor:

> It was slightly rectangular in shape about 12 ft. x 12 ft., and 7 ft. 7 inches in depth. It was protected by a brass railing above. A short flight of four steps led to a small platform from which two flights of six steps one on each side led down to the floor of the crypt. At the eastern extremity was a beautiful marble altar under which was an open grave 6 ft. × 1 ft. and 5 ft. 9 inches deep.[60]

What Fr. Lawrence wanted to do was to create an actual underground compartment, separate from the Cathedral itself, which would allow for more people to visit the tomb at any given time, even while the Cathedral was in use. In his own words:

> And when we started the work, the tomb of St. Thomas, the most important thing, it was just close to the altar ... and people used to go to the tomb from the main nave, only one or two who can go inside at a time, and the tomb was not at all given any importance, it was just like that, neglected ... I know that it was a big disturbance when we have the religious services in the church. A lot of people, tourists and so on, they come and we don't allow them to go to the tomb, and it was a severe problem. Then we got thinking of having a separate entry to the tomb.[61]

Additionally, he hoped to enhance the tomb's sacrality by further demarcating it from the hustle and bustle of the Cathedral grounds and the outside city. A completely separate structure from the Cathedral proper would make the tomb shrine's importance more apparent to pilgrims and tourists. Most of all, Fr. Lawrence wanted to transform the tomb shrine into a more distinctive and novel tourist attraction.

However, the construction work required to make this transformation would potentially put San Thome at great risk, since the building of the new tomb chapel would require the removal of sand and dirt from directly beneath the Cathedral's floor. Fr. Lawrence explains:

> I approached some big construction companies, but they were not will-ing to take [it] up, because it is a risk ... So then I got a hold of one [of] our greatest engineer[s], he is a well-known structural engineer in India and abroad, one Mr. Alex Jacob. So we sat together and designed this one, what we have right now, the tomb chapel. And after designing, we requested the Larsen and Toubro people, L&T, they're supposed to be a big construction company, and initiated their president and after this they took [it] up, and they did that work of digging the underground, because it was a very, very risky thing, because we have these old walls and we are digging inside the old walls ... and also, the seashore, all sand. So, we had a very tough time, of course. Day and night, I had sleepless day[s] and nights, of course, until ... the work got over.[62]

With the completion of phase II of the Cathedral's renovation, phase III could be started, which was by far a simpler task. The last phase of the renovation involved the construction of a brand new building (i.e. the information center) over the tomb shrine's entrance, which was itself placed directly behind the Cathedral's sacristy. This building would also house the new museum, as well as an upstairs mini-auditorium.[63] Fr. Lawrence was both pleased and relieved by the end result, and relished the fact that he was able to accomplish his vision despite all the setbacks he experienced during this project. The newly renovated Cathedral and the freshly built tomb chapel faced its ultimate test in structural integrity when the 2004 tsunami hit Chennai only a couple of weeks after the renovation's completion. Fortunately, despite the crashing waves and the threat of flooding, the Cathedral "miraculously" held firm.

The legacy of San Thome as an apostolic tomb site

As one enters the lobby of the museum/auditorium building, the first thing one sees is a staircase. To the immediate right of the staircase is the entrance to the museum. Upstairs leads to the auditorium, while downstairs leads directly into the tomb shrine of St. Thomas. A few steps down leads to a small landing where directly ahead of it is a long rectangular signboard declaring, "Only three Churches in the whole world are built over the tomb of an Apostle of Jesus Christ." Displayed on this sign board are the three churches: Santiago de Compostela in Spain, St. Peter's Basilica in Rome, and the National Shrine of St. Thomas Basilica in India. In this display,

San Thome is shown alongside Santiago de Compostela and St. Peter's Basilica, both of which are world renowned pilgrimage sites and tourist attractions. By highlighting the Cathedral's illustrious connection to these other two sacred tomb shrines, it is made clear that San Thome is on par with them in terms of historical and spiritual value.

To the right of the sign board that depicts the three apostolic shrines is the official document decreed by the Conference of Catholic Bishops of India that confers upon San Thome the official status of National Shrine. Even before one is able to enter the tomb chapel, both of these displays are in full view in order to demonstrate and validate the significance and prestige of San Thome to every visiting pilgrim and tourist.These exhibits also serve to frame the Church in India and the San Thome parish as important and integral parts of the greater global Catholic community. These displays serve to instil pride into the local community by reaffirming both the heritage and global community aspects of the St. Thomas brand, which as discussed, are integral parts of San Thome's greater agenda for regional identity creation.

The tomb chapel foyer

Heading down from the stairway landing, the next and final set of steps leads into the foyer or lobby of the chapel. Inside the rectangular lobby or foyer, measuring 50 × 20 feet, one is surrounded by a trove of information and visual cues. Straight ahead, hanging on the far wall, is a large reproduction of Caravaggio's *The Incredulity of Saint Thomas*. This striking image depicts the moment when St. Thomas's doubt is transformed into faith as he touches the wounded side of the risen Christ. Written just above the painting, in golden letters and in both English and Tamil, is St. Thomas's faith proclamation, "My Lord and My God" (Figure 4.7). Two tall lamps flank either side of the painting, and on the floor directly in front of the painting is a large basin filled with water and lotus flowers, adding a subtle South Indian flair to the room's presentation. Six information plaques, three on either side of the Caravaggio, provide a historical summary, each in a different language: Hindi, Malayalam, Tamil, English, French, and German. Again, such a selection of languages clearly demonstrates the Cathedral administration's desire to cater to both local and international visitors.

The Doubting Thomas motif is the most common and well-known depiction of St. Thomas the Apostle, and having this literally iconic incident visibly on display makes it clear to any knowing visitor exactly who is being venerated here, and the importance of his connection to Christian myth and history. The emblazoned words, "My Lord and My God" emphasize St. Thomas's proclamation that Jesus is God. Additionally, the main Cathedral structure itself also houses two other depictions of the Doubting Thomas motif. The first is the large stained glass window behind the high-altar (Figure 4.8), which was painstakingly refurbished during

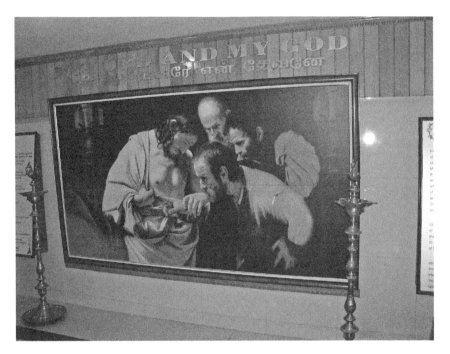

Figure 4.7 Reproduction of Caravaggio's *The Incredulity of Saint Thomas.*
Photo: T. C. Nagy.

the Cathedral's restoration, and the second is a life-sized diorama of the event that was installed at the rear of the Cathedral in 2000 in commemoration of the Great Jubilee, which was a world-wide Catholic event held at the beginning of that year.

Displaying this common motif so prominently throughout the Cathedral's grounds emphasizes the significance of the Saint buried here and his personal connection to the person of Jesus Christ and The New Testament. St. Thomas's faith proclamation is an important part of the greater historical narrative that makes up the Apostle's Indian legacy, which is an integral part of the St. Thomas brand. One may ask why Caravaggio's rendering of the Doubting Thomas story is used when there are many other renderings. This particular painting depicts St. Thomas actually touching the side wound of Jesus, something that is only implied in John 20: 24–29. In other words, this painting makes St. Thomas's physical connection to the resurrected Christ all the more palpable, thus making the direct connection between Jesus and the Indian Christian Church founded by St. Thomas all the more legitimate.

The six information plaques situated alongside Caravaggio's painting give substance to the various aspects that make up St. Thomas's Indian mission and historical narrative. These plaques, which are undoubtedly meant to be

Figure 4.8 Close up of the Cathedral's stained glass mural depicting St. Thomas's
       faith proclamation.
Photo: T. C. Nagy

read while viewing Caravaggio's painting, provide a brief summary of
St. Thomas's Christian and Indian legacy. The information on the plaques
makes clear that the Cathedral is appealing to a wide range of visitors. In a
general sense, it is important to establish that St. Thomas truly visited,
missionized, and was martyred in India. He is also the Apostle who proclaimed
Jesus as God, and is the progenitor of today's Indian Christian faith. One
plaque reads, "We are proud and fortunate to be part of this holy land, which
has been made sacred by the blood of St. Thomas who confessed 'My Lord
and My God.'" The connection is clearly made between St. Thomas's spilled
blood and the land of India, implying indigeneity, and by extending this
connection to the faith proclamation, India is also connected to Jesus through
the person of St. Thomas. For either a pilgrim or a religious tourist, this is vital
information that helps identify the socio-religious and historical significance of
the tomb site they are visiting and it defends the controversial political notion
that there are indigenous Christian communities in India.

Additionally, this sign also touts San Thome's connection with Santiago
de Compostela and St. Peter's Basilica by emphasizing the "international
reputation" garnered from the association, which, once again, highlights
the St. Thomas brand's international character, helping to elevate the site's

prestige in the eyes of all visitors, local and foreign. The last paragraph is aimed more at pilgrims and other spiritually minded visitors, since it is an invitation to participate in the religious act of prayer. From what has already been established through Caravaggio's painting and the first two paragraphs of the plaque, there is reason enough to believe that a figure as important as St Thomas would be able to provide a "powerful intercession" for the answering of petitions.

However, this power is intrinsically tied to the corporeal and real presence of St. Thomas, whose blood was spilled on this land, and whose flesh decomposed in this soil. The plaque capitalizes "Martyr" purposefully, because the legitimacy of this tomb and of an indigenous Christian origin rests on the idea that the "person and presence" of St. Thomas is permanently etched into the soil of India. Thus, the entire right-hand wall is taken up by a life-size diorama of St. Thomas's final moments, as he is about to be murdered while kneeling in prayer on top of what is now known as St. Thomas Mount (see Figure 3.1). In the foreground of the diorama, St. Thomas is kneeling before the Bleeding Cross, St. Thomas Mount's most prized relic. According to local tradition, this stone carving was made by St. Thomas himself and during the Apostle's martyrdom, his blood stained it; since that time this stone cross has been known to miraculously bleed and sweat on a number of occasions, hence its name, the Bleeding Cross.[64] Here we see the narrative detail of St. Thomas's blood staining the Indian soil dramatically portrayed. As mentioned in Chapter 3, St. Thomas's anonymous murderer stands menacingly behind the praying Apostle, his spear raised as he prepares to make the fatal strike. The soldier's cruel intent is visually denoted by a tattoo of a scorpion located just below the wrist of his raised arm. In the background is an artist's rendition of the surrounding area during the first century. The ocean can be clearly seen, visually connecting the site of St. Thomas's martyrdom at St. Thomas Mount to the site of his burial, here at San Thome.

In relation to the concept of a St. Thomas brand, we clearly see that the Church has placed a large emphasis on the Apostle's martyrdom. In terms of identity creation, we can see that the Church is attempting to promote the idea that St. Thomas's blood serves to "root" the Indian Christian community to the soil of India. This imagery clearly echoes Einstein's assertion that brands become a significant factor in personalized identity creation due to feelings of societal "rootlessness," which seems to be an issue the Church in Chennai is attempting to rectify with its promotion of a St. Thomas brand.[65] Finally, in the implicit connection drawn between St. Thomas's martyrdom and the modern-day persecution of Christians in India, the Church is emphasizing the need and possibility for self-sacrifice in a nation where communal and sectarian violence is commonplace. Once again, the Church is attempting to utilize the Apostle's legacy as a martyr in order to promote an Indian Christian identity that stands tall in the face of persecution, and which is willing to make the ultimate sacrifice for its faith.

Directly across from the diorama, on the opposite wall, is a display of more modern significance. Two large poster boards commemorate Pope John Paul II's visit to St. Thomas's tomb in 1986. Both boards are enlarged photographs of the late Pope standing before and praying at the tomb of St. Thomas, as it was before the new underground chapel was built. The figure of Pope John Paul II stands as a popular mainstream religious icon whose legacy has been celebrated the world over, and as Einstein pointed out about faith brands, "More so than with consumer products, spokespeople – pastor, rabbi, or television personality – are an important aspect of the brand."[66] In essence, Pope John Paul II, or at least his memory, acts as a spokesman for both the Church in India and the St. Thomas legacy. As such, the Pope's visit can be seen as an endorsement of the Indian Church's undertakings, as well as for the legitimacy of St. Thomas's tomb as a local heritage site and religious shrine.

The underground tomb chapel and crypt

From the lobby, there are two passageways into the tomb chapel, located on either side of the Caravaggio and information plaques. The chapel room itself measures 72 × 20 feet, and provides a seating capacity of 150 people (Figure 4.9).[67] One of Fr. Lawrence's reasons for creating this new chapel

Figure 4.9 The underground tomb chapel of St. Thomas.
Photo: T. C. Nagy.

was to provide a more comfortable and intimate space for pilgrims and visitors. The chapel is often rented out for private services and functions, and the presence of air conditioning units along the chapel walls provide additional respite from the heat and humidity of Chennai's tropical climate. At the far end of the chapel is the tomb, which also functions as the chapel's altar (Figure 4.10). Above the altar a small window allows visitors to look up into the floor of the Cathedral above. However, it is the layout and design of the tomb altar itself that exemplifies the greater meaning behind St. Thomas's Indian legacy and its significance to Indian Christianity today (Figure 4.11).

There are four main features of the hollow tomb-altar's layout: the gold embossed Persian cross, the life-sized representation of the corpse of St. Thomas, the replica spear or lance, and the glass bottom that shows the exposed sand and soil below the altar. The prominently displayed Persian cross is purposefully reminiscent of the Bleeding Cross at St. Thomas Mount, but also provides a direct connection to the Syrian (Thomas) Christians of Kerala. The Persian cross motif is commonly found in Syrian Christian art and architecture, and is employed by most Thomas Christian denominations in South India. By displaying the connection between St. Thomas's tomb and the history of the Thomas Christians in Kerala, the tomb site is presented as an integral part of Syrian Christian tradition.

Figure 4.10 The tomb chapel's altar.
Photo: T. C. Nagy.

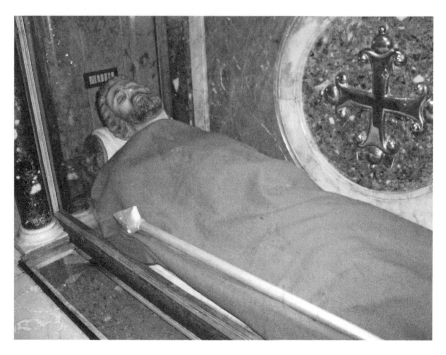

Figure 4.11 Close up of St. Thomas's tomb and altar.
Photo: T. C. Nagy.

Before the 2004 renovation, the tomb of St. Thomas was literally empty, but by adding a life-size statue of the slain St. Thomas, a greater visual dimension was added to the shrine. It is important to note that, regardless of the fact that San Thome no longer possesses any significant portion of St. Thomas's skeletal remains, the site is still adamantly referred to as his tomb. It is probably more accurate to say that San Thome was built over the "original" or "former" tomb site of St. Thomas. As several of San Thome's recent publications have explained, St. Thomas's tomb has been opened several times in the last 2000 years, during which St. Thomas's bones were either translated to a foreign nation, or eventually lost.[68] The Cathedral's official account follows Western European tradition on the whereabouts of St. Thomas's skeletal remains. The majority of St. Thomas's bodily relics were moved to Edessa sometime in the third century. During the Crusades, the relics were moved from place to place in the Holy Land and Europe, before finally arriving at a church in Ortona, Italy in 1258 CE. The majority of the relics remain there to this day, and the only relic that the Cathedral claims to possess was donated by the Ortona Church in 1994.[69] While there is no actual "corpse", the presence of red sand or the supposed remains of the Apostle's decomposed flesh at the site is used to justify the Cathedral's use of the word "tomb" in describing it in the present tense.

The statue of St. Thomas's corpse also reinforces the reality of this shrine as a tomb site. By creating a scenario where one must actually approach the dead Saint, visitors are compelled to take part in an intimate visual and emotional experience that is suggestive of attending a wake. In a sense, the replica of St. Thomas's corpse provides a physical reminder of the site's sacrality, and that the Apostle's body was once truly laid to rest here. Next to the Apostle's body is a spear or lance, the weapon with which St. Thomas was killed and an obvious reminder that St. Thomas was a martyr for the faith. The inclusion of the spear also corroborates the state in which the Portuguese found the tomb. Of all the relics discovered by the Portuguese during their initial excavation, only the spear head they found still exists today. It is currently housed in an ornate reliquary in the Cathedral museum upstairs (Figure 4.12).

Figure 4.12 Reliquary that contains the spear head that was excavated by the Portuguese from St. Thomas's tomb.

Photo: T. C. Nagy.

Once again, the reality of St. Thomas's martyrdom is physically placed on display. As briefly touched upon in Chapter 2, there are several accounts of how the Apostle met his death in India. However, his death with a spear is by far the most popular version, and is what is noted in the Church's official list of martyrs, *The Roman Martyrology*.[70] Depictions of St. Thomas often have him holding a spear, since it is common for martyred saints to include in their iconography the device of their demise (Figure 4.13). Thus, several aspects of the St. Thomas brand are brought together under the auspices of the Apostle's tomb chapel, further showcasing the "source and summit of Indian Christianity," as well as Indian Christian heritage and identity.[71]

However, as demonstrated in previous chapters, the political rhetoric surrounding claims for Indian indigeneity involves an ancient and direct connection to the soil of India, which is why Church administrators emphasize those aspects of St. Thomas's legacy that demonstrate his physical

Figure 4.13 Italian-made statue of St. Thomas located in the Cathedral's threshold.
Photo: T. C. Nagy.

connection to the land of India. Perhaps the most important instance of these aspects is his death as a martyr because, through martyrdom, St. Thomas literally sacrifices his life and sheds his blood on Indian soil. By being buried in Mylapore, his corporeal remains become one with India. The spear emphasizes his martyrdom, but it is the exposed red soil visibly showcased underneath the tomb altar that emphasizes the unity of the Apostle and, by association, of all Indian Christians with India's ancient land. The exposition of the tomb soil has been a facet of St. Thomas's tomb since 1903, but it carries a far older history. Even today the tomb's red sand is touted as the main conduit for St. Thomas's physical presence and spiritual power in India. With this in mind, Fr. Lawrence developed the St. Thomas sand relic card, a novel means to offer tomb sand to pilgrims and tourists keen on taking home with them a piece of St. Thomas.

The development of the St. Thomas sand relic card

The "St. Thomas Relic Card" is a laminated card roughly the shape and size of a typical credit card that holds a relic of St. Thomas by way of a little sand taken from the Apostle's tomb. This bit of sand is classified by the Church as an authentic relic, and thus, the ultimate souvenir of a pilgrimage or visit to the tomb of St. Thomas at San Thome. Priced cheaply at 15 INR, these cards are easily purchased at the Cathedral's gift shop. While there is a certain novelty to the form and substance of this particular souvenir, it is legitimized by ancient tradition. According to both *The Acts of Thomas* and South Indian oral tradition, the king responsible for the death of St. Thomas later had the Apostle's tomb opened so that he might take a bone or some sand from it in order to heal his ailing son.[72]

Furthermore, Marco Polo, the thirteenth-century Venetian merchant and adventurer, visited the tomb of St. Thomas sometime around 1293 to 1295 CE.[73] His memoirs provide historical evidence of a long-standing belief in the tomb sand's healing power, as well as justification for the Cathedral's current utilization of sand relic cards as a way of honouring and advertising the tomb's spiritual legacy. Marco Polo states:

> As I have said, St. Thomas the Apostle was martyred in Maabar [another name for the Coromandel Coast region] in this part of India. His body is kept in a small city which few merchants have cause to visit. But vast numbers of Christians and Saracens go there …. The Christians who make pilgrimage collect earth of a red colour from the spot where he was slain and reverently carry it away with them in the belief that miracles can be performed with it. They also dilute it in water and give it to the sick as a cure for all kinds of disorders.[74]

It is clear from my conversations with many of my informants that the Thomas Christians of Kerala adamantly attest to this tradition and others like it, and are thus the main source of demand for tomb sand at San Thome and holy spring water from Little Mount.

More so, as Fr. Lawrence explained to me, many visiting pilgrims desired to obtain authentic tomb sand for a souvenir or for their own personal use. Initially, pilgrims would take whatever sand they could get from around the tomb, "genuine" or not, but this practice was halted by the parish priest at the time because too much sand was being taken, so he ordered the exposed sandy ground to be covered by a glass panel.[75] Not wanting to have the past repeat itself, Fr. Lawrence understood that his main problem was deciding how to regulate its distribution, because first, it had to be genuine sand from the tomb, and second, there was only so much sand that could go around indefinitely. Fr. Lawrence explained:

> But when we were renovating the Church, I thought we should give something to the people. So, this novel idea was given to me by one Simon; he is a parishioner of San Thome ... so, I thought, why can't we keep this as a relic for the people who come? So, that's how that card was made, and it was very much appreciated by everybody. That card use[s] all the historical details of the thing also, when Thomas came to India, and when he died, where he was buried, all these kind[s] of things are there. Plus the sand is there, and people want to keep it in their pocket, or in their purse, and in their bag, and carry it around [where] they go. And they also pray. In fact, I even heard they sold some of these cards in the U.S. and so on.[76]

Fr. Lawrence also noted the general popularity and desire for souvenirs in India, especially at sacred shrines and temples. He compared the relic card to a popular souvenir given to pilgrims at the Shrine of Our Lady of Vailankanni. It is common practice there to dress the statue of St. Mary in a sari. Afterwards these saris are cut up into tiny pieces and the pieces are distributed to those pilgrims who desire them.[77]

Mr. Zander, who remembers when these cards were first released, agreed with Fr. Lawrence's sentiment about the card's general novelty. During our interview, in order to make a point, Mr. Zander pulled out from his wallet his personal relic card and excitedly said:

> This his sand, St. Thomas really has come out, almost a relic, no? .... This other way of marketing of St. Thomas to spread [the word] about St. Thomas the Apostle. [A person] comes across this thing [pointing to the details on his personal relic card], what is this, what is this? Once he goes through everything [written on the card] then he would like to know more about St. Thomas. And then he would like to have one card like that and then he will like to see the face [of St. Thomas], a bit of marketing![78]

Mr. Zander's use the term "marketing" to describe the Cathedral's release of the relic card was revealing. He clearly recognized that Fr. Lawrence was utilizing a marketing strategy in his promotion of San Thome, and seemed comfortable discussing it in those terms.[79] Also, Fr. Lawrence and Mr. Zander both stressed to me the importance of the card's accessibility, and the ease with which it could be stored or passed around from person to person, thus generating positive word-of-mouth and free advertisement. This understanding demonstrates Fr. Lawrence's sophisticated utilization of marketing techniques, and as Einstein writes, the creation of positive word-of-mouth "is the most effective form of marketing."[80]

As Fr. Lawrence previously mentioned, the idea for the relic card came from a local parishioner by the name of Simon. It is very likely that this Simon is Simon Chumkat, who in January of 2007 presented a research paper on the sand-taking tradition at St. Thomas's tomb at the International Conference on Indian Christianity. This research paper was later excerpted into an article for San Thome's magazine *Voice of St. Thomas*, of which Chumkat is a member of the editorial board.[81] The article sets out to validate the historical and religious significance of the sand taken from St. Thomas's tomb, which is then distributed through the relic card. Chumkat discusses the sand's status as an official third-class relic as categorized by the *Catechism of the Catholic Church* and *Canon Law*, as well the various traditions that have been passed down through written and oral history.

According to this article, first-class relics are usually special items used during or for significant events in the saint's life, as well as the saint's bodily remains. Second-class relics are other such items that were used or worn by the saint during his or her lifetime. Third-class relics, such as the sand from St. Thomas's tomb, are typically items that have been placed in contact with the saint's corpse.[82] As we can see, even though the red sand can also be considered the Apostle's decomposed flesh and blood, it is not classified as an actual bodily remain like a piece of bone. This fact does not seem to have tarnished the significance of this tradition or the relic card's popularity. The sand relic card is incredibly interesting because it represents the repackaging and commodification of an ancient tradition for everyday use in the modern world.

Chumkat's article concludes by celebrating the ingenuity that the relic cards offer for both pilgrims and the preservation of tradition. Chumkat writes

> The long cherished desires of the devotees of St. Thomas was [sic] finally fulfilled when the Shrine made the sand relic available in a convenient credit card format which can always be carried in a wallet or credit card holder. Many miracles, attributed to the sand relic are pouring into the Shrine. The devotion to the sand relic is considered as

a mark of respect to the martyrdom and the bloodshed of St. Thomas on this earth as a witness to the life, teachings, death and Resurrection [of] his Master, Jesus Christ.[83]

Chumkat makes it clear that one of the main purposes behind the creation of the sand card was to emphasize the significance of St. Thomas's spilt blood on Indian soil.

Ultimately, the sand card serves to provide an actual physical product or commodity for the St. Thomas brand that, in and of itself, details the many aspects of St. Thomas's legacy via the card's intriguing layout and design. At the same time, the sand relic card also acts as a conduit for St. Thomas's spiritual power, something that goes well beyond the materials that went into making it and the information shared by it.[84]

The St. Thomas sand relic card as brand commodity

As noted above, the St. Thomas relic card's design and layout resembles that of a typical credit or debit card issued by a bank (Figure 4.14). In fact, Fr. Lawrence admits that this was done on purpose. He explains, "And also, today people like to have something novel, and that was the time everybody was using credit cards and debit cards and so on. So, that's why, if you notice, the whole thing is made just like that."[85] Fr. Lawrence's reasoning indicates that, at the time of the renovation, credit cards were being perceived as "novel" or interesting new devices by Chennai's populace. Credit cards in India are generally associated with upper and middle-class members of society, and as such, can be viewed as an item symbolic of upward mobility. Also, as we know, credit cards are often seen as being synonymous with actual money, and a great deal of it. In other words, a credit card provides its owner with a line of credit that realistically allows one to make purchases of an exorbitant nature. Undoubtedly, there is an obvious correlation between Chennai's economic growth and the rise in popularity of credit cards in the city. Mainly, however, the modern nature of this design demonstrates Fr. Lawrence and Simon Chumkat's innovative and sophisticated use of marketing. It also conveys their understanding of local souvenir culture as a means to create "meaning" through the combination of St. Thomas's legacy and modern financial practices.[86]

It is striking how closely the relic card was designed to mimic an actual credit card. For instance, most credit and debit cards are issued with a sixteen digit number placed horizontally across the face of the card. The sand relic card does this too, only the numbers "0052 0072 0307 2004" are actually a coded reference to four significant dates associated with St. Thomas and San Thome Cathedral. St. Thomas supposedly arrived in India in 52 CE and was then martyred in Mylapore in 72 CE. St. Thomas's feast day is celebrated on July 3rd (0307). Finally, 2004 is the year of the

Figure 4.14 St. Thomas sand relic card front [top] and back [bottom].
Sand relic card: San Thome Cathedral Basilica, Mylapore, Chennai, India, 2009.

Cathedral's renovation, and also the last time the tomb was opened in order for the sand to be collected for use in the relic cards.

Other details that are a part of the relic card's credit card aesthetic include the blue and yellow rectangular logo, which looks to be a direct copy of a former VISA company logo. On closer inspection, instead of the name "VISA," the sand card's logo consists of the four letters "SCBC," which is an acronym for Santhome Cathedral Basilica, Chennai. In place of a "valid thru" date and expiration date is St. Thomas's famous line, "My Lord and my God" from John 20: 28. On the back, there is even a horizontal black line running across the card that mimics the black magnetic strip typical of most credit cards. In all but the last example, the credit card aesthetic is being utilized to convey the finer points of St. Thomas's Indian legacy as it pertains to the historic Cathedral.

More obvious visuals include the background image that depicts a serene day along an unidentifiable section of the Indian coast. At the forefront of the card's left-hand corner is the unmistakable visage of San Thome with its white-washed finish and Gothic features. To the right of this image are four more images that are framed as small snapshots. These four images display the Cathedral's religious and spiritual offerings. First is an image of St. Thomas, the Cathedral's patron saint. Second is a shot of the tomb chapel, the source of St. Thomas's deep connection to the soil of India, and whose physical presence in the sand becomes a real source for grace and spiritual power. Next is Our Lady of Mylapore, San Thome's link to both Mother Mary and St. Francis Xavier. Finally, there is a picture of the Pole of St. Thomas, which stands as the ultimate testimony to St. Thomas's miraculous powers and intercessory hand.

The most important aspect of the relic card is the tomb sand itself. Fr. Lawrence assured me that the sand in the cards was actually sand from the tomb of St. Thomas, since the 2004 restoration work had provided ample opportunity for him to open the tomb and gather as much as was needed.[87] According to historical tradition, St. Thomas's tomb has only been opened four times before the recent renovation. This fifth opening was therefore a very auspicious event, and probably the last time for a while that genuine sand could be removed from the site.

As one can see on the upper right-hand corner of the card, only a small dash of sand is used, thus allowing the Cathedral to make a great number of cards for sale and distribution. The back of the card gives a brief summary of the Apostle's mission in India and his martyrdom. The card continues, "National Shrine of St. Thomas Basilica is built over his tomb. The sand taken from the tomb of St. Thomas is believed to have miraculous healing powers. Keep this card containing the holy sand of St. Thomas in your wallet or credit card holder and carry it always with you." The front of the card goes into more detail as to the benefits of having this card. It states, "May St. Thomas, through his powerful intercession, enable you to be free from fear, anxiety and pain. May you be blessed always with courage, confidence, success, health and happiness." As Chumkat notes, and as Sr. Merrill confirmed to me, there have been several reports of miracles attributed specifically to the sand card.[88] The additional detail and information placed on the card is primarily there to reinforce the legitimacy and potency of the tomb sand's power, and thus, all the emphasized aspects of St. Thomas's brand and legacy. These details are brought together to form a guarantee of sorts that the sand relic card can provide its user with something more than just the sum of its parts and history. The sand card asserts the legitimacy of St. Thomas's spiritual power and, in turn, reaffirms a justifiable faith and belief in St. Thomas's overarching Christian and Indian legacy.

This still begs the question why would one design a holy relic container after something as blatantly worldly and status conscious as a credit card? The answer could simply be, as Fr. Lawrence stated to me, for the novelty. This is certainly a valid enough reason from the perspective of religious tourism and marketing. On the other hand, given that Church administrators mainly wanted to promote and encourage a revival of the cult of St. Thomas, there is probably more to it. Thus, the sand relic card can be seen as a metaphorical credit card, something that offers its holder a spiritual benefit instead of a tangible financial one as would a real credit card. Instead of being issued by a bank or company, the sand relic card is a holy product distributed by a representative of the divine. One could even say that if there are any additional fees beyond the initial monetary price, they could simply be charged to one's faith. The Church is using a well-known material device in order to promote a spiritual belief in the immaterial.

San Thome as heritage site and tourist attraction

Based on my interviews with Church leaders and parishioners, San Thome's renovation seemed to have successfully raised the Cathedral's profile as a pilgrimage site and tourist attraction. However, it is possible that San Thome owes its immediate success more to rising trends in the national and local tourism industry than to the quality of its refurbishment and marketing. As historian and anthropologist Mary Hancock points out, it was only in the 1990s that officials of the Indian government began to really see the financial potential in promoting India's tourism industry. This new vision would see the government-sponsored privatization of India's tourism industry, as well as the creation of a new government-run national ministry in charge of tourism in 1998.[89] Tamil Nadu would also follow suit by creating its own plans for touristic self-promotion in the hope that this would help to bolster its economy and alleviate poverty and unemployment. For the most part, India's efforts have met with success. As Hancock states, "Both central and state plans anticipated major increases in domestic and international tourist arrivals by 2007, and, according to preliminary reports, these goals have been met."[90]

Hancock also discusses the touristic marketing of Tamil Nadu as essentially the creation of its "brand equity" through the branding of Tamil culture.[91] Chennai, as Tamil Nadu's major metropolitan center and international hub, becomes the newly christened "Gateway to Southern India." As Hancock explains, "Chennai's transport, commercial, and administrative services make it a gateway in a practical sense. Beyond that, its sites of public memory function as narrative gateways, framing the pasts that lend value and authenticity to Tamil Nadu's heritage-branded products, services, and knowledge."[92] So too does the newly renovated San Thome Cathedral act in this way as a part of Chennai's historical narrative. Although

Hancock never mentions San Thome as having specifically benefitted from Tamil Nadu's tourism efforts, it is implied from the rise in number of specialized tour packages and circuits that most of Chennai's sites of interest received a boost of some sort in the way of tourist traffic.[93] I, personally, recall the sight of large tour buses parked at San Thome and St. Thomas Mount on several occasions during my time in Chennai.

The official website of the Tamil Nadu Tourism Development Corporation and Department Of Tourism features San Thome several times.[94] Many of the tourism packages offered on this site tend to utilize Chennai as mainly a hub for other destinations around Tamil Nadu state. It seems to only offer a single package for within Chennai called the "half day Chennai city sightseeing tour," however; San Thome is not listed as one of its destinations.[95] Instead, San Thome is highlighted as one of the main attractions of Chennai in the information section, and is included as one of sixteen stops along the special "hop on hop off tour in Chennai city," which is done by bus and organized by the Tamilnadu State Transport Corporation.[96]

All in all, Fr. Lawrence has demonstrated a clear awareness of India's changing attitude towards tourism and heritage preservation. It was the combination of Fr. Lawrence's timing in getting the renovations underway and the overall quality and ingenuity of the Cathedral's work that ultimately got it "put on the world map," as one parishioner wrote of Fr. Lawrence's efforts.[97] Another indication of the above efforts and successes can be found by perusing local tourist guide books from before and after 2004. In *Diaspora of the Gods*, Joanne Waghorne even notes how a 1984 edition of the popular guide book *Lonely Planet Guide* wrote disparagingly about Chennai's (Madras's) touristic appeal.[98]

Before my time in Chennai I acquired a reference guide map of Tamil Nadu published in 1999 by Bharat Graphics. In its section on Chennai's places of interest, which numbered seven sites in total, St. Thomas Mount is only referenced in passing and San Thome is not mentioned at all.[99] During my first trip to Chennai, I came across a more professional looking guide book to the city, published in 2008 by The Times of India. Granted, this publication is both more detailed and concise than the guide map, but it may be that an Indian publication of this calibre did not exist until very recently due to the issues raised above by Hancock. The *Times City Guide-Chennai* includes a list of Chennai's top 40 "must see" sites. San Thome Cathedral is 18th on the list, and St. Thomas Mount comes in at 34th.[100] A number of other Christian sites also make it onto this list, demonstrating the greater variety and depth to which local tourism marketing has progressed over the last decade. Even though San Thome does not make it into the top ten of Chennai's must-see attractions, the fact it is included in the book at all demonstrates, again, that even with the recent growth of Tamil Nadu's tourism industry, Fr. Lawrence's endeavors at San Thome helped to re-establish and confirm the Cathedral's place among Chennai's diverse collection of heritage sites and monuments.

Chapter summary

The Church's aspiration for a big-budget St. Thomas movie much like *The Passion of the Christ* demonstrates the lengths San Thome's administration is willing to go in order to promote and gain exposure for St. Thomas's legacy. It also shows their desire to market St. Thomas as a full-fledged "faith brand," and hopefully reap the same kind of financial and spiritual gain seen with *The Passion*. San Thome's 2004 renovation can be understood in a similar light, but requires the added dimensions of touristic promotion, heritage preservation, evangelization, and pilgrimage in order to solidify this idea.

These dimensions are best exemplified within the context of the original hundred-year-old Cathedral, and by extension, the underground tomb shrine. In terms of branding, it displays what Einstein describes as "making meaning – taking the individual aspects of a product and turning them into more than the sum of their parts."[101] If we look at Schultz and Shultz's list of what brands are meant to accomplish, we see that San Thome's renovation does do some of these things. Fr. Lawrence's appeal and show of goodwill to the parish community "created relationships" with the people most directly involved in the upkeep and promulgation of the site. The renovation as a whole created and highlighted the potential for short and long term "financial value" for the Church and local community by raising the site's profile to generate greater visitor traffic. And with greater traffic in terms of both tourists and pilgrims, the higher quality of facilities and the fostering of interest through published materials created value for the shrine's "customers." Projects that continue on well after the fact, like the bid for a St. Thomas movie, help to maintain, along with the site itself, "long-term income flow." Clearly, the Cathedral's ultimate goal is to become a "cultural icon," and thus a more viable part of mainstream culture. This is something that Fr. Lawrence greatly desired in promoting the veneration of St. Thomas. He also understood that "everyone 'owns' a piece of the brand," and thus targeted his St. Thomas brand to a wider audience that included people who were neither Christian nor religious.[102]

By creating a positive mainstream profile of St. Thomas and Catholicism in India, the Church can better strengthen its position on indigeneity and social justice within India's political landscape. Coupled with the careful presentation of San Thome and other historic Catholic institutions as being an integral compliment to regional and national Indian heritage building and preservation, the Church can also attempt to stave off the criticisms of Hindu nationalist ideologues. Through the development of a St. Thomas brand, Fr. Lawrence and other Church administrators are able to showcase the most significant elements of the Apostle's legacy and transform it into a spiritual, cultural, and historical commodity that has become more easily accessible and consumable by potential converts, pilgrims, and tourists than ever before.

Fr. Lawrence's successes at San Thome and elsewhere have become an influential part of the overall Catholic renewal in Chennai. As the following chapter will demonstrate, San Thome is only a small part of a city-wide Catholic renewal where both older and newer churches in Chennai are going through this process of land and shrine development, as well as exhibiting a greater acceptance of more "popular" forms of Christian devotion. While some internal tensions still persist within the Church regarding popular Christianity, it is mainly due to the Church's own desire to evangelize and guide practitioners of popular religiosity towards a more "Catholic" understanding of their piety. However, due to the vast numbers of potential converts that popular Christianity brings into play, the Church is willing to be more creative with its evangelization strategies.

Notes

1 Pope John Paul II, *Ecclesia in Asia*, http://www.vatican.va/holy_father/john_paul_ii/apost_exhortations/documents/hf_jp-ii_exh_06111999_ecclesia-in-asia_en.html (Accessed August 2, 2011).
2 Interview with Fr. Lawrence Raj, Chennai, June 15, 2009.
3 Ibid.
4 Boris Vukonic, "Religion, Tourism and Economics: A Convenient Symbiosis," *Tourism Recreation Research* 27, 2 (2002): 64.
5 Boris Vukonic, "Sacred Places in the Roman Catholic Tradition," in *Tourism, Religion & Spiritual Journeys*, eds Daniel H. Olsen and Dallen J. Timothy (London and New York: Routledge, 2006), 248.
6 Mary Lee Nolan and Sidney Nolan, "Religious Sites as Tourist Attractions in Europe," *Annals of Tourism Research* 19 (1992): 69.
7 Vukonic, "Religion, Tourism and Economics: A Convenient Symbiosis," 60.
8 Mara Einstein, *Brands of Faith: Marketing Religion in a Commercial Age* (London and New York: Routledge, 2008), 93–94.
9 Quoted in Einstein, *Brands of Faith*, 70.
10 Einstein, *Brands of Faith*, 70.
11 Don Schultz and Heidi Schultz, *Brand Babble: Sense and Nonsense about Branding* (Mason, Ohio: Thompson/ South-Western, 2004), 18.
12 Einstein, *Brands of Faith*, 71.
13 Ibid, 88–89.
14 Ibid, 72–74.
15 *Voice of St. Thomas* 2, 9 (July–September 2011), cover.
16 Vukonic, "Religion, Tourism and Economics: A Convenient Symbiosis," 59.
17 Einstein, *Brands of Faith*, 92.
18 Ibid, 92, 147.
19 Ibid, 93.
20 "The Making of an Epic Film: Tamilnadu Chief Minister, Dr. M. Karunanidhi, is Chief Guest!" *Voice of St. Thomas* 1, 9 (July–September 2008): 26.
21 *TN Church sets Rs 50-cr Budget for Film on St. Thomas*, http://www.indianexpress.com/news/tn-church-sets-rs-50cr-budget-for-film-on-st-thomas/331605/0 (Accessed June 4, 2010). See also: Deccan Chronicle, "Film on St. Thomas: Rajini May Don Role of Tiruvalluvar," http://www.dc-epaper.com/deccanchronicle/default.aspx?BMode=100 (July 2, 2008).
22 Einstein, *Brands of Faith*, 1.

23 Ibid, 4.
24 "The Making of an Epic Film: Tamilnadu Chief Minister, Dr. M. Karunanidhi, is Chief Guest!" 26.
25 Interview with Fr. Lawrence Raj, Chennai, December 15, 2010.
26 Ishwar Sharan, *Madras-Mylapore Archdiocese plans Blockbuster Movie on St. Thomas*, http://apostlethomasindia.wordpress.com/2010/05/11/madras-mylapore-archdiocese-plans-blockbuster-movie-on-st-thomas-%e2%80%93-ishwar-sharan/ (Accessed June 13, 2012).
27 Quoted in Sashi Kala Chandran, "Down Memory Lane with Fr. Lawrence Raj," *Sweet Fruits of God's Harvest on Earth: Rev. Fr. Lawrence Raj Sacerdotal Silver Jubilee Commemorative Souvenir*, edited by Fr. Lawrence Raj Silver Jubilee Souvenir Committee. (Chennai: Fr. Lawrence Raj Silver Jubilee Souvenir Committee, 2007).
28 Interview with Mr. Zander, Chennai, August 5, 2009.
29 Ibid.
30 Ibid.
31 Schultz and Schultz, *Brand Babble*, 18.
32 Lawrence Raj, "A Dream Fulfilled …," *Souvenir San Thome Historic Event 2004* (San Thome Cathedral, Chennai, Tamil Nadu, India: San Thome Cathedral Basilica, 2004).
33 Duncan Forbes, *The Heart of India* (South Brunswick and New York: A. S. Barnes and Company, 1968), 175.
34 Charlie Pye-Smith, *Rebel and Outcasts: A Journey through Christian India* (London: Viking, 1997), 203.
35 Ibid, 203.
36 Interview with Fr. Lawrence Raj, Chennai, June 15, 2009.
37 Interview with Mr. Zander, Chennai, August 5, 2009.
38 Interview with Fr. Lawrence Raj, Chennai, June 15, 2009.
39 Interview with Fr. Lawrence Raj, Chennai, June 30, 2009.
40 Ibid.
41 Ibid.
42 S. J. Anthonysamy, *A Saga of Faith: St. Thomas the Apostle of India* (Chennai: National Shrine of St. Thomas Basilica, 2009), 126.
43 Interview with Mr. Zander, Chennai, August 5, 2009.
44 Interview with Fr. Lawrence Raj, Chennai, June 15, 2009.
45 Ibid.
46 Fr. Lawrence Raj, "A Dream Fulfilled …."
47 Interview with Fr. Lawrence Raj, Chennai, June 15, 2009.
48 Anthonysamy, *A Saga of Faith*, 109–110.
49 Ibid, 125–126. See also: Joe Mannath, "Basilica Par Excellence: An Apostolic Structure & an Architectural Treasure," *Voice of St. Thomas* 1, 1 (July–September 2006): 50.
50 S. Muthiah, *Madras Rediscovered* (Chennai: East West, an imprint of Westland Limited, 2008), 197–198.
51 Ravi Gundu Rao & Associates, "The Restoration Work," *Souvenir San Thome Historic Event 2004* (San Thome Cathedral, Chennai, Tamil Nadu, India: San Thome Cathedral Basilica, 2004).
52 Ravi Gundu Rao & Associates, "The Restoration Work."
53 The Holy See, "Code of Canon Law: Chapter 3, Shrines, Can. 1230," http://www.vatican.va/archive/ENG1104/__P4J.HTM (accessed July 5, 2012).
54 The Holy See, "Code of Canon Law: Chapter 3, Shrines, Can. 1230–1234," http://www.vatican.va/archive/ENG1104/__P4J.HTM (accessed July 5, 2012).
55 Interview with Fr. Lawrence Raj, Chennai, June 15, 2009.

56 Interview with Fr. Lawrence Raj, Chennai, December 15, 2010.
57 Einstein, *Brands of Faith*, 70.
58 Anthonysamy, *A Saga of Faith*, 130.
59 Interview with Mr. Zander, Chennai, August 5, 2009.
60 Anthonysamy, *A Saga of Faith*, 112–113.
61 Interview with Fr. Lawrence Raj, Chennai, June 15, 2009.
62 Ibid.
63 Ibid.
64 Anthonysamy, *A Saga of Faith*, 137–138.
65 Einstein, *Brands of Faith*, 72.
66 Ibid, 92.
67 Anthonysamy, *A Saga of Faith*, 128.
68 See: Anthonysamy, *A Saga of Faith*, 99–103. See also: Simon Chumkat, "Sand from the Tomb," *Voice of St Thomas* 1, 5 (July–September 2007): 10. See also: *National Shrine of St. Thomas Basilica* (Chennai: National Shrine of St. Thomas Basilica, 2009), 4.
69 Anthonysamy, *A Saga of Faith*, 102–103.
70 Published by Order of Gregory XIII, Revised by Authority of Urban VIII and Clement X, Augmented and Corrected in 1749 by Benedict XII, *The Roman Martyrology* (Baltimore, MD: John Murphy Company, 1916), 391.
71 *Voice of St. Thomas* 2, 9 (July–September 2011), cover.
72 Chumkat, "Sand from the Tomb," 10.
73 Leslie Brown, *The Indian Christians of St. Thomas* (Cambridge: Cambridge University Press, 1982), 56. See also: P. J. Podipara, *The Thomas Christians* (Bombay: St. Paul Publications, 1970), 23.
74 Marco Polo, *Journey to the End of the Earth*, translated by Robin Brown (Stroud: The History Press, 2007), 197–198.
75 Interview with Fr. Lawrence Raj, Chennai, June 30, 2009.
76 Ibid.
77 Ibid.
78 Interview with Mr. Zander, Chennai, August 5, 2009.
79 Ibid.
80 Einstein, *Brands of Faith*, 81.
81 Chumkat, "Sand from the Tomb," 10–11.
82 Ibid, 10.
83 Ibid, 11.
84 Einstein, *Brands of Faith*, 70.
85 Interview with Fr. Lawrence Raj, Chennai, June 30, 2009.
86 Einstein, *Brands of Faith*, 70.
87 Interview with Fr. Lawrence Raj, Chennai, June 30, 2009.
88 Interview with Sr. Merrill, Chennai, June 13, 2009.
89 Mary E. Hancock, *The Politics of Heritage from Madras to Chennai* (Bloomington, IN: Indiana University Press, 2008), 129.
90 Ibid.
91 Ibid, 133.
92 Ibid, 135.
93 Ibid, 137–146.
94 Tamil Nadu Tourism, http://www.tamilnadutourism.org/index1.aspx (Accessed May 5, 2014).
95 Tamil Nadu Tourism, "Half Day Chennai City Sight Seeing Tour," http://www.tamilnadutourism.org/Tours/TourFare.aspx?TourId=19 (Accessed May 5, 2014).
96 Tamil Nadu Tourism, "CHENNAI – Gateway to the South: Places of Tourist Interest,"   http://www.tamilnadutourism.org/places/CitiesTowns/chennai01.

aspx?catid=010101P01;pg=2 (Accessed May 5, 2014). See also: Tamil Nadu Tourism, "Hop On Hop Off Tour Of Chennai City," http://tamilnadutourism. org/tnstc-tour.html (Accessed May 5, 2014).

97 Vimala Padmaraj, "A Jubilee Etched in Silver!" *Sweet Fruits of God's Harvest on Earth: Rev. Fr. Lawrence Raj Sacerdotal Silver Jubilee Commemorative Souvenir*, edited by Fr. Lawrence Raj Silver Jubilee Souvenir Committee. (Chennai: Fr. Lawrence Raj Silver Jubilee Souvenir Committee, 2007).

98 Joanne Punzo Waghorne, *Diaspora of the Gods: Modern Hindu Temple in an Urban Middle-Class World* (New York: Oxford University Press, 2004), 3.

99 Reference Guide Map: Tamil Nadu (Chandigarh: Bharat Graphics, 1999), 4–5.

100 Madhulita Mohanty (ed.), "Must See in Chennai," *Times City Guide: Chennai* (New Delhi: Bennett, Coleman & Co., Ltd., 2008), 38, 55, and 68.

101 Einstein, *Brands of Faith*, 70.

102 Schultz and Schultz, *Brand Babble*, 18.

5 A broader view of Catholic renewal in Chennai

A strategy for shrine-based evangelization

Introduction

In an interview published in Fr. Lawrence's 2007 Silver Jubilee souvenir booklet, Fr. Lawrence explained his thoughts on evangelization in India and within the Archdiocese:

> Today we are living in a different context. It is becoming difficult to go ahead and engage in direct evangelization. However … we have many shrines in our Archdiocese. Shrines provide wonderful opportunities for evangelization for people from all religious backgrounds who visit the shrine. Efforts could be taken to proclaim the gospel message more effectively at our shrines.[1]

Thus, Fr. Lawrence holds that the Church should focus on church building and the proper cultivation and promotion of its shrines, because such endeavors provide the perfect backdrop and opportunity for modern-day evangelization.

Missionaries no longer need to go directly to potential converts, because through the development of shrines many potential converts will come to the Church of their own accord. Many non-Christian Indians regularly visit and worship at Catholic shrines all across India. Fr. Lawrence's evangelization strategy combines large-scale shrinal development in tandem with the socio-religious reality of Indian popular religiosity. The adoption of this evangelization strategy demonstrates that Church administrators seek to preserve Catholicism's place in India through compromises and innovations that address the challenges of contemporary Indian society and politics. In this chapter, I argue that Fr. Lawrence's vision for a shrine-based evangelization strategy has already been implemented at shrines throughout the city. This is demonstrated by drawing upon evidence from several of the shrines I encountered during my field work in Chennai. However, it is important to note that the specific ways in which this strategy has been utilized at any given shrine vary according to each particular shrine's history and potential for growth. Officially, the Archdiocese of Madras-Mylapore and the suffragan Diocese of Chingleput are home to at least 14 canonically recognized

Diocesan Shrines, which is in addition to the two National Shrines of San Thome and St. Thomas Mount. Furthermore, this number does not take into account all the unofficial shrines in the Chennai region, as well as any of the official shrines located within the Archdiocese's other three suffragan dioceses. The various shrines I discuss in this chapter represent a good sample of some of Chennai's established, as well as up-and-coming, Catholic shrines, and fall into one of three basic categories.

The first category is that of well-established Catholic sites that are of historical and religious significance, both globally and locally, which is exemplified by San Thome. St. Thomas Mount is the only other site in Chennai that fits into the first category because it reaches the same heights of marketing as San Thome; thus, this chapter treats the Mount as an example of its own. The second category encompasses those shrines that have been well-established for decades and have maintained some local popularity, but are nowhere near as marketable as either San Thome or St. Thomas Mount. Many of Chennai's minor historical churches and long-established sites fall into this category, and through the implementation of Fr. Lawrence's strategy, are currently updating their facilities and making improvements that demonstrate the Church's acceptance of popular piety. The final category includes those churches that are specifically built to become shrines, and as I argue, represents the future of Catholic renewal in India. The case study for this category is the newly built St. Anthony's Seashore Shrine, which is located in the burgeoning suburb of Palavakkam in south Chennai (Figure 5.1).

Popular piety and shrine-based evangelization: a new direction

As Fr. Lawrence stated above, the days of prompting mass conversions in the Indian countryside, a strategy that typified Catholic missionization during the colonial era, are gone. Fr. Lawrence's shrine-based strategy can thus be seen as a form of "indirect" evangelization. According to Fr. Lawrence, the indirectness of this strategy is due to current Catholic attitudes regarding evangelization, or at least those attitudes he personally feels should be adopted. He explains:

> You see, today, at least in the Catholic Church ... we evangelize, yes ... but then we never forcefully convert anybody ... never. If voluntarily they come forward, we think twice about baptism and all those kind of things, and try to instruct them, and then give them baptism after quite some time. Otherwise, we never force anybody to become Christians or Catholics ... certainly we never do that. Now, if you take these shrines, we never call anybody, we never invite anybody, they come on their own.[2]

Fr. Lawrence's emphasis on never "forcefully" converting anybody is a clear reference to the anti-conversion laws introduced in a number of Indian states

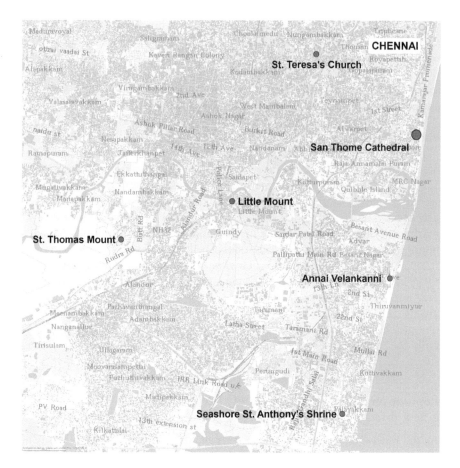

Figure 5.1 A map of Chennai showing the locations of all the various shrines being
discussed in this chapter.

Map: T. C. Nagy using StepMap: Design Your Map, http://www.stepmap.com/.

that specifically target Christian evangelization efforts, such as the one passed
in Tamil Nadu in late 2002.[3] While this law was repealed in mid-2004, when
San Thome's renovation was still underway, its impact has lingered.[4]

The key factor in Fr. Lawrence's strategy is that the Church should no
longer go out and directly seek converts. Instead, it should focus its evangelization efforts on the Hindus and other non-Christians who journey to
Catholic shrines on their own accord, and even then, the road to full
conversion should be responsibly and thoughtfully administered.
Fr. Lawrence's attitude toward conversion is based on both his personal
intuition and the Church's established understanding of popular Christian
piety as a factor of global evangelization. The Church perspective on

popular Christian devotion in South India is outlined by certain Vatican documents, and subsequently maintained by Fr. Lawrence and other Catholic clergy in Chennai. With the reforms of Vatican II, the Church has rethought and reshaped the ways it has traditionally gone about evangelization and missionization in non-Christian lands. Pope Paul VI, in a 1975 Apostolic Exhortation entitled *Evangelii Nuntiandi*, addresses the issue of "popular religiosity" or "popular piety" as "an aspect of evangelization." [5] Pope Paul VI also notes that, "These expressions were for a long time regarded as less pure and were sometimes despised, but today they are almost everywhere being rediscovered," such as in India.[6]

In another Vatican document published in 1988 by the International Theological Commission, entitled *Faith and Inculturation*, the Church's updated understanding of public piety is, "on the one hand, the union of Christian faith and piety with the profound culture, and on the other with the previous forms of religion of populations. It involves those very numerous devotions in which Christians express their religious sentiment in the simple language, among other things, of festival, pilgrimage, dance and song."[7] Here, popular piety is seen as a fusion of Christianity with local and indigenous culture and religion that is commonly expressed through certain forms of ritual piety. However, to what extent does this understanding take into account non-Christian participation in Catholic practice and ritual?

Later in this text, the Commission paraphrases Pope Paul VI's words from *Evangelii Nuntiandi*, which are actually sympathetic to the idea of popular religiosity. In it, Pope Paul VI justifies the use of the phrase popular piety over popular religiosity because he acknowledges the inherent experiential sincerity found in this religious phenomenon, which he views as the "religion of the people, rather than religiosity."[8] However, the Commission and Pope Paul VI agree that there is also a downside to it, and that, if left unchecked, it could result in "the creation of sects and endanger the true ecclesial community." This includes the belief that popular practices can lead to "distortions of religion and even superstitions," and that practitioners will remain "at the level of forms of worship not involving a true acceptance by faith."[9] Thus, popular piety has the potential of becoming a liability for the Church, as well as something entirely alien.

Both documents conclude that the Church must ultimately intervene and properly guide popular practitioners through a "pedagogy of evangelization" that carefully guides them through the stages of conversion.[10] This implies that the practitioner need not be a baptized member of the Church, but anyone who is already participating in Catholic practice. Thus, the Church is able to assume that any practitioner of popular piety is ultimately a potential convert, and that popular piety represents a prime starting point for Catholic evangelization in lands containing a highly ingrained non-Christian religion and culture. It is clear that Fr. Lawrence's shrine-based strategy shares many of the same sentiments expressed by Pope Paul VI and the 1988 International Theological Commission, but that his strategy goes further by accommodating local religious practices. Where better to market, evangelize, and guide practitioners of popular piety than at Catholic shrines especially developed and/or constructed for catering to local and religious popular forms of piety and religiosity? Since much of the information presented in this book represents the perspectives of Church administrators, I employ the terms popular religiosity and popular piety where Church perspectives are being related. Occasionally, I will employ more general terminology in order to convey a basic understanding of popular religious practice by including the word "popular" before typical religious practices such as worship, devotion, or veneration. Generally, however, I understand all such religious practices to be expressions of popular Christianity and Catholicism.

During our interviews, Fr. Lawrence generally discussed popular piety in terms of the large number of Hindus who visit Catholic shrines in Chennai. He stated, "today, if you notice, evangelization through these kind of shrines. If you take Vailankanni's Church Shrine [located on Elliot's Beach in southern Chennai], 80 percent of the people who come there are Hindus and other people. They come on their own; we don't go and force them."[11] Again, he noted, "That's all good, they have faith, they have prayer, that's all ... the Hindus and other people are more attached to these shrines. So ... today is Tuesday, so if you go to St. Anthony's [in Palavakkam], 80 percent of the people will be Hindus. So we don't have any problem at all. With ... a lot of faith, they come and pray."[12] To clarify, Fr. Lawrence is not quoting an exact statistic in his use of "80 percent," but only uses it as an indication of the fact that at any given time, non-Christian visitors tend to out-number Christian ones at certain shrines.

This large traffic of mainly Hindu pilgrims clearly provides the Church with a great opportunity for evangelization, albeit not instantaneously. As Fr. Lawrence's marketing strategy stands, many non-Christian visitors are coming to Catholic shrines without the behest of the Church. It stands to reason that if the Church should encourage this demographic of visitors through religious marketing at its shrines, it could attract an even larger non-Christian audience, which would then enhance the probability for further evangelization, thus sustaining the future of the greater Catholic mission in India. Ultimately, however, such shrines must be prepared and well equipped to handle such a task, and this is why Fr. Lawrence has focused upon greater shrinal development.

Mr. Sam, an engineer originally from Pondicherry, discussed with me the issue of Christian evangelization in India. His insight into this issue is particularly interesting due to his unique religious perspective and positionality. He states:

> Basically, by birth I belong to [the] Hindu religion, but I don't [have] much [of an] inclination to ... [it], because I feel one should not be under some religion. But if he [has] a good heart and if he [has] good principles in life, that's enough, that's what I feel. But I used to go to

church, I pray, I read [the] Bible. I take the words from the Bible, but I ... cannot be called as a Christian.[13]

Mr. Sam's testimony demonstrates that some "Hindu" devotees of Christian saints and shrines are fully aware and proud of the implications surrounding their eclectic identities as practitioners of popular Christian piety. Mr. Sam spoke happily about the countless times he had visited the Vailankanni shrine since his childhood in Pondicherry, and although he does not consider himself either a Hindu or Christian, he was proud to admit that he was a devotee of the Holy Mother. Using the context of Christianity he explains this devotion:

> Jesus Christ ... we don't treat him as a god. We treat him as a mighty messenger who lived here, who died here, had history. Okay, he might [have been] sent by God or anything ... he is a man, he had history and he lived and he died ... but Holy Mother, we treat her as a god, as our own mother.[14]

Mr. Sam also shared the observation that the majority of visitors to Vailankanni were non-Christian, but comprised mainly of Hindus. He was proud of the fact that Vailankanni was one of the few places in India where one could find Hindus, Muslims, and Christians all praying together, "with full faith in their heart[s]," which he considered a testimony to "the great-ness of the Vailankanni Church."[15] For Mr. Sam and many other South Indians, one of the most attractive features of sites like Vailankanni is that they are welcoming to people of all religious faiths. In that sense, such sites represent an ideal and harmonious community of people who are brought together by their religious faith, but no longer fettered by traditional reli-gious boundaries that have so often become a point of contention within India.

In Mr. Sam's opinion, the key to Vailankanni's long-standing pluralistic success lay in the open-mindedness and management skills of the Church administrators. He states:

> I [do] not belong to the Church, I'm an outsider ... but when you come to the Vailankanni, you will not get that poor treatment. At Vailankanni, everyone will be treated equally .... The treatment will be based on only the love and affection. This [is] the success of it ... there are hundreds, thousands of churches in India, but why [has] only Vailankanni become popular in spirit? It is purely because [of] their management only.[16]

Thus, Mr. Sam's praise for Vailankanni stems from its clergy's willingness to accommodate visitors from all religious backgrounds, and undoubtedly, efficiently coordinate and guide the vast number of pilgrims who visit year-round. Mr. Sam has also been witness to the gradual process of Christian conversion that has occurred at Vailankanni. As he describes it, only after a non-Christian family has visited Vailankanni:

> So many times, so many times, then slowly he will think about the conversion thing. I have seen ... I know so many families coming from the south of Tamil Nadu, they visit some two, three generation[s] ... two, three visit[s], or five visit[s], or ten visit[s] ... they slowly adopted this religion [Catholicism] ... that is happening, so many. But, that is not due to any other influence ... it is only due to their ... affection really that is there.[17]

Due to Vailankanni's popularity and long-term successes, it has become something of a model or template for Fr. Lawrence's shrine-based strategy. It serves to indicate that a well-maintained Catholic shrine that can successfully attract non-Christian visitors can also become a prime center for Catholic evangelization.

Fr. Lawrence's shrine-based strategy represents a new direction for Catholic evangelization in India. At the same time, this strategy's foundation is still ultimately rooted in older Catholic missionary models that have been at work in India for centuries. However, some of its more modern and substantive roots can be traced to the innovations of the Second Vatican Council of the 1960s, which eventually led to the development of two new and distinct approaches to Catholic missionary work: the inculturation model and the liberation model. According to Sebastian Kim, "Applied to the issue of conversion, the inculturation movement attempted to synthesise Christian faith with Hindu religion and culture to make change of religion and community avoidable in conversion, and the liberation movement tended to see conversion as a social 'protest' of Dalits and their 'liberation' as a legitimate aim of conversion."[18] As such, Fr. Lawrence's shrine-based strategy represents a combination of the above models in that it does not discriminate between low caste and high caste, but provides a common ground for all interested parties regardless of culture. And while different castes may not choose to interact with each other within any given Catholic shrine, at least it is no longer the policies of the Church that are instigating or encouraging the segregation. Thus, the Church is promoting the spirit of inculturation and indigeneity through its more open acceptance of popular piety, as well as promoting liberation theology and Dalit theology through its continual political presence and emphasis on social justice and equality.

There are also financial advantages to Fr. Lawrence's shrine-based strategy. The great number of popular Christian practitioners in South India alone potentially represents a great source of revenue for Catholic shrines. As Mr. Sam pointed out to me, "For example ... hundred million people they visit [Vailankanni]. If they give one rupee, it's a hundred million ... Indian population is the second in the world ... that comes to uncountable money."[19] Even though most practitioners of popular Christianity have limited financial means, the vast number of such donors at Catholic shrines like Vailankanni can generate considerable revenue for the local Church.

A quick perusal of Vailankanni's webpage gives an indication of the shrine's potential cash-flow. For instance, the website's donation page reveals the Shrine's most current project, the construction of a brand new "mega" church right around the corner from the main basilica. Its seating capacity of over 15,000 people indicates the Shrine's ever growing need to accommodate its many visitors.[20] This new addition to the Vailankanni complex is auspiciously named the "Morning Star Church," in honor of St. Mary. Even though the Church is actively seeking donations, the sheer ambitiousness of this project certainly implies that an undertaking of this magnitude is realistically within the scope of Vailankanni's financial capacity. However, in an urban context like Chennai where space is limited and many local shrines are constrained by their geographical settings, the local Church is inclined to develop more creative and innovative ways of responding to these limitations, which is why shrine-based renewal within the city has taken on a variety of forms.

St. Thomas Mount: shrine and tourist attraction

In the first of three shrinal categories I have identified, it is clear that the ways in which Fr. Lawrence's shrine-based evangelization strategy have been implemented at San Thome and St. Thomas Mount differ significantly from how it would be implemented at other lesser known shrines. What sets this category of shrinal development apart is the implementation of touristic marketing strategies that are geared toward attracting a wider spectrum of visitors that extend beyond only pilgrims and practitioners of popular piety. As its main brochure states, the Mount is the site of "pilgrim fragrance and tourist enticement."[21] Since St. Thomas Mount's shrine is located on top of a largely undeveloped hilltop, it has been afforded a far greater potential for physical expansion from which to better service tourists and pilgrims in the near future. Thus, St. Thomas Mount's room for physical growth and improvement is much more on par with Vailankanni's than with that of San Thome.

In the footsteps of San Thome: physical renovation and media publications

As St. Thomas Mount's recently published information booklet declares, "St. Thomas Mount is a Holy place of international prominence, historical eminence, religious glory and tourist attraction."[22] Due to the Mount's unique status as the site of St. Thomas's martyrdom, it is understandable that its application of Fr. Lawrence's shrine-based marketing strategy would almost be identical with what Fr. Lawrence did at San Thome in

terms of both marketing and audience. St. Thomas Mount is clearly perpetuating the St. Thomas faith brand that was initiated at San Thome, and so
this section of Chapter 5 will also draw from Mara Einstein's understanding of branding, as well as previous ideas borrowed from tourism research.
It is clear that certain elements of St. Thomas Mount's ongoing revival also
exemplify the Church's softened position on popular piety in that some of
the Mount's various projects seem to be explicitly catering to popular
devotion.

Much like San Thome's revival, St. Thomas Mount began its renovation
process with projects aimed at improving its parish facilities, then later
implementing projects that would make the Mount more accessible and
accommodating to pilgrims and tourists alike. First and foremost, there was
the construction of the new parish church, St. Patrick's, located at the
bottom of the Mount. According to Mr. Franks, a long-time parishioner at
St. Thomas Mount, his congregation had outgrown the original
St. Patrick's, so it was deemed necessary to replace it with a larger and more
inspiring church (Figure 5.2).[23] This new church was consecrated in January
of 2008. I was there in 2009 to witness the renovation of the historic
Church of Our Lady of Expectation, as well as the start of other development projects. By the time of my second trip in December of 2010,

Figure 5.2 View of newly built St. Patrick's Church from St. Thomas Mount.
Photo: T. C. Nagy.

St. Thomas Mount had gone through a significant transformation, and it was apparent that there were a number of new projects still underway.

For the most part, St. Thomas Mount's revival closely replicated the marketing strategies and ideas first utilized at San Thome's in 2004. The work at San Thome may not have fully precipitated St. Thomas Mount's revival, since the Mount was already in urgent need of better facilities; nevertheless, it created a template for the Mount's more ambitious projects. The Mount's emulation of San Thome's renovation demonstrates an acceptance of both Fr. Lawrence's evangelization model and marketing practices. By extension, St. Thomas Mount was evidently also buying into Fr. Lawrence's newly established St. Thomas brand.

It is hard to speculate whether or not St. Thomas Mount's revival would have taken place were it not for the initiation of San Thome's own revival. However, due to the chronological progression of events and the fact that the Mount's rector, Fr. G. Backiya Regis, sought out Fr. Lawrence's advice in the first place, it is almost certain that San Thome was used as a model, at least in part, for the Mount's own revival.[24] Fr. Lawrence also spoke well of his management ability, noting his tenacity for getting things done, even in the face of opposition. As Fr. Lawrence noted from his own experiences, the kinds of projects that he and the rector of St. Thomas Mount have undertaken typically instigate some form of opposition from a vocal minority of the local community, which he holds to be just the way of things.[25] To reiterate an important point from the first chapter of this book, it takes a special kind of parish priest to successfully manage and execute renovation and building projects of the magnitude seen at San Thome and St. Thomas Mount. Undoubtedly, Fr. Regis is such an individual, and has thus far demonstrated the drive and ambition to transform St. Thomas Mount into a high profile pilgrimage and tourist destination. [26]

St. Thomas Mount has always been a popular attraction in Chennai due to its panoramic view of the city. However, this aspect of the Mount's vantage point has also earned it a reputation as a popular site for romantic trysts among the city's teenagers and young adults. The Church has gone to some lengths to dissipate this unfortunate reputation, since it is obviously antithetical to the sacrality that many Catholics associate with the Mount's history, and the Church's goal of evangelization.

It was obvious to the Church that something needed to be done, and thus, the Mount's most recent parish priests have made attempts to develop the surrounding landscape into a more pilgrim and tourist accessible shrinal complex. I assert that due to all the additional projects that went into St. Thomas Mount's renovation that were well beyond the basic parish necessities, the Mount's current rector and his predecessor were, in fact, implementing Fr. Lawrence's development strategy. For example, the new St. Patrick's Church was completely rebuilt from the ground up with the addition of several new facilities, which was done just prior to Fr. Regis's tenure in 2008. Since 2009, several additions have been included, such as a large Lourdes grotto, a Eucharistic chapel tower, and a grand flag pole. The hallowed grounds of St. Thomas Mount also saw the construction of new facilities, including another Eucharistic chapel, a canopied amphitheater, a large stage, and a souvenir stall. There are also future plans to add an additional chapel structure directly adjacent to the Church of Our Lady of Expectation (Figure 5.3).[27] As I witnessed on my second trip to Chennai, St. Thomas Mount is currently in the process of clearing out some of the land, most likely in preparation for some future endeavor. All these extra projects, much like at San Thome, help to develop and ensure the future of the parish, as well as create a space more accommodating to evangelization. With regard to the historical nature of the hill-top shrine, not only is it now more pilgrim-friendly in its layout, but also more accessible and enticing for religious tourists.

In line with Fr. Lawrence's understanding of marketing and branding, the rector of St. Thomas Mount sought out ways to raise the shrine's profile as a world-class tourist attraction and as a nationally recognized pilgrimage shrine. Several large sign boards, each in a different language, line the crest of the Mount. One sign, in particular, conveniently lists the great number of attractions associated with this place, dramatically dubbing St. Thomas Mount the "Calvary of St. Thomas," while another sign calls the Mount "the cradle and glory of the Indian Church." The Mount's most prized relic

Figure 5.3 Exterior of Church of Our Lady of Expectation.
Photo: T. C. Nagy.

is the Bleeding Cross, which marks the spot of St. Thomas's martyrdom and is housed inside the equally historic Portuguese Church of Our Lady of Expectation, which was established as early as 1523 (Figure 5.4).[28] In 2009, this old church was renovated from top to bottom. The renovation process included fixing the roof, re-plastering the walls, re-tiling the floor, and installing a generator for modern convenience (Figure 5.5). As with San Thome, the act of renovation was necessary in order to raise the site's standard of quality in terms of management and presentation, as well as stress the significance of Catholic identity and heritage preservation.

St. Thomas Mount has also engaged in different forms of advertisement through various forms of media. As noted earlier, St. Thomas Mount has published, among other things, its own magazine entitled *The Voice from the Hill*, whose name bears a striking similarity to San Thome's magazine *Voice of St. Thomas*. St. Thomas Mount also established several parish organizations in order to diversify its services and streamline its missionary goals. The rector of St. Thomas Mount had the Hill Shrine officially elevated to the status of Diocesan Shrine in 2003, and much later the current rector initiated the shrine's further elevation to National Shrine status, which was given in early 2011, making the Mount only the fourth canonically recognized National Shrine in India to date.[29] It is likely that this recognition was a key factor in the decision to move St. Thomas

Figure 5.4 The Bleeding Cross as it is currently displayed post-renovation.
Photo: T. C. Nagy.

Figure 5.5 Interior of Church of Our Lady of Expectation.
Photo: T. C. Nagy.

Mount's parish out of the jurisdiction of the Archdiocese of Madras-Mylapore and into the newly created suffragan Diocese of Chingleput. The Conference of Catholic Bishops of India would have been hard-pressed to grant National Shrine status to two shrines from within the same diocese. As such, this move could be seen as a small formality or concession in order to obtain for the Chennai region two sites with a National Shrine status.

Another major example of St. Thomas Mount's replication of the San Thome model comes by way of an ambitious new construction project on par with San Thome's underground tomb chapel. As of my last visit to Chennai, this project only existed as a digital mock-up for a newly proposed double-storied church to be built alongside the Church of Our Lady of Expectation. This mock-up was printed for all to see on the back cover of the September 2010 issue of *The Voice from the Hill*.[30] Looking at the mock-up's caption, it seems this new edifice will be composed of two separate chapels. The main structure is called the Holy Apostles Chapel, which will be on the ground floor. The other structure is called the St. Thomas Relic Church, which is described as being a "cave," which seems to imply that this will be an underground facility exactly like Fr. Lawrence's underground tomb chapel at San Thome. Crucially, the Photo-shopped "tourists" on the bottom left-hand side of the mock-up are of a Western, foreign, or non-Indian persuasion, which reinforces the idea that the additional novelty of this proposed structure is meant to foster touristic interest in addition to enticing pilgrims.

Clearly, the proposed construction of a new cave church exemplifies the marketing ethos now shared between the rector of St. Thomas Mount and Fr. Lawrence. More specifically, it underscores the rector's reliance on Fr. Lawrence's marketing strategy, and acceptance of the St. Thomas faith brand with its emphasis on notions of Indian Christian indigeneity. This discourse of indigeneity is already visible in the traditions surrounding the Bleeding Cross, which suggest that it was carved by St. Thomas himself, and that the Apostle's blood was physically shed over it. However, the cave church takes this idea even further. By sharing this underground motif, St. Thomas Mount is maintaining and disseminating the same symbolism and discourses that are apparent at San Thome's tomb chapel, as well as providing a new and inspiring shrine from which to attract potential converts and a popular Christian piety.

Also at St. Thomas Mount, the historical aspects of St. Thomas's life and death are memorialized in ways similar to those found at San Thome, in, for instance, the publication of history books, CDs, and magazine articles devoted to this topic. It is also important to note, that with the renovation of the Church of Our Lady of Expectation, two important dioramas were added to its threshold. The first is of Doubting Thomas kneeling before the risen Lord, and the second is of St. Thomas's final moments before his destined martyrdom (Figure 5.6, see also Figure 3.2). Both of these dioramas are practically identical to their counterparts at San Thome. Moreover, the great lengths to preserve this historic Portuguese church, as well as highlighting its importance, speak volumes about shared Catholic identity and the importance of heritage preservation as a testament to St. Thomas's legacy. Finally, St. Thomas Mount has on display two statues of the Church's most recognizable icons: Pope John Paul II, who visited the Mount during the same trip in which he visited San Thome, and Mother Teresa of Calcutta, who is nationally recognized for her life of service to the poor in India. Once again, by having these statues so prominently displayed on St. Thomas Mount, they serve to provide a kind of endorsement for the legacy of St. Thomas. Thus, these two individuals act as spokespeople for the St. Thomas brand, and due to their mainstream popularity, are also spokespeople for the whole of Catholicism.

Novelty and innovation at St. Thomas Mount

Another facet of St. Thomas Mount's marketing strategy that seems to borrow from San Thome's revival is its use of novelty and not just as a principle *per se*, but in the specific use of materials and ideas first executed at San Thome. For instance, St. Thomas Mount, today, also sells

Figure 5.6 Diorama of St. Thomas's faith proclamation inside the Church of Our
Lady of Expectation. For image of the martyrdom diorama refer to
Figure 3.2.

Photo: T. C. Nagy.

"holy sand." While in its execution it is not as intriguing as San Thome's
relic card, the imitation is rather blatant, but not completely uncalled for.
For the most part, this difference in presentation speaks to St. Thomas
Mount's ability to better cater to popular piety. The first issue of *The Voice
from the Hill* dedicates a page to enumerating the three key characteristics
of a shrine as dictated by the Church in India's "Directory on Popular Piety
and the Liturgy." It states, "Theologically, a shrine, which often derives
from popular piety, is a sign of the active and saving presence of the Lord
in history, and a place of respite," and continues by describing how such
shrines should act as "places of evangelization," "charitable centers," and
"cultural centers."[31] In a later issue, Fr. Regis unequivocally states,

"The Apostolic Hill Shrine of St. Thomas is the first and foremost important spot for [the] Mission in India."[32] Since San Thome is the seat of the Archdiocese, there are principled limitations as to how far it can go in order to cater to popular piety, let alone encourage it. St. Thomas Mount, on the other hand, is in a better position to explore new and innovative ways in order to attract practitioners of popular Christianity.

St. Thomas Mount's "holy sand" is only sold at the top of the Mount, at the Shrine's gift shop and book stall. Unlike San Thome's carefully and strategically designed sand relic card, the Mount's sand is simply sold in a small plastic packet that is stapled to a small laminated bilingual prayer card (Figure 5.7). This sand card's presentation is intriguing, because unlike San Thome's sand card, it stresses the sand's functionality over its packaging. In other words, this "holy sand" is most likely meant to be used in a culturally traditional manner. Predominantly among Keralite Christians, the sand is typically collected and brought back home as a souvenir where it is further venerated or redistributed to other people.[33] It was even mentioned to me that some individuals, not necessarily Christians, consumed the sand in order to take in its power, usually as a medicinal alternative, which coincides with Marco Polo's thirteenth-century testimony.[34] It is also interesting to note that Polo's description states that

Figure 5.7 St. Thomas Mount's "holy sand" with attached double-sided bilingual prayer card in both Tamil [shown] and English [back of card, not shown].

Prayer card: St. Thomas Mount, Ramapuram, Chennai, India, 2010.

pilgrims took sand specifically from the site of the Apostle's martyrdom, and not his tomb. Undoubtedly, San Thome's sand relic card is primarily meant to be used as a personal keepsake or souvenir than as something that can be realistically venerated or physically redistributed, let alone eaten.

As we can see, the way in which St. Thomas Mount's "holy sand" is packaged, as well as the quantity of sand given with each purchase, seems to implicitly cater to local and traditional popular religiosity. Another indication of this possibility lies in the fact that the attached prayer card is bilingual, being written in both English and Tamil, whereas San Thome's sand card is only available in English. This also implies that St. Thomas Mount's administration is more willing to attract and cater to a local demographic that does not necessarily understand English, and are most likely part of the lower stratum of Indian society, which is certainly where the majority of popular Christian practitioners reside. In essence, it could be concluded that St. Thomas Mount's sand is more accessible and functional than San Thome's sand relic card.

Another example of an innovative and novel way in which St. Thomas Mount has attempted to attract more practitioners of popular piety is through the fostering of local Marian devotion. The most obvious indicator of this was the construction of a very prominent Lourdes grotto adjacent to St. Patrick's Church (Figure 5.8). Much like at Vailankanni, this particular apparition of St. Mary is also associated with health and healing, which has always been a prominent aspect of popular Christianity in India, and a major draw for many Indian Christians and Hindus. The topic of Lourdes grottos in Chennai will be further analyzed later in this chapter.

However, the most striking example of a devotional-based innovation to come out of St. Thomas Mount's revival came by way of a newly developed ritual that was implemented for the very first time on December 18, 2010 during the Mount's Festival of Our Lady of Expectation. I was fortunate enough to have been there in 2010 and thus witnessed this brand new processional ritual. Due to its recent development, the Mount's rector had to instruct the audience as to how the ritual would be enacted, which he did in both English and Tamil. He explained:

> Friends, after the final blessing we will be having the solemn procession of the Bleeding Cross of St. Thomas. This is the first of its kind in our Shrine. We have prepared a replica of the Bleeding Cross of St. Thomas, and we will be having the procession. Also, there will be a procession of Our Lady of Expectation. I request all the men to carry this bleeding cross, it's a very heavy one, I request all the strong ones to come and carry it. We need 30 people to carry this cross; this will be about 500 kg [Figure 5.9]. So, I request all the strong men to come and help us, and I request all the ladies to carry the statue of Our Lady of Expectation, especially those who are waiting for marriage and those who are seeking the blessing of our Lord for the gift of a child.

Figure 5.8 Lourdes grotto at St. Patrick's Church, St. Thomas Mount.
Photo: T. C. Nagy.

> These people can come and carry the statue of Our Lady of Expectation
> [Figure 5.10]. Once we turn into the processions, when we having the
> solemn blessing with the relic of the holy relic of St. Thomas, followed
> by the lowering of the flag. I request all of you to participate in this
> procession till we lower the flag. [Repeats above instructions in Tamil]
> Can we stand for the final blessing?[35]

It should be noted that the tradition of honoring the Bleeding Cross on
December 18th, the same day as the Feast of Our Lady of Expectation, goes
as far back as the Portuguese era, when on that same day in 1558 CE it was
said to have miraculously bled or sweated for the very first time. It would
continue to do so for a number of years afterwards until its last recorded
occurrence in 1704 CE.[36] However, from its very first occurrence, the
miraculous nature of St. Thomas's Bleeding Cross would become intrinsically linked to Mother Mary through the auspicious Feast day of Our Lady
of Expectation.

The most interesting aspect of this ritual is that it combines elements of
traditional and popular Indian Catholic Marian devotion with a significant
local symbol of St. Thomas's martyrdom, the Bleeding Cross. In this way,
this ritual is able to accomplish two main things. First, it provides a unique

Figure 5.9. A specially made replica of the Bleeding Cross that was carried around
the campus of the St. Thomas Mount hilltop shrine as part of a newly
developed ritual.

Photo: T. C. Nagy.

ritual specific to St. Thomas Mount that is fundamentally geared towards
the religious sensibilities of Indian Marian devotees, and by extension,
popular devotion in general. Second, it helps to raise St. Thomas's regional
profile by associating his symbol of martyrdom with that of Mother Mary,
a saint who is extremely popular in South India. Additionally, there are
other significant ritual and symbolic elements that also cater to the religious
sensibilities of local popular Catholicism, such as the ritual's defined gender
roles, and the juxtaposed symbols of birth and death that are signified by
the pregnant St. Mary and the martyred Apostle.

As we can see, this innovative emphasis on the person and power of St. Mary
at a site associated with St. Thomas's Indian legacy greatly mirrors San Thome's

Figure 5.10 The palanquin carrying the statue of a pregnant St. Mary, otherwise known as Our Lady of Expectation.
Photo: T. C. Nagy.

own specialized recognition of its unique Marian incarnation Our Lady of Mylapore. As described in Chapter 4, Fr. Lawrence implemented several new features at San Thome that revolved around Our Lady of Mylapore. For instance, he provided greater community awareness for her week-long festival, and built an outdoor prayer grotto to her, and finally, had a newly designed display alter installed inside the Cathedral in order to better showcase the venerable statue from which this incarnation of St. Mary originated. However, while I argue that this ritual represents the continued emulation of San Thome's 2004 revival, I also believe that it helps to set St. Thomas Mount's revival apart from San Thome's. In terms of ritual innovation, I am not aware that Fr. Lawrence ever initiated anything of this sort; instead, he chose to focus more on up-scale building projects. As explained before, St. Thomas Mount is in a better position to cater to popular piety, which, in turn, allows for a greater breadth for religious innovation such as that seen on December 18, 2010. This is also true socio-economically, as Mylapore is a more up-scale neighborhood than the areas immediately surrounding the Mount.

Furthermore, there is a lot to be said about the significance of the festival context in relation to popular piety and Catholic evangelization. Margaret Meibohm's ethnography of Vailankanni has noted the Shrine's wide appeal in South India, especially during its main festival in September. What she has witnessed there is a shared meeting ground between Hindus and Catholics that offers both parties a new and refreshing look at their eclectic and modern Indian religious identities. Meibohm explains:

> I have proposed that the festival blends past and present along more than one dimension, making possible the construction of an integrated, multifaceted sense of Indian identity. Along the religious dimension, the Vailankanni festival provides a hybridity of Hindu and Catholic that appeals to wide range of people and helps to foster a sense of Indian Catholicism. In sharing elements with Hindu temple festivals, the Vailankanni festival makes use of the recognized religious past and surrounding cultural present of Indian Catholics. It also, however, combines these elements with Catholic ones or opens the door to new interpretations with a Christian theme.[37]

In other words, Indian Catholics are treated to expressions of their former Hindu selves through various cultural customs, which are then organized in terms of Catholic symbols and faith, thus being indicative of their present Catholic selves. Hindus, on the other hand, are presented with many traditional sights and customs, which are then accentuated with a uniquely Catholic flair. While Meibohm may not be writing about this issue in terms of potential Hindu converts, what she has to say about the complexities of Vailankanni's mass appeal relates to what Church administrators hoped to emulate at other Catholic shrines. The strategic combination of Catholic and Hindu elements at such shrines could open the doors to much more than just "new interpretations," but to an Indian identity that underlines the Christian more than the Hindu.

Once again we see the motif of St. Thomas's martyred blood highlighted by the Church in Chennai. Previous chapters have demonstrated how San Thome Cathedral has taken this concept and used it within several of its renewal and revivalist evangelizing and developmental strategies. This chapter has already shown how St. Thomas Mount has perpetuated San Thome's discourse via its own holy sand and the plans for a uniquely designed shrine, and with the ritual above, how the Mount has added its own religious innovation in order to better showcase its prized relic the Bleeding Cross. For a site like St. Thomas Mount, which is invested in attracting popular devotion, what exactly could the blood of St. Thomas come to symbolize for a non-Christian visitor or devotee? According to Indologist David Shulman, traditional Tamil mythology is filled with stories that tell of various Hindu gods who have sanctified land through sacrifice and the spilling of their blood. He writes:

> Blood, then, comes to be a conventional symbol of sanctity in the Tamil origin myths. It appears because of an act of violence, usually an attack

upon the deity himself. The god is in some way wounded, and this fact acquires a decisive significance in defining his local character and the manner of his revelation.[38]

Additionally, the sanctity of holy blood is also understood by Tamils as a symbol of fertility, or more to the point, as Shulman notes, "The Tamils of the Caṅkam period regarded blood as the source of life. Life (*uyir*) resides in the blood, and escapes with the blood poured out from a wound."[39] In other words, St. Thomas could possibly be viewed in a similar way by non-Christian worshippers, as a deity or holy man who sacrificed his life's blood, which, in turn, sanctified the hilltop of St. Thomas Mount and thus, imbued its soil with sacred power having to do with life and fertility. In this way, even a non-Christian Tamil could view St. Thomas as a "divine exemplar" due to his noble sacrifice.[40]

At first glance, the Tamil Hindu understanding of spilled or sacrificial blood differs greatly from traditional Abrahamic notions of blood and sacrifice that are prevalent in the Catholic Church's long-standing veneration of the cult of martyrs. However, St. Thomas in Chennai has come to represent a merging of these two notions that is not necessarily due to the Tamil cultural context. In one sense, St. Thomas is already identified alongside spiritual concepts of fertility, such as in his connection with St. Mary in the ritual above. San Thome's quarterly magazine has even included within its pages, on several occasions, testimonials that explicitly state that after having prayed for a child at the tomb of the Apostle they, or someone else in their family, became pregnant. However, the simplest explanation comes by way of my informant Brother Joe, who states:

> Here, because of … St. Thomas's martyrdom, Christianity flourished, here in Chennai in Tamil Nadu, because the blood of the martyrs [is the] seed of Christianity …. St. Thomas, his blood, even his preaching … flourished here and there in India. Christianity grow[s] because one of the 12 Apostles who came to India, the one who doubted the resurrection of Christ, who put his finger in the side when he said my Lord and my God. So, that faith is here, the growth of Christianity, the seed of St. Thomas blood.[41]

The key sentence in Brother Joe's explanation is the line, "the blood of the martyrs [is the] seed of Christianity." This same expression was quoted to me on several occasions by different Catholic informants and is in fact a popular Christian epitaph taken from one of the works of the well-known Christian theologian and apologist Tertullian.[42] None of the informants who recited this line attributed it to Tertullian, which suggests that this quotation has become part of the Indian Catholic mainstream consciousness and explains much of St. Thomas's blood and soil imagery that is present in Chennai due to purely Western and Catholic traditions, and not necessarily the context of Tamil and Hindu culture.

All in all, the layout and design of St. Thomas Mount's shrinal complex has significantly changed over the course of the last five years or so, becoming more accessible to pilgrims and tourists alike. Many of these recent improvements come by way of emulation of Fr. Lawrence's endeavors at San Thome, as well as the adoption of his shrine-based evangelization strategy, which is becoming more common with the Church in Chennai and possibly the rest of South India. Much like San Thome and Vailankanni, St. Thomas Mount has also utilized its traditional festival calendar in order to better reach out to the local community and attract popular piety. As this section has demonstrated, St. Thomas Mount is inherently marketable with its historic architecture, ancient relics, and the impressive panoramic view of the city. However, the majority of Catholic shrines in Chennai do not have the kind of history and novelty that St. Thomas Mount possesses, and thus, must make greater use of smaller construction projects in order to implement a shrine-based strategy and improve their facilities.

Recent development projects at some of Chennai's minor shrines

The majority of Catholic shrines in Chennai fall within my second shrinal category, which encompasses various kinds of smaller development projects that are intended to cater to their already established communities. For instance, this section will discuss the Annai Vailankanni Shrine near Elliot's Beach in the district of Besant Nagar, and St. Teresa's Church in Nungambakkam. I would also include in this category the third St. Thomas site, the Shrine of Our Lady of Good Health at Little Mount (Figure 5.1). Such communities tend to include sizeable numbers of non-Christian participants in popular Christian piety, which increases during festival times. Thus, in order to better facilitate the Church's new shrine-based strategies, these shrines must rely on smaller building projects that take into consideration their limited space and capacity. Many of these shrines do not have the same level of historical significance as San Thome or St. Thomas Mount, but through various circumstances have garnered some level of success in attracting a popular following. More than anything discussed in this chapter so far, these shrines serve to demonstrate some of the tensions that are still prevalent within shrines that attract and invite non-Christian participation at their festivals and services.

The development of Annai Vailankanni shrine with brief comparisons to Little Mount

This particular Chennai shrine truly exemplifies the growing popularity of St. Mary in India and how her particular incarnation at Vailankanni is steadily becoming a mainstay of South Indian religiosity. Annai Vailankanni Shrine was erected in 1971–72 in the image of the original

Vailankanni shrine in Nagapattinam, and thus represents an early attempt to cultivate devotion to Our Lady of Vailankanni in Chennai, which it seems to have succeeded in doing. According to its parish website, Annai Vailankanni's local popularity spiked during the 1990s, and thus, it needed to expand its facilities in order to accommodate the growing crowds.[43] It was no coincidence that in 1993 Fr. Lawrence Raj was named parish priest of Annai Vailankanni, and for the next seven years he set about transforming and expanding its grounds into a more pilgrim-accommodating space.[44]

Fr. Lawrence's assignment was most likely intentional on the part of the Archdiocese, which was familiar with, and therefore confident in, the Father's managerial abilities. As we already know, Fr. Lawrence was assigned to San Thome in 2000, thus making Annai Vailankanni his last project before taking on the monumental renovation of the Cathedral and St. Thomas's tomb. Fr. Lawrence, and later his immediate successor, helped to improve Annai Vailankanni's facilities, thereby transforming it from a simple city church into a full-fledged shrine, which was accomplished through the use of various smaller-scale building projects in order to better attract shrinal popular devotion. With the new improvements and additions in place, Annai Vailankanni was elevated to Diocesan Shrine status in 2005, and currently boasts of being the "largest and most popular" shrine dedicated to Our Lady of Vailankanni outside of Nagapattinam.[45]

Before Fr. Lawrence's time at Annai Vailankanni, the church complex consisted of two main structures, the original chapel built in 1972 (Figure 5.11) and a larger church building that was added in 1985. As with previous and future endeavors, Fr. Lawrence's stewardship involved a complete renovation of these two structures. He had the lobby of the shrine chapel extended, and added a decorative commemoration archway to the entrance of the larger church. In addition, he also had a new community hall constructed, along with various stalls and classrooms, all of which is in keeping with Father's main *modus operandi* that, first and foremost, seeks to provide and improve the church's basic facilities.[46]

However, Fr. Lawrence's most ambitious project at Annai Vailankanni required the acquisition of additional land for the parish. After securing nearly eight new plots of adjacent land, Fr. Lawrence initiated the construction of a large outdoor stage, along with fifteen enclosed dioramas depicting the Mysteries of the Holy Rosary.[47] These dioramas depict specific important moments in the life of St. Mary that are meant to be meditated upon during one's recitation of the Rosary prayer cycle. Most significant is the vast amount of space left empty in order to create a courtyard large enough to accommodate the great number of pilgrims that visit during the festival season in August. The new stage and courtyard were completed in 2000.[48]

The construction of Marian dioramas in Chennai is not unique to Annai Vailankanni, which demonstrates that this kind of edifice is representative of local minor-shrinal development, as well as the growing popularity of

Figure 5.11 Annai Vailankanni Shrine.
Photo: T. C. Nagy.

St. Mary. As we know, her reputation as a powerful source of miraculous healing is at the core of her mass popularity. For many practitioners of popular piety, Our Lady of Vailankanni is also commonly associated with the Tamil/ Hindu goddess Mariamman.[49] Both St. Mary and Mariamman maintain the dual roles of mother figure and healer, and I wonder if there is any coincidence in the similarities between their names. However, it is certain that these dioramas were erected with popular piety in mind, which is evident in the fact that each station's description is written in both English and Tamil. These dioramas provide a visual focal point for the recitation of the Rosary and general Marian veneration, which is very fitting for shrines dedicated to Mother Mary. Such additions certainly help to educate and encourage parishioners and visitors to pray the Rosary, a doctrinally recognized form of Marian devotion, in the wake of more popular forms of worship.

After Fr. Lawrence's departure from Annai Vailankanni, his successor Fr. Bernard oversaw the addition of several new significant structures in the Church's ever-developing grounds. Fr. Bernard's very first construction project was the installation of a Eucharistic chapel. His most time-consuming project, however, involved the erection of a new convent, which required the purchase of even more land for the parish. At the same time, a new chapel and square was dedicated to the many officially recognized incarnations of Mother Mary from around the world (Figure 5.12).[50] This particular presentation of Our Lady of Vailankanni situates her within the global context of the Catholic Church's four most recognized apparitions of St. Mary: Our Lady of Guadalupe from Mexico, Our Lady of Fatima from Portugal, Our Lady of La Salette and Our Lady of Lourdes, both from France. Undoubtedly, Annai Vailankanni's Mother Mary's Square is meant to showcase the validity of India's very own Marian apparition as part of a greater tradition within global Catholicism. It should also be noted that of the four globally accepted incarnations of St. Mary listed above, Our Lady of Lourdes is by far the most similar to Vailankanni, mainly due to their shared association as places for miraculous healing.

This presentation of St. Mary also raises some concerns. Because of its close association with local forms of popular worship, the Vatican does not officially recognize Our Lady of Vailankanni as a legitimate manifestation of the Virgin Mary. Thus, by presenting Our Lady of Vailankanni alongside the four official Marian apparitions, Annai Vailankanni's administration is actually attempting to reinforce the validity of Vailankanni as an equally authentic incarnation of Mother Mary. Another

Figure 5.12 Annai Vailankanni's Mother Mary's Square and Reconciliation Chapel.
Photo: T. C. Nagy.

Figure 5.13 Vailankanni "grotto" at Annai Vailankanni Shrine.
Photo: T. C. Nagy.

case in point is Fr. Bernard's construction of a Vailankanni "grotto" prior
to this, something that is traditionally constructed in honor of Our Lady
of Lourdes (Figure 5.13).[51]

Clearly, many within the Church in India hope to one day see
Vailankanni fully recognized as an authentic apparition of Mary by the
Vatican, since it would be a boon for the Indian Church and most likely
open the doors for a greater global awareness of Indian Christianity.
However, even though Church attitudes in India regarding popular piety
have softened, Vailankanni's non-Christian popularity is still a point of
contention for many in the Church hierarchy because it is unlikely that
non-Catholic practitioners of popular Christianity fully recognize the religious authority of either the Church or the Pope. The greatest evidence for
this particular hierarchal concern can be seen in the Indian Church's
propensity towards the erection of Lourdes grottos all throughout
Chennai, and possibly throughout all of South India. As previously
implied, it is probably no coincidence that the Church in India would
favor the one European based apparition of St. Mary that shares a key
spiritual asset with Our Lady Vailankanni, namely a reputation for divine
healing.

Lourdes grottos in Chennai: St. Mary as a
symbol of papal authority

A Lourdes grotto is simply a dioramic monument dedicated to the specific apparition of St. Mary that appeared several times in 1858 to a young girl named Bernadette who was from the small town of Lourdes, France. News of Bernadette's visions eventually spread, and almost instantly made her and the Lourdes region into a focal point for local popular religiosity and devout Marian veneration that is still prevalent to this day. What makes Lourdes interesting is that the Church was quick to validate its legitimacy, and with this support, Lourdes was able to become a "modern pilgrimage shrine" that could accommodate and service both tourists and pilgrims *en masse*.[52] A key aspect of the Church's acceptance and support related to the fact that according to Bernadette's visions, St. Mary proclaimed to her, "I am the Immaculate Conception."[53] In 1854, four years before Bernadette's visions, Pope Pius IX (reigned 1846–1878) issued an Apostolic Constitution that officially laid out a new dogma pronouncing St. Mary as having been immaculately conceived.[54] Thus, Bernadette's vision served to confirm Pope Pius IX's proclamation.[55] Additionally, in 1869, only 11 years after Bernadette's visions, the First Vatican Council was opened. The most significant result of this meeting was the promulgation of papal infallibility, which "defined all papal *ex cathedra* declarations as dogma and represented the Pope as an absolute monarch in both the spiritual and temporal domains."[56] Many Catholics, especially proponents of the Immaculate Conception and Marian devotion, supported this doctrine and saw it as a necessary first step towards "Catholic renewal" in Europe, which Lourdes ultimately helped to foster.[57] It is no wonder then that the Church would actively promote and encourage the development of Lourdes into a highly visible pilgrimage site for Catholics the world over. To this day, Lourdes remains a popular pilgrimage and tourist destination, seeing an estimated 6 million visitors a year.[58]

Today, in Chennai and other parts of South India, Lourdes grottos have become a common architectural fixture of typical church parish landscaping (Figure 5.14). Indeed, this over-abundance of Lourdes grottos is arguably unique to South India. Within the rest of the Catholic world Lourdes grottos are typically found only at churches dedicated to Our Lady of Lourdes or have some special connection to France, not commonly in all parishes. In South India, these grottos serve to symbolically reinforce papal and Church authority in a country where a great deal of popular Catholic worship takes place without the auspices of the hierarchy, who, as Selva Raj points out, often "deliberately distance themselves from popular practices."[59] Furthermore, Tamil Nadu's past and present socio-religious context already lends itself to the regional acceptance of such a figure as Mother Mary. The Tamil/ Hindu goddess Mariamman establishes a precedence of sorts in Tamil Nadu for divine mother figures who specialize in healing.[60]

Figure 5.14 Lourdes grotto at Little Mount.
Photo: T. C. Nagy.

Wide-spread poverty and the relative high-cost of medical care may also help to explain why such figures as St. Mary, at both Vailankanni and Lourdes, and Mariamman attract such a large following in South India.

More importantly, Our Lady of Lourdes serves as a canonically and universally recognized alternative to the locally popular Our Lady of Vailankanni, seeing as both Shrines are primarily reputed for offering the same spiritual and physical benefits associated with good health and divine healing. We can also assume that the abundance of Lourdes grottos is partly due to the popularity of St. Mary, since Vailankanni and Lourdes are incarnations of the same Catholic saint.

This attitude regarding the "unified diversity" of local and popular gods and goddesses is prevalent in Hindu worship.[61] Anthropologist Stanley N. Kurtz notes the prevalence of this particular attitude among devotees of the goddess Santoshi Ma. For Kurtz, this issue arose out of his attempt to understand how Santoshi Ma, as a very recent addition to the Hindu pantheon (c. 1970s), was able to become so popular in such a short amount of time. Ultimately, Kurtz deduced that for his Hindu informants it was never an issue of newness or emergence, but that Santoshi Ma, and all other Hindu goddesses for that matter, was always a significant part of the "same larger Goddess: 'All of the goddesses are one.'"[62] As Kurtz explains:

I had to grant my informants, moreover, that in actual worship the "all are one" theme did seem to win out. In her temples as well as in private homes, worship of Santoshi Ma was part and parcel of the worship of the great Goddess in all her forms. In these contexts, as we have already seen, Santoshi Ma's identity was blended inextricably with that of other goddesses.[63]

As we can see, it is not unusual for Hindus to identify and find personal significance with various different incarnations of the same larger deity. Thus, St. Mary and all her incarnations easily fit into Hindu modes of worship, and for many of her popular devotees, Mother Mary also represents yet another inextricable part of the greater unified Goddess.

The dramatic display of piety associated with the Lourdes grotto clearly show how the foreign and global character of the Roman Catholic Church is fully acknowledged through the construction of such grottos throughout India. Just as the Lourdes grotto represents a physical transplantation of France onto Indian soil, so too can the Roman Catholic Church be seen as a religion that has been transplanted all across the globe. For example, in Figure 5.14 is a Lourdes grotto that is typical of the grottos found in Catholic churches all across Chennai. Such Indian grottos tend to be approximate replicas of the original Lourdes grotto in France, utilizing the specified depiction of Our Lady of Lourdes in statue form, which is then usually housed within a rocky edifice made up of various sized boulders. More often than not, there is also an accompanying statue of Bernadette, kneeling in prayer before the Virgin. Many of the grottos I came across in Chennai were also surrounded or decorated with greenery or running water, most likely to add to the ambiance of the display.

The grotto pictured above is located at Little Mount and it has been there since 1993, although there has supposedly been one at that site since the 1960s.[64] But, as Brother Joe was quick to exclaim, "Every parish has it, a Lourdes grotto … purposefully they built that because … every church, the parish, have a Lady of Lourdes [grotto]."[65] In other words, it has become so common in South India that it has become almost customary. While it is unlikely that every single Catholic church in India has one, it is certainly a structure that can be found in the majority of Catholic churches in Tamil Nadu, and according to my Malayali informant, Catholic churches all across Kerala as well.[66] However, unlike at Little Mount, a number of the Lourdes grottos in Chennai are fairly recent additions to their respective parishes.

Fr. Lawrence also recognized the aesthetic value that Lourdes grottos offered Catholic shrines in India. As stated in the previous chapter, Fr. Lawrence had a grand-sized Lourdes grotto installed at the main entrance to San Thome Cathedral during its renovation (see Figure 4.5). This particular grotto is impressive with its lush greenery and pond, creating a garden-like ambiance rare in the drab concrete jungle of Chennai city. It is interesting to point out that within San Thome's immediate parish are two other Lourdes grottos, one at the local high school, and another at the Archdiocesan Pastoral Center, which was still being installed during my last days in Chennai in 2009. By 2010, it was fully built and as lush as San Thome's grotto (Figure 5.15).

St. Thomas Mount also erected an impressive Lourdes grotto in 2009 as part of the new St. Patrick's Church complex (see Figure 5.8). While not as lush as the ones at San Thome parish, it boasts a statue of St. Mary acquired directly from Lourdes, whose consecration was officiated by Cardinal Simon Lourdusamy (d. 2014). Cardinal Lourdusamy, at that time of my data collection, was one of only four Indian Cardinals within the Catholic hierarchy, as well as the first Tamil clergyman to be elevated to that rank. Additionally, it is clear that his ordination name "Lourdusamy" already represented for him a long-standing personal devotion to Our Lady of Lourdes (Figure 5.16). At a site as high profile as St. Thomas Mount, the symbolic addition of a Lourdes grotto is intrinsically tied to Church author- ity and the transplantation of Western Catholic traditions. Additionally, the Lourdes grottos at San Thome, the Archdiocesan Pastoral Center, and at St. Thomas Mount underscore the fact that the Church in India has, and will continue to erect Lourdes grottos as a matter of local custom, global tradition, and hierarchal commitment.

Figure 5.15 Recently completed Lourdes grotto at the Archdiocesan Pastoral Center, San Thome, c. 2010.

Photo: T. C. Nagy.

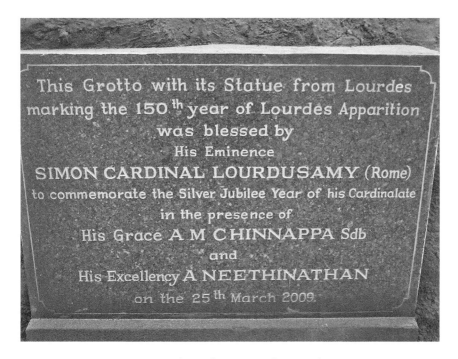

Figure 5.16 Commemoration plaque for St. Patrick's Lourdes grotto.
Photo: T. C. Nagy.

On the other hand, as stated before, the Church's current shrine-based strategy for evangelization in India allows for a softer stance on issues concerning popular piety, especially with regard to St. Mary and Vailankanni Shrine, since they are both immensely popular with non-Christian Indians. As demonstrated with Annai Vailankanni Shrine, we are now seeing Vailankanni "grottos" or monuments being built at a number of churches in Chennai. Upon my arrival to Chennai in early 2009, while driving down Nungambakkam High Road, one of the city's major roads, it was hard not to notice a highly ornate shrine located adjacent to the grounds of St. Teresa's Church (Figure 5.17). As it turned out, St. Teresa's was Fr. Lawrence's current post as parish priest, which he accepted after completing his tenure at San Thome in 2007. As he would explain, building this mini-shrine to Our Lady of Vailankanni was practically the very first thing he did as the Church's new parish priest:

> Yes, yes, as soon as I came. You see, that is because that corner was very, very dirty … so I thought something should be done there to [make] the place clean first of all, and also, personally I have a belief, once Our Lady comes into the campus, a lot of good things will happen.

Figure 5.17 Our Lady of Vailankanni "grotto" at St. Teresa's Church.
Photo: T. C. Nagy.

So that was also my idea. And also, there are two bus stands out there. And this [Nungambakkam High Road] is the only commercial road in the city where we have so many vehicles passing through. So on, many of our people they have a lot of devotion to Our Lady of Vailankanni. So, I thought it was this also a kind of evangelization, by looking at the statue for one second anybody will be touched for that matter, you know.[67]

As Fr. Lawrence notes, his initial reason for erecting this shrine was to do something about the undeveloped bit of land at the corner of St. Teresa's grounds. The ultimate purpose for the construction, however, was to encourage local piety and thus precipitate evangelization.

Once again, Fr. Lawrence was doing his part to execute his shrine-based strategy for evangelization. When his time at San Thome was ending, he was offered a list of other parishes he could be transferred to. He purposefully chose St. Teresa's because he had previously noted that it needed work and that it had potential due to its centralized location within the city. Fr. Lawrence explains:

> That is one of my very big ambitions, and that was one of the reasons why I came, also, here [St. Teresa's] .... And since, this being in the heart of the city, there's a possibility to attract much more crowds, and not only Catholics, many other people. See, putting up that small grotto over there on the main floor, which attracts so many people, so many people come and pray there day and night, and many people talk about it. And all those who travel by the way, just for that, this one second they look at the statue and then say something, no? So many people go to these hospitals, yet they come and pray there. It is just on the road, so it is very, very convenient for people. And so many miracles do take place.[68]

Above, Fr. Lawrence noted that many people pray before this shrine in addition to going to the hospital. In this way, we can see how such grottos are seen by many Indians as being complimentary to modern medical care. Clearly, Fr. Lawrence's marketing mentality was at the forefront of his thinking. Not only was the location a significant factor, but also the goal of generating positive word-of-mouth, which as Mara Einstein notes, "is the most effective form of marketing."[69] Ultimately, Our Lady of Vailankanni is slowly becoming a symbol of Indian Catholicism, and for Church administrators like Fr. Lawrence, Vailankanni offers the Church in India a possible way to attract new converts, as well as promote the heritage and longevity of Indian Christianity to the rest of the world. In essence, through the use of a "grotto" motif, the Church in India is attempting to legitimize Vailankanni as an authentic Marian apparition, so that it too can enjoy the global popularity and spiritual reputation found at Lourdes. It is unsurprising that the Church in India often refers to Vailankanni as the "Lourdes of the East."[70]

The addition of any Marian-centric structure to any parish grounds makes sense in the context of St. Mary's mass appeal in India. However, it is an entirely different case with regard to another common feature of South Indian Catholic churches and shrines: the Eucharistic adoration chapel. The significance of this particular kind of chapel and the specific Catholic devotion it inspires goes well beyond any specific church, and thus, represents a growing trend in contemporary Indian Catholic devotion and evangelization that can be seen all across South India, speaking directly to the issues of religious persecution, popular piety, and the fear of Catholicism's dwindling numbers in India.

Eucharistic adoration chapels: an Indian Catholic innovation

Based on the field research and interviews I collected in Chennai, it is clear that the Eucharistic adoration chapel is quickly becoming a permanent fixture of both Roman Catholic architecture and religiosity in India today. In this context, the Eucharist refers to the host or bread that is transubstantiated into the literal body of Jesus Christ during the Catholic mass in emulation of the Last Supper. Due to the Catholic belief in transubstantiation, the Eucharist can become a focal point for worship and adoration.[71] In the Exposition of the Blessed Sacrament, the transubstantiated host is placed in a special container called a monstrance, whereby it is placed on display in a chapel or other such place to be viewed by the faithful (Figure 5.18).[72] For the Catholic Church in India, special chapels are built for the sole purpose of Eucharistic Exposition and adoration. Due to the specific religious function of Eucharistic chapels and the significance of Eucharistic adoration to the Catholic faith, the construction of such edifices should be viewed as a unique expression and assertion of Indian Roman Catholic religiosity and identity that is distinct from most of the other Indian Christian churches and sects that currently populate India.

There are several reasons why the Church in India would embrace such a devotionally-specific structure, even in urban Chennai where churches are already contending with issues of space and general upkeep. First and foremost, these buildings are viewed as means to extend the Kingdom of God. According to Fr. Lawrence, "By developing all these places ... we are building churches, we are building God's kingdom, and we attract more people, and more people come to know about God and Christ. And as a priest, I suppose, that's one of my primary duties, also...it is not the building, through the building you are building people and building God's kingdom."[73] The inspiration for building Eucharistic chapels came directly from the Vatican. In 2003, Pope John Paul II published an encyclical letter entitled *Ecclesia de Eucharistia* that explained to the faithful the importance of the Eucharist as a foundation for belief and Church teachings.[74] Simply, it was a call for the universal revival of Eucharistic adoration within the Catholic Church. A year later, the Council for Divine Worship and the Discipline of the Sacrament published the *Redemptionis Sacramentum*, which was a set of instructions and guidelines for the implementation of Eucharistic revival at the Diocesan and parish levels.[75]

Finally, in order to initiate the Pope's call for revival, the Vatican designated October 2004–2005 as the "Year of Eucharist." Some Eucharistic chapels were present in South India before this time. For example, San Thome has had a Eucharistic chapel since the time of Archbishop Arulappa, who was Archbishop of Madras-Mylapore from 1966–1987. At some point during his tenure, the north-side sacristy was converted into the current side-chapel. In 1986, during the papal visit, Pope John Paul II came to pray at San Thome's Eucharistic chapel, and to this day, an empty

Figure 5.18 Monstrance used during Eucharistic Procession at San Thome during Feast of St. Thomas July 5, 2009.

Photo: T. C. Nagy.

chair has been placed before the tabernacle in memory of the late pope's visit [Figure 5.19].[76] Nevertheless, the widespread construction of Eucharistic chapels in South India dates from 2003. These new structures can be seen as an innovative solution that goes beyond the requirements outlined in *Redemptionis Sacramentum*.

According to the *Redemptionis Sacramentum*, "It is highly recommended that at least in the cities and the larger towns the diocesan Bishop should designate a church building for perpetual adoration."[77] There is no mention of new chapels, only that a pre-existing church building should be utilized in such a way. As Fr. Lawrence explained, certain bishops decided that new chapels were a good idea, and this idea eventually won the approval of the Archbishop of Madras-Mylapore. Some priests voiced concern about the

Figure 5.19 Eucharistic chapel at San Thome.
Photo: T. C. Nagy.

actual need for new structures, since churches were already like Eucharistic chapels.[78] Nevertheless, the idea of building Eucharistic chapels throughout the country was fully adopted by the Church in India. Fr. Lawrence, who had first-hand knowledge of this process, explains:

> When we had the Year of the Eucharist … a lot of things were spoken about the Eucharist and the importance of the Eucharist in the Christian life. And the main idea is to have these Eucharistic chapels in shrines. Because in shrines all sorts of people go there and the Blessed Sacrament is always kept in the center and the Hindus and Muslims they don't know what it is. As a reason, they go and desecrate, no, we don't say it like that, but they simply walk like that [gesturing], you know, without any reverence and so on. We don't blame them because they don't know what it is. For them [Hindus] the statues are more important. So, therefore, we said we will put up separate Eucharistic chapels … so that only Christians will be able to go and pray there. And other people, they can go to the statue in the shrine and pray, that was the idea.[79]

As we can see, there were two main reasons as to why the Indian Church adopted this idea. First, to promote Eucharistic adoration among the faithful, and second, to fully separate and delineate the Catholic-specific ritual of Eucharistic adoration from the many practitioners of popular piety that frequent Catholic shrines in India. I would add to this list other Indian Christian (Protestant) visitors who do not hold the Eucharist in the same esteem as members of the Catholic Church. I assert that the Church's latter reason should be viewed as a distinctive Roman Catholic response to popular piety that is entirely unique to the context of India's modern-day eclectic and socio-religious landscape.

While this particular solution may imply a certain level of tension between the Church and popular piety, it is simultaneously indicative of the Church's more mindful attitude towards local expressions of popular practice. In other words, the Church has become more willing to go the extra mile in order to accommodate both practitioners of popular piety and each respective parish's established Catholic community. For example, at Little Mount a great deal of effort must have been necessary for the installation of its Eucharistic chapel, which was built in spite of the Shrine's space limitations in 2006. It was built to replicate the Portuguese mission style of the historic Shrine of Our Lady of Good Health, which it is situated against (Figure 5.20). St. Thomas Mount boasts two separate Eucharistic chapels, one at the top of the Hill Shrine and a second on the grounds of St. Patrick's Church at the bottom of the mount. The

Figure 5.20 Shrine of Our Lady of Good Health (left) and Eucharistic chapel (right) at Little Mount.

Photo: T. C. Nagy.

hilltop chapel was constructed in 2006, and much like Little Mount's chapel, was built in the Portuguese mission style so as to complement the historic Our Lady of Expectation chapel which it neighbors. St. Thomas Mount's more recent Eucharistic chapel was most likely started in 2010, since it was still under construction when I visited it in December of that same year. This particular chapel is an impressive tower-like structure that adds grandeur to St. Patrick's campus (Figure 5.21). But, more than anything else, it demonstrates the great significance that the Church in India attributes to Eucharistic adoration and the strategy of shrinal development.

The need for Eucharistic chapels, especially at popular shrines, demonstrates a tension between the established Catholic community and practitioners of popular Christian piety. These structures do not cater to popular religiosity, but are intended to inspire the Catholic faithful and new converts to the Church. According to Little Mount's parish priest, the

Figure 5.21 Eucharistic chapel at St. Patrick's Church, St. Thomas Mount.
Photo: T. C. Nagy.

Church's emphasis on the Eucharist and the building of adoration chapels can also be seen as a strategy for the prevention of "sheep stealing." In his opinion, the Catholic Eucharist is something other Christian denominations cannot compete against, and through the reinforcement and reemphasizing of this fact, fewer Catholics will be inclined to leave the Church. As discussed in previous chapters, this perspective is prominent among the hierarchy, whose emphasis on shrine-based revival includes strategies for preserving Catholic numbers in the wake of Pentecostalism and other such factors. [80]

Mr. Mark, a Thomas Christian from Kerala, interpreted the recent revival of Eucharistic adoration as an organized counter against the demoralizing violence perpetrated by the Hindu right against Indian Christian communities. Mr. Mark explains:

> You know, in the last five years or six years, if you take the history, several churches have been directly attacked. Earlier Christians, now the churches and even the Blessed Sacrament, you know. They demolish the statues, statues of Mary, Jesus, saints; they've all been desecrated. So people started losing reverence towards it. Anyone can go and just destroy, there's no power (as it is). We believe that Jesus is present there, so people need to be given that feeling that we just don't proclaim that Jesus is there, we also want to propagate that Jesus is still there. So we, more forcefully, we come out and propagate that Jesus is present there and we want to really show that, exhibit that through this expositions, through this physical structures that are made ... that is the only reason: the persecution, the attack against churches specifically ... [the Catholic Church] if it is not protected with these structures, after all it is in the church we really worship God, and without them, for us, there is no civil sign of God here on earth.[81]

The Indian Church is well aware of the purposeful desecration of Christian churches and symbols on the part of the Hindu right. Fr. Lawrence even noted the issue of accidental desecration caused by unknowing practitioners of Christian popular piety. As such, due to the unpredictability of India's Hindu Right and Christianity's minority status in India, many Indian Christians perceive a threat to their religious identity. Thus, the construction of Eucharistic adoration chapels is viewed by some as a symbol of perseverance, preservation, and re-sacralization in the wake of targeted violence, polemics, and dwindling numbers.

St. Anthony's Seashore Shrine: a suburban made-to-order Catholic shrine

The third of my shrinal categories is exemplified by the recently constructed St. Anthony's Seashore Shrine. This shrine can be viewed as a product of

India's growing economy and booming middle class, which are most apparent in many of Chennai's outer suburbs, such as Palavakkam where St. Anthony's is located. C. J. Fuller and Joanne Waghorne have both argued that contemporary Hindu temple construction and revival in Tamil Nadu is intrinsically tied to the patronage of the nation's growing middle class.[82] In the same way, several of the Catholic shrines discussed in this book have prospered due to the patronage of middle-class parishioners, converts, and devotees of popular Christian worship. Fuller and Waghorne have identified and implied several pertinent socio-religious characteristics unique to Indian middle-class urban religiosity. In other words, due to India's growing economy and the recent burgeoning of this social class, many middle-class Indians – Hindu and Christian alike – are discovering new ways of expressing their religiosity that is a direct reflection of their new financial status in society.[83] Some of the distinctive Indian middle-class religious features that Fuller and Waghorne have identified can also be found at certain Catholic shrines in India, especially at newly constructed suburban parishes like St. Anthony's Seashore Shrine. Through the analysis of some of St. Anthony's specific design aspects and physical features, it becomes apparent that the Church has come to understand popular piety not as a religious phenomenon only partaken by low-caste or low-class members of society, but also as an avenue for middle-class religious expression.

The development of St. Anthony's Seashore Shrine

St. Anthony's can be best described as a made-to-order shrine because all the elements that have gone into the refurbishment of older shrines like St. Thomas Mount and Annai Vailankanni have been included in St. Anthony's construction from almost the very beginning. Furthermore, there are several elements in place that solidify this newly constructed church into a full-fledged shrine that conforms to Fr. Lawrence's shrine-based evangelization strategy, especially in its ability to attract and accommodate popular devotion. As St. Anthony's website even states, "Seashore St. Antony at Palavakkam is a very popular saint not only among Catholics, but among all religious people. People of all walks flock to St. Antony for his powerful intercession as well as to thank him for all the favors received through him …. [St. Anthony's] attracts pilgrims in a large number throughout the year."[84]

It is clear that Fr. Lawrence and other Church administrators are well aware of India's economic trends, as well as the financial capabilities of their parishioners. More importantly, recognizing such trends allowed the Church to determine potential sites for future parishes, especially in newly developed regions like Palavakkam, where new neighborhoods are being created in order to facilitate Chennai's up-and-coming middle class. St. Anthony's Seashore Shrine was built to purposefully provide the area with an official shrine that could fundamentally cater to Palavakkam's diverse and expanding community. As St. Anthony's website explains, when the parish first started it was made up of about three hundred families who were originally a part of a parish in Vettuvankeni, but this parish could no longer accommodate its growing community, and quite possibly, could not reflect the community's greater sense of prosperity.[85]

As with many other local projects, Fr. Lawrence also played a significant role in the construction of St. Anthony's. While beginning his tenure at San Thome, Fr. Lawrence also held the position of Diocesan properties in-charge, and thus, was tasked with raising the funds to build this new church. Construction started in 2000 and the church was consecrated by early 2002, and is now a part of the Chingleput Diocese. St. Anthony's website boasts, "He [Fr. Lawrence] along with the devotees raised funds indigenously and built the Church without any foreign funds," which suggests that the local community donated a great deal towards this project.[86] With this task accomplished, Fr. Lawrence's part was done, and from that point on it would be the job of the parish priest to popularize this site and make it shrine-worthy. St. Anthony's would be declared an official Diocesan Shrine by 2009, only nine years after breaking ground, which the Church's website notes as being "a miracle in itself."[87]

Clearly, there are many factors that make this Shrine's development and situation very different from many of the other shrines already discussed in this chapter. Most significant is the relative newness of this particular shri-nal complex. At the time of my first trip to Chennai, St. Anthony's was not even a decade old. Another major difference is the Shrine's location in an up-and-coming middle-class suburban neighborhood, from which one can infer that a good portion of the congregation must belong to this social status. The fact that St. Anthony's was completely built without the aid of foreign funds and only with money "indigenously" raised in a very short period of time seems to attest to the financial capabilities of the parish community. Furthermore, when we look at the parish grounds, we see that all the basic edifices and shrinal structures that have come to partly define Catholic renewal in Chennai have been built as part of the Shrine's initial layout, and not piecemeal as seen with other older and more established parishes. What makes this all the more remarkable is that St Anthony's was given official shrine status so swiftly, which can also be seen as an indicator of St. Anthony's well-to-do community and its financial ability to give this new shrine all the modern amenities necessary to further the Church's shrine-bases evangelization strategy. Thus, it is fair to infer that, due to St. Anthony's local popularity and the prosperity of the parish community, this particular church was intended from its conception to be developed into a canonically recognized shrine.

Middle-class aesthetics as fixtures for popular Catholicism

St. Anthony's grounds are crowded with all the fixtures expected of a modern Indian Catholic church, as well as additional structures and ornamentation that makes this parish church a multi-functional shrine. As expected, it is well maintained and highly decorated with Catholic symbols and lush greenery. The route to St. Anthony's is fairly direct. Going down the long stretch of highway towards Palavakkam, St. Anthony's is only a short distance from the side of the road, but far enough away so as not to be visible from the road. Travelers are greeted by a large gate reminiscent of the Dravidian-style gates that surround most Hindu temples in South India (Figure 5.22). Within the church complex are several fixtures of modern Indian Catholic popular devotion. Since St. Anthony is the patron saint of this shrine, he has his own outer "grotto" (Figure 5.23). Situated just behind this grotto is the Shrine's Lourdes grotto (Figure 5.24). Possibly the most impressive structure on the grounds is the Shrine's Eucharistic chapel. However, this is not merely a chapel, but a 100-foot tall Eucharistic tower (Figure 5.25). Its ornate design is meant to resemble a larger than life monstrance, and was constructed in 2005 in honor of the Catholic "Year of the Eucharist."

These structures can be viewed as products geared towards attracting popular Christian devotion to St. Anthony's Seashore Shrine, as well as to elicit symbols of popular Catholic piety. Both Fr. Lawrence and the parish priest of Little Mount suggested to me that the two most popular Catholic saints in India are first and foremost St. Mary, and in a distant second place, St. Anthony.[88]

Figure 5.22 Entrance gate to St. Anthony's Seashore Shrine.
Photo: T. C. Nagy.

Figure 5.23 St. Anthony statue display.
Photo: T. C. Nagy.

Figure 5.24 Lourdes grotto at St. Anthony's Seashore Shrine.
Photo: T. C. Nagy.

Figure 5.25 Eucharistic tower at St. Anthony's Seashore Shrine in the form of a monstrance.

Photo: T. C. Nagy.

The Eucharistic tower can be seen as a means to attract and educate visitors about Eucharistic adoration, and the fact that it is possibly the tallest structure in the immediate area, could lead to it being considered a tourist attraction as well. Although I have categorized St. Anthony's as a middle-class parish, this does not mean that its community is uninterested in attracting practitioners of popular piety from all stratums of society. It is easy to assume that most practitioners of popular piety are from the lower spectrum, however, this does not seem to be necessarily the case.

From my many conversations with my Catholic informants in Chennai, it seems that there is a great deal of mixing between various social classes at most shrines. This is most likely a product of the Church's push for caste equality, which is easier to implement within an urban context. Fr. Lawrence has implied that practitioners of popular Christian piety in Chennai tend to freely shop around when it comes to Catholic shrines, and that something as simple as the attractiveness of a church's statuary, or the appearance of "new products on the market," can provide enough incentive for a visit.[89] Of course, more likely reasons include the convenience of location, or a pre-existing devotion to a particular saint. St. Anthony's location is, as with many of Fr. Lawrence's projects, adjacent to the coastline, which also serves to add another level of attractiveness. Thus, I do not believe popular Christian devotion is uniquely a phenomenon associated with low-caste and low-class Indians; it clearly extends to middle-class Indians as well. As Meera Nanda observes, one of the more intriguing characteristics of Hindu middle-class religiosity is its embrace of more ritualistic and popular forms of Hindu worship. She states, "The new Hindu elite and middle classes revel in ritualism, idol worship, fasts, pilgrimages, and other routines of popular, theistic Hinduism, sometimes mixed with new age spirituality."[90] On a more personal observation, recall my informant Mr. Sam, who considers himself neither Hindu nor Christian, but a devotee of Mother Mary. He is undeniably a participant in the popular worship and veneration of St. Mary at Vailankanni, but he is also a member of India's middle class who holds a PhD in engineering and who travels regularly to Saudi Arabia for work. Although more data would be needed to establish this conclusively, I believe that there is indeed both Catholic and Hindu middle-class religious participation within the realm of popular Christian piety and ritual in India, and that this could very well be the result of social mobility, where the status of the practitioners may improve, but their religious practice and devotion stays fundamentally the same.

Continuing onward to St. Anthony's Church, we see that this structure is noteworthy, in and of itself, due to its practical and space-efficient design (Figure 5.26). It is a double-tiered building, with a multi-purpose hall on the ground level, and the main church on top. It is very likely that this structural design is becoming the favored build for new Catholic churches in India because it essentially combines two buildings into one, which allows the Church to make the most of any given plot of land. Many of the churches that Fr. Lawrence has had a hand in building or renovating utilize this double-tier concept. Fr. Lawrence showed me the blueprint for the future St. Teresa's, and if all goes according to his plans, it will also be a double-tiered structure like St. Anthony's, which makes practical sense considering St. Teresa's location in the heart of the city.

The building's interior was closed off to photography, so I was unable to take any pictures. However, there were several notable features of St. Anthony's interior that are worth discussing. In terms of design, the main church seems to have been built with maintaining good air circulation in mind, which accounts for its high ceilings, multiple ceiling fans, and spacious floor plan. It seems that something as simple as the more efficient use of space and the up-keep of general cleanliness can be understood as a hallmark of Indian middle-class sensibilities. In Waghorne's *Diaspora of*

Figure 5.26 St. Anthony's Seashore Shrine, Palavakkam.
Photo: T. C. Nagy.

the Gods, she is cautious about her application and categorization of anything pertaining to Indian middle-class sensibilities, because she is aware of its ambiguity with regard to the constantly changing face of modern-day Indian socio-religious identity.[91] However, she does take note of several changes in attitude and common trends distinct to contemporary middle-class Hindu temple construction and community formation.

As Waghorne relates, a couple of the newly built Hindu temples she researched were organized around the "like-mindedness" of its committee members, and not by their separate caste distinctions or similarities. She further explains:

> This like-mindedness, however, was a trait they had in common with the middle-class devotees of Madhya Kailas. Both temples had the same openness, both social and spatial – clean architectural lines, open proportions, sunlight shining on polished floors …. I saw such design elements repeatedly in many of the new suburban temples.[92]

She goes on to suggest the existence of an "unwritten 'code' of modern temples in Chennai" that many of these new temples have conformed to, which includes, "revere cleanliness, foster a serene atmosphere, and create openness in a broad space that welcomes a wider public, which sometimes extends beyond the middle class...."[93] While some of these aspects seem obvious for any newly built edifice, within the context of Chennai's growing urbanization issues such as cleanliness become more vital. This is also seen at St. Thomas Mount, where a local Sister commenting on the new changes at the Hill Shrine writes, "Their [the priests] first priority is towards cleanliness .... Hordes of people are assigned to cleaning the premises .... That obvious difference is noted and appreciated by one and all and that indeed was the start to the numerous changes that are to follow."[94] We can see how the traditional notion of building an open-air temple is less desirable amidst the pollution of an industrialized modern city; however, it is clear that indoor temples are designed to emulate the open-air aspects of older temples with the use of high walls and open architecture.

In various ways, some of the recently built and refurbished Catholic shrines in Chennai also conform to this middle-class sensibility. It seems likely that Fr. Lawrence had guidelines such as these in mind when he began to seriously implement a shrine-based evangelization strategy in Chennai, and that he may have been ultimately influenced by such growing middle-class trends within the city. St. Anthony's provides a prime example of this aesthetic due to its recent inception, and as we can see, it has certainly attempted to present itself as a physically and socially open space that is welcoming to everyone regardless of caste or class.

As Waghorne reiterates in a later section of her book, "even the architecture both of the space and the polity of new temples reflects democratic models of civic organizations, which leads to new space for meetings, lectures, and education."[95] It seems that the Church would already be inclined towards a more democratic arrangement within the parish organization, especially when we take into consideration the Church in Chennai's recent attempts to foster a greater sense of urban egalitarianism through various development and revivalist projects throughout the city. Thus, St. Anthony's stands as a clear indication of the kinds of brand new parishes and shrines that the Church hopes to build in the near future. While older sites have been busily catching up to this ideal, new parishes like St. Anthony's are being constructed and organized to reflect certain middle-class sensibilities from the very beginning as a part of a larger Catholic renewal movement, which in turn, is taking place within the greater backdrop of Indian urban religious renewal and transformation in Chennai.

One last significant feature of St. Anthony's interior is a prominent side chapel that is dedicated to Our Lady of Vailankanni. Its presentation was very much in line with the "grottos" built at Annai Vailankanni Shrine and St. Teresa's Church. Behind St. Anthony's were other edifices, such as dioramic displays of all the Stations of the Cross. I visited St. Anthony's in mid-2009, and during this time its grounds were bustling with craftsmen and other workers busily assembling and securing various other projects not written about here. Undoubtedly, this extra work was a result of St. Anthony's newly acquired status as a Diocesan Shrine. Reflecting on this memory, it seems as if the title of shrine has become synonymous with parish development, modernization, and "kitschy" representations of popular Catholic religiosity, and may very well be an honest reflection of Indian Catholic middle-class sensibilities, which are ultimately derived from the recently acquired sense of national economic prosperity. The Church's shrine-based strategy for evangelization, revival, and renewal relies upon this new-found national sense, and shrines like Seashore St. Anthony's represents the culmination and future of this strategy in India.

Chapter summary and final thoughts

The contemporary Catholic renewal strategy of shrine building has devloped out of Fr. Lawrence and other Church administrator's desire to precipitate evangelization in a manner suited to modern-day India's political climate. This recent evangelization strategy relies upon the multitudes of non-Catholics who participate and worship at Catholic shrines throughout India, and thus, the Church in India has slowly softened its original hard-line stance against popular religiosity. The key to this shrine-based strategy involves the maintenance and development of Catholic shrines in order to better attract and accommodate popular religiosity, while at the same time improving and preserving the faith of the already established parish community, and somehow managing both these agendas without compromising Catholic doctrine and authority.

As this chapter has discussed, this shrine-based strategy involves different kinds of projects depending on the nature of the shrine in question. Historically significant and well-established shrines like San Thome and St. Thomas Mount require a greater marketing scheme in order to reach their potential as world-class pilgrimage and tourist sites. More typical of Catholic shrines in India are sites like Annai Vailankanni Shrine and Little Mount, which are lesser known, but still maintain a respectable level of popularity. Such sites require proper expansion and smaller projects that serve to better highlight their spiritual significance.

The future of Catholic renewal in India relies, to some extent, upon the patronage of India's growing middle class. As we can see with St. Anthony's Seashore Shrine, a shrinal mold has been created that takes several aspects of popular Catholic religiosity and then places them under a single roof. Such a church is undoubtedly an inevitable product of so-called middle-class consumer sensibilities that appear to play a large part in up-and-coming urban districts such as Palavakkam.[96] This is also seen at the long-established St. Teresa's parish in Nungambakkam, where the initial plan involves the demolition of its original heritage church in order to build a bigger, more modern complex in order to better overcome the inherent space limitations that come from being located in the heart of Chennai.

While such a location ultimately hinders expansion, it also provides a great deal of exposure for Fr. Lawrence's projects, such as his Vailankanni grotto, which has, in essence, transformed a simple parish church into some semblance of a minor shrine.

However, if we are to discuss this strategy in terms of marketing, then we can consider a possible key consequence of the Church's recent reliance on shrinal development. As mentioned before, St. Anthony's was calling itself a shrine from the very beginning without having yet received its canonical recognition. Fr. Lawrence points out:

> If they are not officially declared as shrines, the parish priest declares shrines. In what way that is going to help, you know, whether it is a church or a shrine? So, if these are places where a lot of people go that have real devotion, then it is okay ... but everyday these popular devotions are picking up. Some new devotions, they are starting. A difference, sort of like the new products on the market, you know.[97]

It seems there is nothing stopping any parish priest from calling his church a shrine, something Fr. Lawrence believes to be justifiable under the correct circumstances.

It is interesting that Fr. Lawrence even noted the abundance of new shrines as being "like the new products on the market," which continues to highlight the fact that in many ways the Church's shrine-based evangelization strategy can be viewed in marketing terms, and that the Church's administration most likely views it this way; Fr. Lawrence certainly does. A possible consequence of this strategy is that the Church could theoretically over-saturate the market with "shrines," and this would ultimately dilute the spiritual significance of the term, as well as over-extend the financial and managerial abilities of the administration. As Fr. Lawrence mentioned, "See, what happens here actually, last week we had a meeting of the priests and the Bishop, so that the Bishop was telling, 'You don't simply name all the churches shrines, because if everybody makes shrines, shrines, shrines, shrines!'"[98] It seems at least one bishop in Chennai has expressed his fears over this issue, and this could mean that the shrinal-market in Chennai is already beginning to be over-saturated.

Notes

1 Quoted in Sashi Kala Chandran, "Down Memory Lane with Fr. Lawrence Raj," *Sweet Fruits of God's Harvest on Earth: Rev. Fr. Lawrence Raj Sacerdotal Silver Jubilee Commemorative Souvenir*, edited by Fr. Lawrence Raj Silver Jubilee Souvenir Committee. (Chennai: Fr. Lawrence Raj Silver Jubilee Souvenir Committee, 2007).
2 Interview with Fr. Lawrence Raj, Chennai, June 15, 2009.
3 Laura Dudley Jenkins, "Legal Limits on Religious Conversion in India," *Law and Contemporary Problems* 71, 109 (Spring 2008): 119.

4 Ibid.

5 Pope Paul VI, *Evangelii Nuntiandi*, http://www.vatican.va/holy_father/paul_vi/apost_exhortations/documents/hf_p-vi_exh_19751208_evangelii-nuntiandi_en.html (Accessed February 2, 2013).

6 Ibid.

7 International Theological Commission, *Faith and Inculturation*, http://www.vatican.va/roman_curia/congregations/cfaith/cti_documents/rc_cti_1988_fede-inculturazione_en.html (Accessed August 19, 2012).

8 Pope Paul VI, *Evangelii Nuntiandi*.

9 Ibid.

10 Ibid.

11 Interview with Fr. Lawrence Raj, Chennai, June 15, 2009.

12 Interview with Fr. Lawrence Raj, Chennai, June 30, 2009.

13 Interview with Mr. Sam, Chennai, March 27, 2009.

14 Ibid.

15 Ibid.

16 Ibid.

17 Ibid.

18 Sebastian C. H. Kim, *In Search of Identity: Debates on Religious Conversion in India* (New Delhi: Oxford University Press, 2005), 110.

19 Interview with Sam, Chennai, March 27, 2009.

20 Shrine Basilica of Our Lady of Health Vailankanni: The Place of Our Lady's Apparitions, "Donation," http://www.vailankannishrine.org/donation.php (Accessed September 30, 2012).

21 P. John Bosco, *St. Thomas Mount-Chennai-South India: The Spot of the Heroic Martyrdom of St. Thomas the Apostle and the Cradle and Glory of the Indian Church* (Chennai: Apostolic Hill Shrine of St. Thomas, St. Thomas Mount, 2010), 26.

22 Ibid, 6.

23 Interview with Mr. Franks, Chennai, July 16, 2009

24 Interview with Fr. Lawrence Raj, Chennai, December 15, 2010.

25 Ibid.

26 G. Backiya Regis, "From the Editor's pen." *The Voice from the Hill* 1, 1 (July 2010): 3.

27 *The Voice from the Hill: Spiritual Magazine-Monthly* 1, 3 (September 2010), back cover.

28 S. J. Anthonysamy, *A Saga of Faith: St. Thomas the Apostle of India* (Chennai: National Shrine of St. Thomas Basilica, 2009), 146.

29 Oddly enough, according to the cover insert of issue 3 of *The Voice from the Hill*, St. Thomas Mount was elevated to "Regional Shrine" status in 2010 by the Tamil Nadu Bishops' Council. This particular level is not specified in the *Code of Canon Law*, which seems to imply that it was purely a creation of the Church in India. Perhaps it was a pre-requisite for National Shrine status, or possibly, a quick and easy way to assign certain shrines a status greater than Diocesan Shrine status. See also: Gcatholic.org, "National Shrines: India, Bhutan," http://www.gcatholic.org/churches/data/shrineINX.htm (accessed April 14, 2016). The above website is the only list of Catholic international and national shrines I could find, but it is updated regularly.

30 *The Voice from the Hill* 1, 3 (September 2010), back cover.

31 "Characteristics of Shrines," *The Voice from the Hill* 1, 1 (July 2010): 2.

32 G. Backiya Regis, "From the Editor's pen," *The Voice from the Hill* 1, 4 (October 2010): 3.

33 Simon Chumkat, "Sand from the Tomb," *Voice of St Thomas* 1, 5 (July–September 2007): 10–11.

34 Marco Polo, *Journey to the End of the Earth*, trans. by Robin Brown (Stroud: The History Press, 2007), 197–198.
35 Field Notes, Chennai, December 18, 2010.
36 Bosco, *St. Thomas Mount-Chennai-South India*, 15.
37 Margaret Meibohm, "Past Selves and Present Others: The Ritual Construction of Identity at a Catholic Festival in India," in *Popular Christianity in India. Riting between the Lines*, eds Selva J. Raj and Corinne G. Dempsey (Albany, NY: State University of New York Press, 2002), 66.
38 David Shulman, *Tamil Temple Myths: Sacrifice and Divine Marriage in the South Indian Śaiva Tradition* (Princeton, NJ: Princeton University Press, 1980), 107.
39 Ibid, 91.
40 Ibid, 92.
41 Interview with Brother Joe, Chennai, June 11, 2009.
42 Tertullian lived during the late second and early third centuries CE and hailed from the ancient city of Carthage. In Chapter 50 of his *Apologeticus* he states to his Pagan audience, "We [Christians] multiply whenever we are mown down by you; the blood of Christians is seed." Tertullian, *Apology* and *De Spectaculis*, translated by T. R. Glover (London: Heinemann, 1931), 227. For the most part, my informants have correctly captured Tertullian's sentiments within their own phrasing of his words, which demonstrates a wholly Christian understanding of martyrdom that includes an allusion to the idea of fertility and the creating of new life, or Christians, through the spilled blood of a martyr's sacrifice.
43 Annai Vailankanni Shrine, "About Us," http://www.vailankannishrinechennai.org/vailankanni/about.html (Accessed October 11, 2012).
44 Interview with Fr. Lawrence Raj, Chennai, December 15, 2010.
45 Archdiocese of Madras-Mylapore, "Annai Vailankanni Shrine," http://www.archdioceseofmadrasmylapore.org/parish_view1.php?uid=P015 (Accessed October 11, 2012). See also: Annai Vailankanni Shrine, "About Us."
46 Annai Vailankanni Shrine, "About Us."
47 Ibid.
48 Ibid.
49 Paul Younger, *Playing Host to Deity: Festival Religion in the South Indian Tradition* (Oxford: Oxford University Press, 2002), 112–115.
50 Annai Vailankanni Shrine, "At the Shrine," http://www.vailankannishrinechennai.org/vailankanni/shrine.html (Accessed October 11, 2012).
51 Annai Vailankanni Shrine, "About Us."
52 Suzanne Kaufman, *Consuming Visions: Mass Culture and the Lourdes Shrine* (Ithaca and London: Cornell University Press, 2005), 2.
53 Ruth Harris, *Lourdes: Body and Spirit in the Secular Age* (New York: Viking, 1999), 14.
54 Pope Pius IX, *Ineffabilis Deus*, http://www.newadvent.org/library/docs_pi09id.htm (Accessed October 23, 2012).
55 Harris, *Lourdes*, 14.
56 Ibid, 221.
57 Ibid.
58 Mary of Nazareth: Her Mystery, Her Museum, Her Site, "Lourdes," http://www.mariedenazareth.com/7410.0.html?&L=1 (Accessed October 23, 2012).
59 Selva J. Raj, "Transgressing Boundaries, Transcending Turner: The Pilgrimage Tradition at the Shrine of St. John de Britto," in *Popular Christianity in India: Riting between the Lines*, eds Selva J. Raj and Corinne G. Dempsey (Albany, NY: State University Press of New York, 2002), 97, and 102–103. Over the course of several individual articles, Selva Raj has provided a keen insight into the complex positionality of Tamil Catholic priests within the hybridized

socio-religious milieu of popular Christian practice in South India. It probably helps that Selva Raj was, for the bulk of his academic career, a practicing Catholic priest. See also: Selva J. Raj, "Ethnographic Encounter with the Wondrous in a South Indian Catholic Shrine," in *Miracle as Modern Conundrum in South Asian Religious Traditions*, eds Corinne G. Dempsey and Selva J. Raj (Albany, New York: State University Press, 2008), 156–160. Selva J. Raj, "Public Display, Communal Devotion: Procession at a South Indian Catholic Festival," in *South Asian Religions on Display: Religious Processions in South Asia and in the Diaspora*, ed. Knut A. Jacobson (London and New York: Routledge, 2008), 87–89.

60 Younger, *Playing Host to Deity*, 112–115.
61 Stanley N. Kurtz, *All the Mothers Are One: Hindi India and the Cultural Reshaping of Psychoanalysis* (New York: Columbia University Press, 1992), 7.
62 Ibid, 14.
63 Ibid, 14–15.
64 Interview with Brother Joe, Chennai, June 11, 2009.
65 Ibid.
66 Interview with Mr. Mark, Chennai, July 23, 2009.
67 Interview with Fr. Lawrence Raj, Chennai, June 15, 2009.
68 Interview with Fr. Lawrence Raj, Chennai, December 15, 2010.
69 Mara Einstein, *Brands of Faith: Marketing Religion in a Commercial Age* (London and New York: Routledge, 2008), 81.
70 Interview with Fr. Lawrence Raj, Chennai, June 15, 2009.
71 Joseph Pohle, "The Real Presence of Christ in the Eucharist," http://www.newadvent.org/cathen/05573a.htm (Accessed October 26, 2012).
72 Herbert Thurston, "Exposition of the Blessed Sacrament," http://www.newadvent.org/cathen/05713a.htm (Accessed October 26, 2012).
73 Interview with Fr. Lawrence Raj, Chennai, December 15, 2010.
74 Pope John Paul II, *Encyclical Letter: Ecclesia de Eucharistia*, http://www.vatican.va/holy_father/john_paul_ii/encyclicals/documents/hf_jp-ii_enc_17042003_ecclesia-de-eucharistia_en.html (Accessed October 26, 2012).
75 Council for Divine Worship and the Discipline of the Sacrament, *Redemptionis Sacramentum: On certain matters to be observed or to be avoided regarding the Most Holy Eucharist*, http://www.vatican.va/roman_curia/congregations/ccdds/documents/rc_con_ccdds_doc_20040423_redemptionis-sacramentum_en.html (Accessed October 26, 2012).
76 Interview with Fr. Lawrence Raj, Chennai, June 30, 2009.
77 Council for Divine Worship and the Discipline of the Sacrament, *Redemptionis Sacramentum: On certain matters to be observed or to be avoided regarding the Most Holy Eucharist*.
78 Interview with Fr. Lawrence Raj, Chennai, June 30, 2009.
79 Ibid.
80 In addition to my above points, historian of religion Mathew Schmalz, in some recent publications, offers a couple of examples of how the exposed host via Eucharistic adoration has been utilized by Charismatic Catholic healers in North India as a source for their spiritual gifts. See: Mathew N. Schmalz, "A Catholic Charismatic Healer at Play in North India," in *Sacred Play: Ritual Levity and Humor in South Asian* Religions, eds Selva J. Raj and Corinne G. Dempsey (Albany, NY: State University of New York Press, 2010), 187 and 200. Mathew N. Schmalz, "Boundaries and Appropriations in North Indian Charismatic Catholicism," in *Engaging South Asian Religions: Boundaries, Appropriations, and Resistances*, eds Mathew N. Schmalz and Peter Gottschalk (Albany, NY: State University of New York Press, 2011), 87–91.
81 Interview with Mr. Mark, Chennai, July 23, 2009.

82 See: C. J. Fuller, *The Renewal of the Priesthood: Modernity and Traditionalism in a South Indian Temple* (Princeton and Oxford: Princeton University Press, 2003), 37–42. See also: Joanne Punzo Waghorne, *Diaspora of the Gods: Modern Hindu Temple in an Urban Middle-Class World* (New York: Oxford University Press, 2004), 35–74.

83 Meera Nanda makes note in her book, *The God Market*, that the religiosity of many of India's religions have been positively affected by the nation's economic boom. She states, "Hindus are not the only ones becoming more religious. The 2007 State of the Nation Survey shows that 38 per cent of Indian Muslims, 47 per cent of Christians, and 33 per cent of Sikhs, as compared to 27 per cent Hindus, claim to have become more religious in the last five years." Meera Nanda, *The God Market: How Globalization is making India more Hindu* (Noida, Uttar Pradesh: Random House India, 2009), 70.

84 Palavakkam: Seashore St. Anthony's Shrine: The Diocese of Chingleput, http://www.seashorestanthony.org/index.html (Accessed October 30, 2012).

85 Palavakkam: Seashore St. Anthony's Shrine: The Diocese of Chingleput, "Mother Parish," http://www.seashorestanthony.org/about-shrine.html (Accessed October 30, 2012).

86 Palavakkam: Seashore St. Anthony's Shrine: The Diocese of Chingleput, "Church Construction," http://www.seashorestanthony.org/about-shrine.html (Accessed October 30, 2012).

87 Palavakkam: Seashore St. Anthony's Shrine: The Diocese of Chingleput, http://www.seashorestanthony.org/about-shrine.html (Accessed October 30, 2012).

88 Interview with Fr. Lawrence Raj, Chennai, December 15, 2010. See also: Field notes, Chennai, December 16, 2010.

89 Interview with Fr. Lawrence Raj, Chennai, December 15, 2010.

90 Nanda, *The God Market*, 62.

91 Waghorne, *Diaspora of the Gods*, 20–21.

92 Ibid, 30.

93 Ibid.

94 Angel Mary, "Apostolic Hill Shrine of St. Thomas: A Beacon of Spirituality," *The Voice from the Hill* 1, 1 (July 2010): 12.

95 Waghorne, *Diaspora of the Gods*, 236.

96 Ibid, 37–41.

97 Interview with Fr. Lawrence Raj, Chennai, December 15, 2010.

98 Ibid.

6 Conclusion
Catholic renewal in Chennai

Introduction

I have argued that in the context of Chennai's growing economy and urbanization, contemporary Catholic renewal can be seen through the construction and refurbishment of new and old church edifices of varying historical significance. According to Mary Hancock, Chennai "is one of India's mega-cities and one of the nodes through which forces of neoliberal globalization are transforming the country .... the city is poised to follow other South Indian metropoles as a center for global software production, export processing, and back-office services."[1] Only as recently as the mid 1990s has Chennai fully embraced and transformed itself into a modern city befitting its burgeoning economy and growing middle class. Chennai has also seen the development of new forms of local religiosity that implement more modernized forms of urbanization and technology, directly reflecting its higher quality of living. In this context, Catholic renewal and revival are movements initiated by members of the Church hierarchy, using various marketing strategies, towards the goals of evangelization, faith preservation, and fostering global awareness.

In this book I have endeavored to answer the following sets of questions regarding Catholic renewal and the revival of St. Thomas in Chennai: What contemporary strategies have been employed by the Roman Catholic Church in Chennai, India for religious revival and maintenance in the face of various political and social issues that have developed and evolved out of the context of India's unique political and religious history? How have these strategies been utilized, how have they been informed by local culture and customs, and why were certain specific strategies adopted over others?

Using these questions as guidelines, I have demonstrated that the Church in Chennai has adopted several significant revivalist marketing strategies in order to promulgate the Indian legacy of St. Thomas, and to precipitate Catholic evangelization and renewal throughout the city with the hope of extending these goals throughout India and across the globe. Fr. Lawrence's prominent role demonstrates that it is primarily from the parochial level of local Church hierarchy that religious renewal and revival is implemented within the urban context of Chennai. Church administrators have utilized various forms of media to portray St. Thomas's death and burial as a new myth of origin for Tamil Catholics. The additional context of Hindu right politics and ideology has also come to inform Catholic renewal in Chennai. Finally, Church administrators at San Thome and St. Thomas Mount have effectively created a St. Thomas "faith brand" from which to market and streamline the Apostle's Indian legacy. Ultimately, the revivals at San Thome and other such shrines demonstrate that Catholic renewal is taking place throughout Chennai.

Furthermore, I have endeavored in this book to avoid certain theoretical and methodological pitfalls, namely the typical post-colonial and postmodern discourses that are prevalent in the academic study of modern-day India. I do not state that such discourses are wholly unnecessary, but that they are inadequate when applied to certain post-colonial communities, such as the urban Indian Catholics of Chennai, who maintain a generally positive and optimistic view of their colonial heritages. As the historian Richard Eaton pointed out, the inadequacy of postmodern and post-colonial theory and discourse was made painfully clear with the eruption of communal violence in India during and after the Babri Masjid incident of 1992.[2] With this event and the continued use of Hindutva and nationalist rhetoric by the Hindu right in India, it has also become clear that the language of post-colonial theory has been appropriated by such groups in order to justify and sow anti-minority sentiment within the country.[3] However, more importantly, such rhetoric – political and academic – has ultimately denied minority communities, such as the Indian Christians, personal agency with regard to their communal and individual religious destinies. I hope, above all else, that my book has successfully presented in a fair light the communal agency of Indian Catholics in Chennai, and the personal religious agency of individuals such as Fr. Lawrence, Sr. Merrill, Mr. Sam, and Mr. Zander.

Competition and challenges

To quote Roger Hedlund again, "More than any other city, Chennai is the home of indigenous Christian action, organizations and churches."[4] Hedlund's observation makes it clear that Chennai is an important city for the study of Christianity in India, and that my research on Catholic renewal is a small, but pivotal, part of this larger picture. Within this urban context, many Christian denominations and indigenous organizations have set about their own attempts at religious revival and renewal. The Catholic Church is not alone in its utilization of religious marketing for the purposes of evangelization and preservation. For the Church in Chennai, these other denominations represent competition for both converts and space. In a conversation I had with the rector of Little Mount, I recall him bemoaning the fact that two new churches had been built in the vicinity of Little Mount. The first was a Mormon church, and the second was a large Pentecostal church belonging to the Assemblies of God.

In Fr. Lawrence's opinion, the rapid growth of Pentecostalism is the most significant challenge that the Church in India is currently facing. Stanley Burgess, a specialist on Pentecostal and Charismatic Christianity, estimates that the number of Indian Pentecostals reached about 33.5 million people in the year 2000.[5] This figure is incredible, especially when we take the Census of India into consideration, which placed the *total* number of Indian Christians at nearly 28 million in 2015.[6] As noted in Chapter 1, both Michael Bergunder and Robert Frykenberg agree with the disparity of census figures, and that this purposeful refusal by the Indian government to recognize the growing number of Indian Christians could potentially lead to some dire socio-political upheavals within India in the near future.[7]

Regardless of the exact figures, Pentecostalism is on the rise and is perceived by many Indian Catholics as a threat to Catholic evangelization and socio-political stability. Mr. Zander said to me, "if you come and visit again, you should pray that the number of Catholics should not diminish. We don't know [how] to increase the number of Catholics, at least more Catholics should not be converted into Protestant Evangelicals."[8] Most of all, there is the fear that many Catholics, especially the younger generation, are being lured away from the Church by the more ecstatic forms of Pentecostal worship. According to Bergunder's statistical data, this accusation of "sheep-stealing" seems to be exaggerated on the part of Catholics, and is most likely due to anecdotal evidence.[9] Undoubtedly, this strong impression has much to do with Chennai's centrality to India's growing Pentecostal movement, where new meeting places and non-Catholic houses of worship seem to spring up every other day.

The Church in Chennai has certainly taken notice of this burgeoning movement and has actively sought to strengthen Catholic devotion by emphasizing and marketing its most unique and enduring aspects. Some examples include the Church's longevity, its global connections, its many shrines and notable saint cults, as well as its commitment to caste equality, education, and health services. Obviously, the legacy of St. Thomas also represents one of Indian Catholicism's most enduring aspects. Even with these various selling points, the Church may begin to stagnate or decline in places, but it may also prosper, as sites like Vailankanni have demonstrated. In the end, the determining factor for stimulating consistent growth may be a church's ability to attract more Hindus. The Catholic Church has its shrines and its cult of the saints, while Pentecostalism has its ecstatic forms of worship and Gifts of the Spirit. The continued growth of India's economy and the subsequent wider distribution of wealth could provide local Christian denominations better opportunities for expansion and preservation; but at the same time, these same opportunities could also serve to benefit the Hindu nationalist cause in South India.

The Church in Chennai has had to be especially wary of not inciting the ire of the Hindu right, and recognizes that Hindutva represents a serious threat to Indian Christian identity and the future of the Church in India. India's political future is uncertain, as are its inevitable effects on the future of Indian Christianity. According to C. J. Fuller, Hindu nationalism is gaining momentum in Tamil Nadu; however, it is of a distinctly moderate nature that is free of the fundamentalist excesses commonly associated with the more militant aspects of the movement.[10] Nevertheless, for many of the Indian Roman Catholics I spoke with in Chennai, the BJP still maintains such a reputation for religious intolerance and for turning a blind eye to communal violence that even a politically moderate BJP-led government would result in hardship for India's Christian minority.

Now with the outcome of the 2014 election behind us, India's economic aspirations appear to have overshadowed the rhetoric of the extreme Hindu right, with issues pertaining to India's future with regard to economic revitalization, infrastructure development, modernization, and globalization taking center stage. However, the national emphasis on the economy ultimately resulted in a landslide victory for the BJP. More concerning is the political background of India's newly instated Prime Minister Narendra Modi. His strong ties to the RSS go back to his teenage years, and more significantly, he was chief minister of Gujarat during the 2002 anti-Muslim riots. However, like many of his BJP compatriots, he has since distanced himself politically from the RSS, while still retaining a moderate Hindu nationalist agenda.[11] As Michael Kugelman, a senior programs associate for South and Southeast Asia at the Woodrow Wilson Center for Scholars, explains, "The magnitude of his [Modi] victory suggests that the Indian voting public was willing to overlook Modi's baggage. For many Indians, the immediate concern for economic progress, better governance – the things Modi has promised – have trumped any concerns about his past."[12] Clearly, the large numbers of upper and middle-class voters who have participated in this election have become accustomed to India's economic prosperity, and are thus more invested in a political leadership that can revitalize and increase the nation's wealth than on preserving religious ideals.[13] If this is the case, the Church stands to also benefit and prosper under Modi's new BJP-led government; however, only time will tell if Modi and his new regime have truly distanced themselves from the militant Hindu fundamentalist mind-set of the RSS and its ilk.

Role of church administrators and the nature of urban Catholic renewal

For Fr. Lawrence, St. Thomas can become a rallying point for all Indian Catholics, but first the Church must become more active in it promulgation of St. Thomas's legacy. He has stated many times that it is the duty of the bishops and parish priests to raise St. Thomas's profile and curb the threat of Pentecostalism. Only time will tell if the Church's claim to an ancient Christian origin will become ingrained in the hearts and minds of Chennai's Indian Catholics. If and when such a claim can be firmly established within Chennai's Christian communities, it is possible that the ethnic and indigenous significance of St. Thomas's local legacy of martyrdom and burial will spread to other parts of Tamil Nadu, and perhaps even the rest of India. According to Fr. Lawrence, the responsibility for ensuring the maintenance and promulgation of St. Thomas's legacy falls to the Archbishop of Madras-Mylapore, but more decisively, to the bishops and priests of Chennai, especially those who are directly associated with one of the three St. Thomas shrines.[14] Without their leadership and drive, it is possible for St. Thomas to once again fall into obscurity and for his sacred sites in Chennai to fall into disrepair. However, due to the limited tenure of Catholic priests at any given parish, there is always a degree of unpredictability associated with what can be realistically accomplished by the priest and his community.

Another significant concern for the Church's shrinal development strategy resulting from the limited tenure periods of its parish priests is that, as posited in Chapter 1, the execution and success of many of these recent shrinal revivals relies on the personal effort and skill of the managing parish priest. Thus, the future of Catholicism in India and the Church's current shrine-based evangelization strategy will mainly be determined by the continued effort of such individuals within the parochial hierarchy. As this book has demonstrated, Fr. Lawrence is one such priest who has been called upon by the Church numerous times to help in developing and renovating both established and up-and-coming shrines around Chennai. The rectors of St. Thomas Mount and Little Mount have proven their managerial and organizational skills also. However, such men within the Church are few.

It seems, as I mused with Sr. Merrill, that the enthusiastic praise that Fr. Lawrence received from the laity for his dynamism and strong work ethic is ultimately due to the common impression that the majority of parish priests in the area have nowhere near the level of Fr. Lawrence's dedication. As previously implied, Mr Zander, a long-time parishioner at San Thome, also made this observation with regard to the future of San Thome. He stated, "Everything depends upon a [single] thing, I pray that people like ... priests like [Fr.] Lawrence, some more [Fr.] Lawrence[s] will come and some more people who are really interested in getting involved in church activities will come and do some, some more on us. Pray some more priests like Father Lawrence have to come."[15] For Mr. Zander, the key to Fr. Lawrence's success was his ability to motivate and work with parishioners in giving back to the parish community. Thus, as Mr. Zander explained, with Fr. Lawrence no longer at San Thome, the community was "slowly getting detached" from church involvement.[16]

Fr. Lawrence also expressed his concerns about the current state of San Thome. In his opinion, the current parish administration was not doing everything in its power to maintain the momentum he created during his tenure. From Fr. Lawrence's words, it seemed that he was more critical of the Cathedral's basic up-keep, which includes everything from refurbishing the continually weather-battered exterior, to replacing burned out light bulbs. He was also fearful that not enough effort was being put towards motivating the parish community into becoming more active in the daily running of the Cathedral, especially with regard to promoting its sacrality to new visitors and potential converts. It is hard to say for sure whether or not San Thome is on the decline, but that seems to be Fr. Lawrence and Mr. Zander's impression. This begs the question: Can we call the events at San Thome and St. Thomas Mount revivals?

In most instances, revival implies success or a case where it is undeniable that a community has experienced awakening or religious rejuvenation. I believe that San Thome, St. Thomas Mount, and other shrines in Chennai have experienced revivals to different extents. Within the crowded urban context of Chennai, with its pollution and humidity, perhaps the first steps towards spiritual renewal is being able to see the physical renewal of one's community and sacred places. As my informants can attest, many of the sites I have discussed have changed drastically and are being more consistently maintained now than they were before the last decade, which demonstrates a commitment from each respective community.

It may be that Fr. Lawrence and Mr. Zander's dismay at the current state of San Thome is simply a reflection of their more stringent standards. My personal observation, as someone who visited San Thome years after Fr. Lawrence's tenure, is that the community is doing well, far better than how it supposedly was before 2004. While it may take another personality as charismatic as Fr. Lawrence to replicate the positive atmosphere that existed during the renovation, I believe that a solid foundation has been laid at San Thome that will allow it to be better maintained and rejuvenated in the years to come. This foundation includes, but is not limited to, the underground tomb chapel, the various publications, the museum, and the recent memory of what Fr. Lawrence was able to accomplish there in 2004. The San Thome community is also more aware now than they have ever been in recent times about the apostolic legacy of their Archdiocese.

It is hard to imagine that St. Thomas will ever be as popular as St. Mary, but that is a moot point. I would assert that St. Thomas's profile has been raised both locally and internationally. A recent article of *National Geographic* featured an article entitled "In the Footsteps of the Apostles."[17] As the title suggests, this article, which was also the magazine's cover story, investigates the missionary journeys of Jesus' Apostles and what became of them after the Crucifixion. Situated prominently in this article is the story of St. Thomas's voyage to India, which is placed alongside the reports of religiously motivated violence against Christians in India today. The article declares, "Of all the Apostles, Thomas represents most profoundly the missionary zeal associated with the rise of Christianity – the drive to travel to the ends of the known world to preach a new creed."[18] There is certainly a correlation between the Church in Chennai's revival of St. Thomas, the great Indian missionary, and its desire to maintain his spirit of missionary zeal as a part of its own renewal and evangelization efforts across India.

Local concerns and global church

Hindutva rhetoric, coupled with India's recent history of religiously moti-vated communal violence, has clearly demonstrated to the Church the precarious position they are faced with when evangelizing to Hindus and other non-Christians in India. This complex political and socio-religious context has made apparent the need for a more subdued evangelization strategy, such as the shrine-based strategy currently being implemented by the Church in Chennai. While the Church has traditionally looked down on popular religiosity, this current shrine-based strategy allows the Church, at least in Chennai, to accommodate and guide practitioners of popular piety towards a more doctrinally acceptable Catholic practice. This accommoda-tion is seen all over Chennai at several different Catholic shrines that have all recently undergone some form of renovation or upgrade. Additionally, some recent construction trends, such as Lourdes grottos and Eucharistic chapels, demonstrate the doctrinal precariousness that inevitably arises due to the Church's more lenient attitude towards popular Christianity. The number of officially designated Catholic shrines in Chennai has grown significantly within the last decade, so much so that some Church officials worry that they are ultimately diminishing the significance of this recogni-tion by, in essence, over-saturating the market. However, for now, it appears to be the best strategy available that takes into consideration India's political climate and its theological diversity.

The level of success that the Church hopes to achieve through its strategy of shrinal development is reliant upon India's growing economy and the support of the nation's burgeoning middle class, but more importantly on how convincing the Church is able to be in proliferating its socio-religious and political messages. Primarily, the Church in Chennai is utilizing the legacy of St. Thomas in order to validate and propagate a claim towards Indian Christian indigeneity, or at least, a pre-colonial origin. With this message, the Church is better able to engage such political issues as caste equality, social justice, and gender equality, all the while attempting to counter the more anti-Christian elements of Hindu nationalism and Hindutva ideology.

Furthermore, the Church has had to also contend with the issue of its foreign colonial heritage, as well as maintain its character as a global and doctrinally homogenous institution, something that can be very difficult considering the prevalence of popular Christian piety at Catholic shrines across India. In most instances, this colonial heritage is downplayed, but there are exceptions to this trend, such as the memorialization of the missionary legacies of St. Francis Xavier and St. John de Britto. Ultimately, from Fr. Lawrence's perspective, the concerns of the global Church are secondary to the concerns of the Indian Church. On many occasions, he expressed his disappointment in the Archbishop and some of the policies enacted in the name of the Vatican, which seems to demonstrate a wariness towards Church bureaucracy. Fr. Lawrence's opinion is that the global Church should leave local affairs to the locals, because they (he) knew best. This is not to say that Fr. Lawrence does not desire new converts to the Church to become doctrinally proper Catholics, but that conversion on their own terms came first and everything after would hopefully later fall into place.

Clearly, the Indian Church is attempting to rectify two primary concerns. The first is to preserve and spiritually strengthen its established communities, and second, is to evangelize and missionize throughout India. In order to do the former, the Church has utilized the legacy of St. Thomas's death and martyrdom as a means to validate an indigenous Indian Christian origin and thus fortify Tamil Catholic identity. The need for this validation is due to Hindutva's claim that Hindu-ness and being Indian are synonymous and exclusive concepts. The Church has become invested in the issue of indigeneity due to the fear that one day a Hindutva government could take away from the Indian Christian community many of the liberties promised them under the constitution. To some extent, the Church's claim for religious indigeneity acts to safeguard the Indian Christian community's rights as citizens within the Indian nation.

On the surface, the Church's emphasis on indigeneity does not seem to coincide with its espousal of a global and universal Catholicism. In light of Vatican II, the secularization of the West, and the rise of several third-world churches, the long established centers of the Catholic Church are being replaced by peripheral ones. As such, even with the Church in India's strong hierarchal ties, priests like Fr. Lawrence are looking to local concerns first. However, the doctrines and dogmas of the Church are still retained and preserved, and their presentation is given a local flair or modified for local consumption. In this way, the universality of the Church is still being maintained as a kind of meta-Catholicism. The figure of St. Thomas as one of the Twelve Apostles is both Indian and universally Christian. His individual significance acts as a bridge between Indian Christianity and global Christianity.

With regard to the latter concern, the Church has had to accept the necessity of developing new and more creative strategies as a response to India's shifting religious and socio-political landscape. What makes this complex process so interesting is that it is indicative of a uniquely contemporary post-colonial attitude with regard to religion in India. This is an attitude that resists Hindutva discourses on the Church and colonialism, identity and religion. It is a growing eclectic urban middle-class attitude that is no longer interested in deconstructing or shedding the influence of European colonialism, but instead accepts and celebrates this heritage through the construction of shrines and edifices that are now the hallmarks of a socio-religious identity permanently intertwined with the history and diversity of the Indian soil.

Future research and final thoughts

I have made it clear from the beginning of this book that my research was focused on the top-down perspective of the Catholic hierarchy within the Chennai Church. Of course, by maintaining this focus throughout the entire book one is left with a sense that the bottom-up perspective of Indian Catholic laity and practitioners of popular Catholicism are undoubtedly required for obtaining a more complete understanding of Catholic shrine-based evangelization and religious marketing in Chennai. This bottom-up or grassroots perspective is definitely a potential topic of research that would complement my current book. After all, in terms of marketing, it is important to collect customer feedback from the target audience in question. Additionally, Chennai is a big place brimming with unique forms of Indian Christian expression and religiosity. There are many minor Catholic shrines scattered throughout the Chennai region that were not discussed in this book. Clearly, each and every one of them has a story to tell. However, the Catholic Church is not the only Christian denomination engaged in evangelization and religious marketing within the city. It would be interesting to see what the Church of South India may be doing in competition with the Catholic Church, as well as the many strategies adopted by the various independent Pentecostal groups that can be found throughout Chennai's urban landscape, let alone all of India.

Finally, it should be noted that it has been several years since the research for this book was collected to the time of its publication as a book. During this time, Fr. Lawrence and the Chennai Church have seen the fruition of several new projects, experienced some failures, and are also, most likely, devising new and innovative ways for marketing Catholicism and spreading the message of India's apostolic legacy. It should prove interesting to see what becomes of the three St. Thomas sites in the years to come, especially as knowledge of St. Thomas's Indian legacy becomes more mainstream, and India's burgeoning role as a center for global Christian missionization begins to take root.

Notes

1 Mary E. Hancock, *The Politics of Heritage from Madras to Chennai* (Bloomington, IN: Indiana University Press, 2008), 9.
2 Richard M. Eaton, "(Re)imag(in)ing Otherness: A Postmortem for the Postmodern in India," *Journal of World History* 11, 1 (Spring 2000): 65.
3 See: Arun Mukherjee, *Postcolonialism: My Living* (Toronto: TSAR Publications, 1998).
4 Roger E. Hedlund, *Quest for Identity, India's Churches of Indigenous Origin: The "Little Tradition" in Indian Christianity* (Chennai: MIIS/ ISPCK, 2000), 196.

5 Stanley M. Burgess, "Pentecostalism in India: An Overview," *Asian Journal of Pentecostal Studies* 4, 1(2001): 85.
6 Office of the Register General & Census Commissioner, India, "Census of India 2011: C-1 Population by Religious Community," http://www.censusindia.gov.in/2011census/C-01.html (Accessed October 8, 2015).
7 Michael Bergunder, *The South Indian Pentecostal Movement in the Twentieth Century* (Cambridge: Wm. B. Eerdmans Publishing Co., 2008), 18. See also: Robert Eric Frykenberg, *Christianity in India: From Beginning to the Present* (New York: Oxford University Press, 2008), 463–464.
8 Interview with Mr. Zander, Chennai, August 5, 2009.
9 Bergunder, *The South Indian Pentecostal Movement in the Twentieth Century*, 231–232.
10 C. J. Fuller, *The Renewal of the Priesthood: Modernity and Traditionalism in a South Indian Temple* (Princeton and Oxford: Princeton University Press, 2003), 142.
11 Jason Burke, "Narendra Modi: India's Saviour or its Worst Nightmare?" http://www.theguardian.com/world/2014/mar/06/narendra-modi-india-bjp-leader-elections (Accessed June 10, 2014).
12 Quoted in Michael Pizzi, "In Modi, Indians hope for an Economic Miracle-worker," http://america.aljazeera.com/articles/2014/5/16/india-modi-election.html (Accessed June 10, 2014).
13 Jagdish Bhagwati and Arvind Panagariya, "The Bells Toll for India's Congress Party," http://www.project-syndicate.org/print/the-bell-tolls-for-india-s-congress-party (Accessed December 1, 2012).
14 Interview with Fr. Lawrence Raj, Chennai, December 20, 2010.
15 Interview with Mr. Zander, Chennai, August 5, 2009.
16 Ibid.
17 Andrew Todhunter, "In the Footsteps of the Apostles," *National Geographic* 221, 3 (March 2012): 38–65.
18 Ibid, 48.

Bibliography

Primary Sources

Adaikalam, A. J. *The St. Thomas' Cathedral Museum*. Madras: San Thome, 1985.

Andrade, Alberto Pereira de. *Our Lady of Mylapore and St. Thomas the Apostle*. Madras: San Thome, 1956.

Anthonysamy, S. J. "A Saga of Faith Part I." *Voice of St. Thomas* 1, 2 (October–December 2006): 14–15.

———. "A Saga of Faith Part IV." *Voice of St. Thomas* 1, 5 (July–September 2007): 12–13.

———. "A Saga of Faith Part V." *Voice of St. Thomas* 1, 6 (October–December 2007): 12–13.

———. "A Saga of Faith Part XV." *Voice of St. Thomas* 2, 5 (July–September 2010): 10–11.

———. *A Saga of Faith: St. Thomas the Apostle of India*. Chennai: National Shrine of St. Thomas Basilica, 2009.

Bosco, P. John. *St. Thomas Mount-Chennai-South India: The Spot of the Heroic Martyrdom of St. Thomas the Apostle and the Cradle and Glory of the Indian Church*. Chennai: Apostolic Hill Shrine of St. Thomas, St. Thomas Mount, 2010.

Carvalho, James and Francis Carvalho. "Song of India." In *At the Feet of St. Thomas*. Translated by Rick Weiss. Chennai: National Shrine of St. Thomas Basilica, 2004.

Chandran, Sashi Kala. "Down Memory Lane with Fr. Lawrence Raj." In *Sweet Fruits of God's Harvest on Earth: Rev. Fr. Lawrence Raj Sacerdotal Silver Jubilee Commemorative Souvenir*, ed. Fr. Lawrence Raj, Silver Jubilee Souvenir Committee. Chennai: Fr. Lawrence Raj Silver Jubilee Souvenir Committee, 2007.

———. "Feast of St. Thomas-The Apostle," *Voice of St. Thomas* 2, 5 (July–September 2010): 14–15.

"Characteristics of Shrines," *The Voice from the Hill* 1, 1 (July 2010): 2.

Chumkat, Simon. *St. Thomas: Monuments in Chennai, India*. Chennai: IRIS SOFTEK.

———. "Sand from the Tomb." *Voice of St. Thomas* 1, 5 (July–September 2007): 10–11.

———. "The Miraculous Pole." *Voice of St. Thomas* 1, 6 (October–December 2007): 10–11.

Clarence, Mukti. "My Experience of the First 48 hours of Kandhamal Violence." *Voice of St. Thomas* 2, 7 (January–March 2011): 6–8.

Concessao, Vincent M. "In the Face of Communal Violence: What can the Church do?" *The New Leader* 121, 20 (October 16–31, 2008): 10–11.

Disciples of St. Thomas. "What do you know about St. Thomas?" *Voice of St. Thomas* 1, 12 (April–June 2009): 17.

———. "St. Thomas Quiz-II." *Voice of St Thomas* 2, 6 (October–December 2010): 18–19.

D'Souza, Herman. *In the Steps of St. Thomas*. Chennai: National Shrine of St. Thomas Basilica, 2009.

———. *In the Steps of St. Thomas*. Chennai: Diocese of Chingleput, Apostolic Hill Shrine of St. Thomas, 2010.

Forum for Catholic Unity. "Corruption Charges against the Archbishop of Madras-Mylapore." *Metamorphose* (October 2009): 1–6.

Goel, Sita Ram. *Papacy: Its Doctrine and History*. New Delhi: Voice of India, 1986.

———. *History of Hindu Christian Encounters: AD 304 to 1996*. New Delhi: Voice of India, 2010.

"Golden Flagstaff for Santhome Basilica." *Voice of St. Thomas* 2, 9 (July–September 2011): 16.

Hosten, Henri. *Antiquities from San Thome and Mylapore, the Traditional Site of the Martyrdom and Tomb of St. Thomas the Apostle*. Calcutta: Baptist Mission Press, 1936.

Joseph, Josephine. "Festivity to Honour the Apostle of India." *Voice of St. Thomas* 1, 9 (July–September 2008): 16–17.

Mannath, Joe. "Basilica Par Excellence: An Apostolic Structure & an Architectural Treasure." *Voice of St. Thomas* 1, 1 (July–September 2006): 50–52.

Mary, Angel. "Apostolic Hill Shrine of St. Thomas: A Beacon of Spirituality," *The Voice from the Hill* 1, 1 (July 2010): 12.

Michael, Joseph. "A Priestly Jubilee." In *Sweet Fruits of God's Harvest on Earth: Rev. Fr. Lawrence Raj Sacerdotal Silver Jubilee Commemorative Souvenir*, ed. Fr. Lawrence Raj Silver Jubilee Souvenir Committee. Chennai: Fr. Lawrence Raj Silver Jubilee Souvenir Committee, 2007.

National Shrine of St. Thomas Basilica. Chennai: National Shrine of St. Thomas Basilica, 2009.

Padmaraj, Vimala and Josephine Joseph. "Celebrating the Ninth Beatitude." *Voice of St. Thomas* 1, 2 (October–December 2006): 10–12.

———. "A Jubilee Etched in Silver!" In *Sweet Fruits of God's Harvest on Earth: Rev. Fr. Lawrence Raj Sacerdotal Silver Jubilee Commemorative Souvenir*, ed. Fr. Lawrence Raj Silver Jubilee Souvenir Committee. Chennai: Fr. Lawrence Raj Silver Jubilee Souvenir Committee, 2007.

———. "Living the Faith: A Touching Account of the Feast of Saint Thomas AD 2007." *Voice of St. Thomas* 1, 5 (July–September 2007): 14–15.

"Poignant Handing-Over and Taking Charge." *Voice of St. Thomas* 1, 5 (July–September 2007): 25.

Quintana, Pedro López. "Homily of the Apostolic Nuncio: On the Occasion of the Consecration of the Renovated San Thome Cathedral, Archdiocese of Madras-Mylapore December 12, 2004." In *Souvenir—San Thome Historic Event 2004*. San Thome Cathedral, Chennai, Tamil Nadu, India: San Thome Cathedral Basilica, 2004.

Raj, Lawrence. "A Dream Fulfilled … ." In *Souvenir—San Thome Historic Event 2004*. San Thome Cathedral, Chennai, Tamil Nadu, India: San Thome Cathedral Basilica, 2004.

———. "With a Grateful Heart! The Jubilarian Thanks." In *Sweet Fruits of God's Harvest on Earth: Rev. Fr. Lawrence Raj Sacerdotal Silver Jubilee Commemorative Souvenir*, ed. Fr. Lawrence Raj Silver Jubilee Souvenir Committee. Chennai: Fr. Lawrence Raj Silver Jubilee Souvenir Committee, 2007.

Ravi Gundu Rao & Associates. "The Restoration Work." In *Souvenir—San Thome Historic Event 2004*. San Thome Cathedral, Chennai, Tamil Nadu, India: San Thome Cathedral Basilica, 2004.

Regis, G. Backiya. "From the Editor's Pen." *The Voice from the Hill* 1, 1 (July 2010): 3.

———. "From the Editor's Pen." *The Voice from the Hill* 1, 4 (October 2010): 3.

Ribeiro, Julio. "The Testimony of One Christian: Religion was in the Private Domain. No One Made Me Feel 'Different.' Until Now." *Voice of St. Thomas* 1, 12 (April–June 2009): 19.

"Saints are Heavenly Intercessors for us." *Voice of St. Thomas* 2, 4 (April–June 2010): 27.

San Thome Cathedral Basilica: A Quick Introduction. Chennai: San Thome Cathedral Basilica.

San Thome Cathedral Basilica: Rich in History, Steeped in Faith. Chennai: San Thome Cathedral Basilica.

Sharan, Ishwar. *The Myth of Saint Thomas and the Mylapore Shiva Temple*. New Delhi: Voice of India, 1995.

Simon, C. A. "In Memory of a Slain Saint." In *The Myth of Saint Thomas and the Mylapore Shiva Temple*, ed. Ishwar Sharan, 151–154. New Delhi: Voice of India, 1995.

Souvenir San Thome Historic Event 2004. San Thome Cathedral, Chennai, Tamil Nadu, India: San Thome Cathedral Basilica, 2004.

"The Making of an Epic Film: Tamilnadu Chief Minister, Dr. M. Karunanidhi, is Chief Guest!" *Voice of St. Thomas* 1, 9 (July–September 2008): 26.

The Voice from the Hill: Spiritual Magazine-Monthly 1, 1–4 (2010).

Victor, Grace. "Blessed are the Santhomites!" In *Souvenir—San Thome Historic Event 2004*. San Thome Cathedral, Chennai, Tamil Nadu, India: San Thome Cathedral Basilica, 2004.

Victoria, M. Nevis. *Brief History of St. Thomas and Little Mount*. Chennai: Centurion, 2010.

Voice of St. Thomas: A Quarterly Magazine from the National Shrine of St. Thomas Basilica 1, 1–12 (2006–2009).

Voice of St. Thomas: A Quarterly Magazine from the National Shrine of St. Thomas Basilica 2, 1–11 (2009–2012).

"Web Television from Basilica." *Voice of St. Thomas* 2, 9 (July–September 2011): 10.

"What they say…" *Voice of St Thomas* 1, 5 (July–September 2007): 24.

Xavier, Loreto A. "Rally-cum-Demonstration: To Condemn Orissa Violence." *Voice of St. Thomas* 1, 11 (January–March 2009): 21.

Secondary Sources

Ali, Daud. "Introduction." In *Invoking the Past: The Uses of History in South Asia*, ed. Daud Ali, 1–12. New Delhi: Oxford University Press, 1999.

Andersen, Walter K. and Shridhar D. Damle. "RSS: Ideology, Organization, and Training." In *The Sangh Parivar: A Reader*, ed. Christophe Jaffrelot, 23–55. New Delhi: Oxford University Press, 2005.

Barrier, N. Gerald (ed.). *The Census in British India: New Perspectives*. New Delhi: Manohar Publications, 1981.

Bayly, Susan. *Saints, Goddesses and Kings: Muslims and Christians in South Indian Society 1700–1900*. New York: Cambridge University Press, 1989.

Bergunder, Michael. "Contested Past: Anti-Brahmanical and Hindu Nationalist Reconstructions of Early Indian History." *Historiographia Linguistica* 31, 1 (2004): 59–104.

———. *The South Indian Pentecostal Movement in the Twentieth Century*. Cambridge: Wm. B. Eerdmans Publishing Co., 2008.

Bhatt, Chetan. *Hindu Nationalism: Origins, Ideologies and Modern Myths*. Oxford and New York: Berg, 2001.

Blackburn, Stuart. "The Legend of Valluvar and Tamil Literary History." *Modern Asian Studies* 34, 2 (May, 2000): 449–482.

Brown, Leslie. *The Indian Christians of St. Thomas*. Cambridge: Cambridge University Press, 1982.

Burgess, Stanley M. "Pentecostalism in India: An Overview." *Asian Journal of Pentecostal Studies* 4, 1 (2001): 85–98.

Clarke, Sathianathan, Deenabandhu Manchala and Philip Vinod Peacock (eds). *Dalit Theology in the Twenty-first Century: Discordant Voices, Discerning Pathways*. Oxford: Oxford University Press, 2010.

Cover page. *Frontline: India's National Magazine* 26, 11 (May 23–June 5, 2009).

Daughrity, Dyron B. "The Indianness of Christianity: The Task of Re-imagination." In *Re-imagining South Asian Religions: Essays in Honour of Professors Harold G. Coward and Ronald W. Neufeldt*, eds Pashaura Singh and Michael Hawley, 245–269. Leiden: Brill, 2013.

Dempsey, Corinne G. *Kerala Christian Sainthood: Collisions of Culture and Worldview in South India*. New York: Oxford University Press, 2001.

———. "Lessons in Miracles from Kerala, South India: Stories of Three "Christian" Saints." In *Popular Christianity in India: Riting Between the Lines*, eds Selva J. Raj and Corinne G. Dempsey, 115–139. Albany, NY: State University of New York Press, 2002.

Doniger, Wendy. "Foreword: The View from the Other Side: Postpostcolonialism, Religious Syncretism, and Class Conflict." In *Popular Christianity in India. Riting between the Lines*, eds Selva J. Raj and Corinne G. Dempsey, xi–xix. Albany, NY: State University of New York Press, 2002.

Eaton, Richard M. "(Re)imag(in)ing Otherness: A Postmortem for the Postmodern in India." *Journal of World History* 11, 1 (Spring 2000): 57–78.

Einstein, Mara. *Brands of Faith: Marketing Religion in a Commercial Age*. London and New York: Routledge, 2008.

Forbes, Duncan. *The Heart of India*. South Brunswick and New York: A. S. Barnes and Company, 1968.

Frenz, Matthias. "The Virgin and Her 'Relations': Reflections on Processions at Catholic at a Catholic Shrine in Southern India." In *South Asian Religions on Display: Religious Processions in South Asia and in the Diaspora*, ed. Knut A. Jacobson, 92–103. London and New York: Routledge, 2008.

———. "The Illusion of Conversion: Śiva meets Mary at Vēḷāṅkaṇṇi in Southern India." In *Asia in the Making of Christianity: Conversion, Agency, and Indigeneity, 1600s to the Present*, eds Richard Fox Young and Jonathan A. Seitz, 373–401. Leiden: Brill, 2013.

Frykenberg, Robert Eric. *Christianity in India: From Beginning to the Present*. New York: Oxford University Press, 2008.

Fuller, C. J. "The 'Vinayaka Chaturthi' Festival and Hindutva in Tamil Nadu." *Economic and Political Weekly* 36, 19 (May 12–18, 2001): 1607–1609, 1611–1616.

———. *The Renewal of the Priesthood*. Princeton and Oxford: Princeton University Press, 2003.

George, Jacob. *The Trails of St. Thomas: 2000 Years of Christianity in India*. Charleston, SC: Create Space Inc., 2014.

Hancock, Mary E. *The Politics of Heritage from Madras to Chennai*. Bloomington, IN: Indiana University Press, 2008.

Harding, Christopher. *Religious Transformation in South Asia: The Meaning of Conversion in Colonial Punjab*. Oxford: Oxford University Press, 2008.

Harris, Ruth. *Lourdes: Body and Spirit in the Secular Age*. New York: Viking, 1999.

Hebden, Keith. *Dalit Theology and Christian Anarchism*. Farnham: Ashgate, 2011.

Hedland, Roger E. *Quest for Identity: India's Churches of Indigenous Origin: The "Little Tradition" in Indian Christianity*. Chennai: MIIS/ISPCK, 2000.

"India: Compounding Injustice: The Government's Failure to Redress Massacres in Gujarat." *Human Rights Watch* 15, 4 (C) (July 2003).

Jaffrelot, Christophe. "The Sangh Parivar Between Sankritization and Social Engineering." In *The BJP and the Compulsions of Politics in India*, eds Thomas Blom Hansen and Christophe Jaffrelot, 22–71. New Delhi: Oxford University Press, 2001.

———. "The BJP at the Centre: A Central and Centrist Party?" In *The BJP and the Compulsions of Politics in India*, eds Thomas Blom Hansen and Christophe Jaffrelot, 315–369. New Delhi: Oxford University Press, 2001.

———. "The RSS: A Hindu Nationalist Sect." In *The Sangh Parivar: A Reader*, ed. Christophe Jaffrelot, 56–102. New Delhi: Oxford University Press, 2005.

———. "Introduction: The Invention of an Ethnic Nationalism." In *Hindu Nationalism: A Reader*, ed. Christophe Jaffrelot, 3–25. Princeton, NJ: Princeton University Press, 2007.

———. "Conversion and the Arithmetic of Religious Communities." In *Hindu Nationalism: A Reader*, ed. Christophe Jaffrelot, 233–254. Princeton, NJ: Princeton University Press, 2007.

———. *Religion, Caste and Politics in India*. New York: Columbia University Press, 2011.

Jenkins, Laura Dudley. "Legal Limits on Religious Conversion in India." *Law and Contemporary Problems* 71, 109 (Spring 2008): 109–127.

Jeremiah, Anderson H. M. *Community and Worldview among Paraiyars of South India: "Lived" Religion*. London: Bloomsbury Academic, 2013.

Kaufman, Suzanne. *Consuming Visions: Mass Culture and the Lourdes Shrine*. Ithaca and London: Cornell University Press, 2005.

Keay, John. *India: A History*. London: Harper Collins Publishers, 2001.

Kenoyer, Jonathan Mark and Kimberly Heuston. *The Ancient South Asian World*. New York: Oxford University Press, 2005.

Kim, Sebastian C. H. *In Search of Identity: Debates on Religious Conversion in India*. New Delhi: Oxford University Press, 2005.

—— (ed.). *Christian Theology in Asia*. Cambridge: Cambridge University Press, 2008.

Klijn, A. F. J. (ed.). *The Acts of Thomas: Introduction, Text, and Commentary*. Leiden: Brill, 2003.

Kollaparambil, Jacob. *The Babylonian Origin of the Southists Among the St. Thomas Christians*. Rome: Pont. Institutum Studiorum Orientalium, 1992.

Kurikilamkatt, James. *First Voyage of the Apostle Thomas to India: Ancient Christianity in Bharuch and Taxila*. Bangalore: Asian Trading Corporation, 2005.

Kurtz, Stanley N. *All the Mothers are One: Hindi India and the Cultural Reshaping of Psychoanalysis*. New York: Columbia University Press, 1992.

Loomba, Ania. *Colonialism. Postcolonialism*. London and New York: Routledge, 2004.

McKean, Lise. *Divine Enterprise: Gurus and the Hindu Nationalist Movement*. Chicago: University of Chicago Press, 1996.

Meibohm, Margaret. "Past Selves and Present Others: The Ritual Construction of Identity at a Catholic Festival in India." In *Popular Christianity in India. Riting between the Lines*, eds Selva J. Raj and Corinne G. Dempsey, 61–83. Albany, NY: State University of New York Press, 2002.

——. "Cultural Complexity in South India: Hindu and Catholic in Marian Pilgrimage." Ph.D. dissertation, University of Pennsylvania, 2004.

Mines, Mattison. *Public Faces, Private Voices: Community and Individuality in South India*. Berkeley and Los Angeles, CA: University of California Press, 1994.

Mines, Mattison and Vijayalakshmi Gourishankar. "Leadership and Individuality in South Asia: The Case of the South Indian Big-man." *Journal of Asian Studies* 49, 4 (November, 1990): 761–786.

Missick, Stephen A. "Mar Thoma: The Apostolic Foundation of the Assyrian Church and the Christians of St. Thomas in India." *Journal of Assyrian Academic Studies* XIV, 2 (2000): 33–61.

Mohanty, Madhulita (ed.). "Must See in Chennai," *Times City Guide: Chennai*, 38–71. New Delhi: Bennett, Coleman & Co., Ltd., 2008.

Moraes, George Mark. *A History of Christianity in India: From Early Times to St. Francis Xavier: A.D. 52–1542*. Bombay: P. C. Manaktala and Sons Private LTD, 1964.

Mosse, David. "Catholic Saints and the Hindu Village Pantheon." *Man* 29, 2 (1994): 301–332.

——. "Idioms of Subordination and Styles of Protest Among Christian and Hindu Harijan Castes in Tamil Nadu." *Contributions to Indian Sociology* 28, 1 (1994): 67–106.

——. "The Politics of Religious Synthesis: Roman Catholicism and Hindu Village Society in Tamil Nadu, India." In *Syncretism/ Anti-Syncretism: The Politics of Religious Synthesis*, eds Charles Stewart and Rosalind Shaw, 85–107. London and New York: Routledge, 1994.

——. "Honour, Caste and Conflict, The Ethnohistory of a Catholic Festival in Rural Tamil Nadu (1730–1990)." In *Altérité et identité Islam et Christianisme en Inde*, eds Jackie Assayag and Gilles Tarabout, 71–120. Paris: Ehess, 1997.

——. *The Saint in the Banyan Tree: Christianity and Caste Society in India*. Berkeley and Los Angeles, CA: University of California Press, 2012.

Mukherjee, Arun. *Postcolonialism: My Living*. Toronto: TSAR Publications, 1998.

Mundadan, A. M. *History of Christianity in India Volume I: From the Beginning up to the Middle of the Sixteenth Century.* Bangalore: Theological Publications in India, 1984.

———. *Indian Christians: Search for Identity and Struggle for Autonomy.* Bangalore: Dharmaram Publications Dharmaram College, 2003.

Muthiah, S. *Madras Rediscovered: A Historical Guide to Looking Around, Supplemented with Tales of 'Once upon a City.'* Chennai: East West, an imprint of Westland Limited, 2008.

Nanda, Meera. *The God Market: How Globalization is Making India more Hindu.* Noida, Uttar Pradesh: Random House India, 2009.

Narayanan, Indira and Susheela Raghavan. "Geography." In *Madras/Chennai: A 400-Year Record of the First City of Modern India: The Land, The People & Their Governance*, ed. S. Muthiah, 1–52. Chennai: Palaniappa Brothers, 2008.

Narayanan, Vasudha. "Afterward: Diverse Hindu Responses to Diverse Christianities in India." In *Popular Christianity in India. Riting between the Lines*, eds Selva J. Raj and C. Dempsey, 255–267. Albany, NY: State University of New York Press, 2002.

Neill, Stephen. *A History of Christianity in India: The Beginnings to AD 1707.* Cambridge: Cambridge University Press, 1984.

———. *A History of Christianity in India: 1707–1858.* Cambridge: Cambridge University Press, 1985.

Nesbitt, Eleanor. "South Asian Christians in the UK." In *South Asian Christian Diaspora: Invisible Diaspora in Europe and North America*, eds Knut A. Jacobsen and Selva J. Raj, 17–38. Farnham: Ashgate, 2008.

Nolan, Mary Lee and Sidney Nolan. "Religious Sites as Tourist Attractions in Europe." *Annals of Tourism Research* 19 (1992): 68–78.

Olsen, Daniel H. and Dallen J. Timothy. "Tourism and Religious Journeys." In *Tourism, Religion & Spiritual Journeys*, eds Daniel H. Olsen and Dallen J. Timothy, 1–21. London and New York: Routledge, 2006.

Pandian, M. S. S. "Tamil-Friendly Hindutva." *Economics and Political Weekly* 35, 21/22 (May 27–June 2, 2000): 1805–1806.

Panikkar, K. M. *Malabar and the Portuguese.* New Delhi: Voices of India, 1997.

Pearson, M. N. *The Portuguese in India.* Cambridge: Cambridge University Press, 1987.

Perumalil, A. C. *The Apostles in India.* Bangalore: St. Paul Press Training School, 1971.

Podipara, P. J. *The Thomas Christians.* Bombay: St. Paul Publications, 1970.

Polo, Marco. *Journey to the End of the Earth.* Translated by Robin Brown. Stroud: The History Press, 2007.

Pope Gregory XIII, Urban VIII, Clement X, and Benedict XII. *The Roman Martyrology.* Baltimore, MD: John Murphy Company, 1916.

Pye-Smith, Charlie. *Rebel and Outcasts: A Journey Through Christian India.* London: Viking, 1997.

Raj, Selva J. "The Ganges, the Jordan, and the Mountain: The Three Strands of Santal Popular Catholicism." In *Popular Christianity in India: Riting between the Lines*, eds Selva J. Raj and Corinne G. Dempsey, 39–60. Albany, NY: State University of New York Press, 2002.

———. "Transgressing Boundaries, Transcending Turner: The Pilgrimage Tradition at the Shrine of St. John de Britto." In *Popular Christianity in India: Riting between the Lines*, eds Selva J. Raj and Corinne G. Dempsey, 85–111. Albany, NY: State University of New York Press, 2002.

———. "Shared Vows, Shared Space, and Shared Deities: Vow Rituals among Tamil Catholics in South India." In *Dealing with Deities: The Ritual Vow in South Asia*, eds Selva J. Raj and William P. Harman, 43–64. Albany, NY: State University of New York Press, 2006.

———. "Ethnographic Encounter with the Wondrous in a South Indian Catholic Shrine." In *Miracle as Modern Conundrum in South Asian Religious Traditions*, eds Corinne G. Dempsey and Selva J. Raj, 141–165. Albany, NY: State University Press, 2008.

———. "Public Display, Communal Devotion: Procession at a South Indian Catholic Festival." In *South Asian Religions on Display: Religious Processions in South Asia and in the Diaspora*, ed. Knut A. Jacobson, 77–91. London and New York: Routledge, 2008.

———. "Serious Levity at the Shrine of St. Anne in South India." In *Sacred Play: Ritual Levity and Humor in South Asian* Religions, eds Selva J. Raj and Corinne G. Dempsey, 21–36. Albany, NY: State University of New York Press, 2010.

Raj, Selva J. and Corinne G. Dempsey (eds). *Popular Christianity in India. Riting between the Lines*. Albany, NY: State University of New York Press, 2002.

———. "Introduction." In *Popular Christianity in India. Riting between the Lines*, eds Selva J. Raj and Corinne G. Dempsey, 1–7. Albany, NY: State University of New York Press, 2002.

Rajkumar, Peniel J. R. *Dalit Theology and Dalit Liberation: Problems, Paradigms and Possibilities*. Farnham: Ashgate, 2010.

Ramaswamy, Sumathi. *Passions of the Tongue: Language Devotion in Tamil Nadu, 1891–1970*. New Delhi: Munshiram Manoharlal Publishers Pvt. Ltd., 1997.

Reference Guide Map: Tamil Nadu. Chandigarh: Bharat Graphics, 1999.

Robinson, Rowena and Joseph Marianus Kujur (eds). *Margins of Faith: Dalit and Tribal Christianity in India*. New Delhi: SAGE Publications India Pvt Ltd, 2010.

Said, Edward W. *Culture and Imperialism*. New York: Alfred A. Knopf, Inc., 1993.

Samuel, Manohar. "Christianity." In *Madras/Chennai: A 400-Year Record of the First City of Modern India: The Land, The People & Their Governance*, ed. S. Muthia, 160–184. Chennai: Palaniappa Brothers, 2008.

Santos, Xosé M. "Pilgrimage and Tourism at Santiago de Compostela." *Tourism Recreation Research* 27, 2 (2002): 41–50.

Sastri, K.A. Nilakanta. *The Illustrated History of South India: From Prehistoric Times to the Fall of Vijayanagar*. Oxford: Oxford University Press, 2009.

Savarkar, Vinayak Damodar. "Extract from *Hindutva: Who is a Hindu?*" In *Hindu Nationalism: A Reader*, ed. Christophe Jaffrelot, 87–96. Princeton, NJ: Princeton University Press, 2007.

Schmalz, Mathew N. "A Catholic Charismatic Healer at Play in North India." In *Sacred Play: Ritual Levity and Humor in South Asian* Religions, eds Selva J. Raj and Corinne G. Dempsey, 185–204. Albany, NY: State University of New York Press, 2010.

———. "Boundaries and Appropriations in North Indian Charismatic Catholicism," in *Engaging South Asian Religions: Boundaries, Appropriations, and Resistances*, eds Mathew N. Schmalz and Peter Gottschalk, 85–111. Albany, NY: State University of New York Press, 2011.

Schultz, Don and Heidi Schultz. *Brand Babble: Sense and Nonsense about Branding.* Mason, OH: Thompson/ South-Western, 2004.

Seneviratne, H. L. "Identity and Conflation of Past and Present." In *Identity, Consciousness and the Past: Forging of Caste and Community in India and Sri Lanka,* ed. H. L. Seneviratne, 3–22. New Delhi: Oxford University Press, 1997.

Sharma, Jyotirmaya. *Hindutva: Exploring the Idea of Hindu Nationalism.* New Delhi: Penguin Books India/ Viking, 2003.

Shaw, Rosalind and Charles Stewart. "Introduction: problematizing syncretism." In *Syncretism/ Anti-Syncretism: The Politics of Religious Synthesis,* eds Charles Stewart and Rosalind Shaw, 1–26. London and New York: Routledge, 1994.

Shulman, David. *Tamil Temple Myths: Sacrifice and Divine Marriage in the South Indian aiva Tradition.* Princeton, NJ: Princeton University Press, 1980.

Singh, Kumar Suresh. "Introduction," in *People of India,* ed. Kumar Suresh. Calcutta: Anthropological Survey of India, 1992.

Sinha, Vineeta. *Religion and Commodification: 'Merchandizing' Diasporic Hinduism.* New York: Routledge, 2011.

Smith, Jonathan Z. *Drudgery Divine: On the Comparison of Early Christianities and the Religions of Late Antiquity.* Chicago: University of Chicago Press, 1990.

Srinivas, Tulasi. "Traditions in Transition: Globalisation, Priests, and Ritual Innovation in Neighbourhood Temples in Bangalore." *Journal of Social and Economic Development* 6, 1 (Jan.–June, 2004): 57–75.

Subramanyam, Ka Naa. *The Catholic Community in India.* Madras: MacMillan and Company Limited, 1970.

Tertullian. *Apology* and *De Spectaculis.* Translated by T. R. Glover. London: Heinemann, 1931.

Thangaraj, M. Thomas. "South Asian Christianity: Practising Tradition Today." In *South Asian Religions: Tradition and Today,* eds Karen Pechilis and Selva J. Raj, 160–191. London and New York: Routledge, 2013.

Thekkedath, Joseph. *History of Christianity in India Volume II: From the Middle of the Sixteenth Century to the End of the Seventeenth Century.* Bangalore: Theological Publications in India, 1982.

Timothy, Dallen J. "Sacred Journeys: Religious Heritage and Tourism." *Tourism Recreation Research* 27, 2 (2002): 3–6.

Todhunter, Andrew. "In the Footsteps of the Apostles," *National Geographic* 221, 3 (March 2012): 38–65.

Vadakkekara, Benedict. *Origin of Christianity in India: A Historiographical Critique.* Delhi: Media House, 2007.

van der Veer, Peter. "The Foreign Hand: Orientalist Discourse in Sociology and Communalism." In *Orientalism and the Postcolonial Predicament: Perspectives on South Asia,* eds Carol A. Breckenridge and Peter van der Veer, 23–44. Philadelphia: University of Pennsylvania Press, 1993.

Vazhuthanapally, Joseph. *The Biblical and Archaeological Foundations of the Mar Thoma Sliba.* Kottayam, Kerala: Oriental Institute of Religious Studies India Publications, 1990.

Vellian, Jacob. *Syrian Church Series Volume XVII: Knanite Community: History and Culture.* Kerala: Jyothi Book House, 2001.

Vukonic, Boris. "Religion, Tourism and Economics: A Convenient Symbiosis." *Tourism Recreation Research* 27, 2 (2002): 59–64.

———. "Sacred Places in the Roman Catholic Tradition." *Tourism, Religion & Spiritual Journeys*, eds Daniel H. Olsen and Dallen J. Timothy, 237–253. London and New York: Routledge, 2006.

Waghorne, Joanne Punzo. *Diaspora of the Gods: Modern Hindu Temple in an Urban Middle-Class World*. New York: Oxford University Press, 2004.

Wingate, Andrew. *The Church and Conversion: A Study of Recent Conversions to and from Christianity in the Tamil Area of South India*. Kashmere Gate, Delhi: ISPCK, 1999.

Young, Richard Fox (ed.). *India and the Indianness of Christianity: Essays on Understanding—Historical, Theological, and Bibliographical—in Honor of Robert Eric Frykenberg*. Grand Rapids, MI: Wm. B. Eerdmans Publishing Co., 2009.

Younger, Paul. *Playing Host to Deity: Festival Religion in the South Indian Tradition*. New York and Oxford: Oxford University Press, 2002.

Internet Sources

ActaIndica: The St. Thomas in India Swindle, "Articles on the Dubious Saint Thomas in India Legend by Noted Historians, Researchers, and Journalists," http://apostlethomasindia.wordpress.com.

Annai Vailankanni Shrine, "About Us," http://www.vailankannishrinechennai.org/vailankanni/about.html.

———, "At the Shrine," http://www.vailankannishrinechennai.org/vailankanni/shrine.html.

Archaeological Survey of India, "About Us," http://asi.nic.in/asi_aboutus.asp.

Archdiocese of Madras-Mylapore, "Annai Vailankanni Shrine," http://www.archdioceseofmadrasmylapore.org/parish_view1.php?uid=P015.

———, "History," http://www.archdioceseofmadrasmylapore.org/about_us.php.

———, "Conservation and Preservation," http://asi.nic.in/asi_cons_prev.asp.

BBC News, "Factfile: Roman Catholics around the world," http://news.bbc.co.uk/2/hi/4243727.stm.

———, "India Christians Shelter in Camps," http://news.bbc.co.uk/2/hi/7591217.stm.

———, "Orissa Mob Attacks Police Station," http://news.bbc.co.uk/2/hi/south_asia/7618031.stm.

Bhagwati, Jagdish and Arvind Panagariya. "The Bells Toll for India's Congress Party," http://www.project-syndicate.org/print/the-bell-tolls-for-india-s-congress-party.

Bhardwaj, Prabha. "Book Barons of Delhi: Decades-old Publishing Dynasties Protect, Promote and Preserve Dharma," http://www.hinduismtoday.com/modules/smartsection/item.php?itemid=4583.

Burke, Jason. "Narendra Modi: India's Saviour or its Worst Nightmare?" http://www.theguardian.com/world/2014/mar/06/narendra-modi-india-bjp-leader-elections.

Carvalho, Nirmala. *Tamil Nadu: police Arrests then Releases Bishops and Faithful Marching for Christian Dalit Rights*, http://www.asianews.it/news-en/Tamil-Nadu:-police-arrests-then-releases-bishops-and-faithful-marching-for-Christian-Dalit-rights-17808.html.

Council for Divine Worship and the Discipline of the Sacrament, *Redemptionis Sacramentum: On certain matters to be observed or to be avoided regarding the Most Holy Eucharist*, http://www.vatican.va/roman_curia/congregations/ccdds/documents/rc_con_ccdds_doc_20040423_redemptionis-sacramentum_en.html.

Disciples of St. Thomas, http://www.santhome.org/.

Deccan Chronicle, "Film on St. Thomas: Rajini May Don Role of Tiruvalluvar," http://www.dc-epaper.com/deccanchronicle/default.aspx?BMode=100.

Elst, Koenraad. *St. Thomas and Anti-Brahmanism*, http://apostlethomasindia.wordpress.com/2010/08/17/st-thomas-and-anti-brahminism-koenraad-elst/.

Gcatholic.org, "National Shrines: India, Bhutan," http://www.gcatholic.org/churches/data/shrineINX.htm

George, Nirmala. *Catholic Church says have more Children*, http://www.stuff.co.nz/world/asia/5771731/Catholic-church-says-have-more-children.

Hinduism Today, "Interview with Voice of India," http://www.scribd.com/doc/42222793/14/Interview-with-Voice-of-India.

India Today Bureau, "CAG report, India Today poll survey: BJP all set to take on Congress in 2014 elections," http://indiatoday.intoday.in/articlePrint.jsp?aid=213765.

International Theological Commission, *Faith and Inculturation*, http://www.vatican.va/roman_curia/congregations/cfaith/cti_documents/rc_cti_1988_fede-inculturazione_en.html.

Isaacs, Dan. "What is Behind Hindu-Christian Violence," http://news.bbc.co.uk/1/hi/world/south_asia/7214053.stm

Jayaseelan, K.S. "BJP tries hard to get Jaya into NDA fold," http://www.deccanchronicle.com/channels/nation/north/bjp-tries-hard-get-jaya-nda-fold-772.

Lal, Vinay. *Anti-Christian Violence in India*, http://www.sscnet.ucla.edu/southasia/History/Current_Affairs/Current_affairs.html.

Malhotra, John. "Indian Christians seek protection from Hindu nationalist government," http://www.christiantoday.com/article/indian.christians.seek.protection.from.hindu.nationalist.government/25760.htm.

Mary of Nazareth: Her Mystery, Her Museum, Her Site, "Lourdes," http://www.mariedenazareth.com/7410.0.html?&L=1.

NDTV Correspondent, "Tamil Nadu Election Results: Jayalalithaa's Massive Comeback," http://drop.ndtv.com/ndtv/articles/tamil-nadu-election-results-jayalalithaas-massive-comeback-105402.html?pfrom=home-Top-Stories&cp.

News Feature, *Church in India Responds to Pentecostalists*, http://www.catholicculture.org/news/features/index.cfm?recnum=4866.

Nussbaum, Martha. *A cloud over India's Muslims*, http://www.latimes.com/newsopinion/commentary/la-oe-nussbaum30-2008nov30,0,2188189.story.

Office of the Register General & Census Commissioner, India, "Census of India 2011: C-1 Population by Religious Community," http://www.censusindia.gov.in/2011census/C-01.html.

One News Now, "India Braces for More Violence against Christians," http://www.onenewsnow.com/Persecution/Default.aspx?id=312620.

Palavakkam: Seashore St. Anthony's Shrine: The Diocese of Chingleput, http://www.seashorestanthony.org/index.html.

———, "Church Construction," http://www.seashorestanthony.org/about-shrine.html.

———, "Mother Parish," http://www.seashorestanthony.org/about-shrine.html.

Pizzi, Michael. "In Modi, Indians hope for an Economic Miracle-worker," http://america.aljazeera.com/articles/2014/5/16/india-modi-election.html.

Pohle, Joseph. "The Real Presence of Christ in the Eucharist," http://www.newadvent.org/cathen/05573a.htm.

Pope John Paul II, *Ecclesia in Asia*, http://www.vatican.va/holy_father/john_paul_ii/apost_exhortations/documents/hf_jp-ii_exh_06111999_ecclesia-in-asia_en.html.

———, *Encyclical Letter: Ecclesia de Eucharistia*, http://www.vatican.va/holy_father/john_paul_ii/encyclicals/documents/hf_jp-ii_enc_17042003_ecclesia-de-eucharistia_en.html.

Pope Paul VI, *Evangelii Nuntiandi*, http://www.vatican.va/holy_father/paul_vi/apost_exhortations/documents/hf_p-vi_exh_19751208_evangelii-nuntiandi_en.html.

Pope Pius IX, *Ineffabilis Deus*, http://www.newadvent.org/library/docs_pi09id.htm.

Sabastian, Don. "Did Thomas the Apostle visit South India?" http://www.dnaindia.com/dnaprint.asp?newsid=1066746.

Sahu, Sandeep. "Riots Grip India's Orissa Region," http://news.bbc.co.uk/2/hi/south_asia/7582887.stm.

Santhome Church, http://www.santhomechurch.com/.

Santhome Church TV, http://www.santhomechurch.tv/a/.

Sepe, Crescenzio. *St. Thomas, Apostle 1,950 Years Ago; St. Francis Xavier 450 Years Ago*, http://www.catholicculture.org/culture/library/view.cfm?recnum=4580.

Sharan, Ishwar. *Kapaleeswara Temple Memorial Plaque*, http://apostlethomasindia.wordpress.com/2010/04/17/kapaleeswara-temple-plaque-ishwar-sharan/.

———. *Madras-Mylapore Archdiocese plans Blockbuster Movie on St. Thomas*, http://apostlethomasindia.wordpress.com/2010/05/11/madras-mylapore-archdiocese-plans-blockbuster-movie-on-st-thomas-%e2%80%93-ishwar-sharan/.

Shrine Basilica of Our Lady of Health Vailankanni: The Place of Our Lady's Apparitions, "Donation," http://www.vailankannishrine.org/donation.php.

———, "Shrine History," http://www.vailankannishrine.org/history.php.

Special Correspondent, *Archbishop Chinnappa puts Onus of Dalit Liberation on Christian Leaders*, http://www.thehindu.com/todays-paper/tp-national/tp-tamilnadu/article626427.ece.

Special Correspondent, *Stress on Holistic Approach to Dalit Liberation*, http://www.hindu.com/2011/05/02/stories/2011050253160300.htm.

Sridhar, V. *Communalism: A Numbers Game*, http://www.frontlineonnet.com/fl1625/16250930.htm.

Srinivasan, Rajeev. *Ishwar Sharan Interview*, http://bharatabharati.wordpress.com/ishwar-sharan-interview.

StepMap: Design Your Map, http://www.stepmap.com/.

Tamil Nadu Tourism, http://www.tamilnadutourism.org/index1.aspx.

———, "CHENNAI—Gateway to the South: Places of Tourist Interest," http://www.tamilnadutourism.org/places/CitiesTowns/chennai01.aspx?catid=010101P01;pg=2.

———, "Half Day Chennai City Sight Seeing Tour," http://www.tamilnadutourism.org/Tours/TourFare.aspx?TourId=19.

———, "HOP ON HOP OFF TOUR IN CHENNAI CITY," http://tamilnadutourism.org/tnstc-tour.html.

The Hindu, "St. Teresa's Church Spruced Up," http://www.thehindu.com/news/cities/chennai/chen-downtown/st-teresas-church-spruced-up/article4200756.ece.

The Holy See, "Code of Canon Law: Chapter 3, Shrines, Can. 1230–1234," http://www.vatican.va/archive/ENG1104/__P4J.HTM.

The Ishwar Sharan Archive, "About Us," http://ishwarsharan.wordpress.com/about-us/.

The New Ishwar Sharan Archive, *The Myth of Saint Thomas and the Mylapore Shiva Temple* 3rd Revised Edition, http://ishwarsharan.wordpress.com.

The New Ishwar Sharan Archive, *The Myth of Saint Thomas and the Mylapore Shiva Temple* 3rd Revised Edition, http://ishwarsharan.wordpress.com/introduction-ishwar-sharan/.

Thomas, P.V. "Church Watches Anxiously as General Election Begins," http://www.ucanews.com/story-archive/?post_name=/2009/04/16/church-watches-anxiously-as-general-election-begins&post_id=713.

Thurston, Herbert. "Exposition of the Blessed Sacrament," http://www.newadvent.org/cathen/05713a.htm.

Times of India Agencies, "BJP-AIADMK alliance on the cards?" http://www.timesnow.tv/BJP-AIADMK-alliance-on-the-cards/articleshow/4393724.cms.

TN Church sets Rs 50-cr Budget for Film on St. Thomas, http://www.indianexpress.com/news/tn-church-sets-rs-50cr-budget-for-film-on-st-thomas/331605/0.

Viswanathan, S. "A Decree on Animal Sacrifice," http://www.frontlineonnet.com/fl2020/stories/20031010001205000.htm.

World Christian Database, http://www.worldchristiandatabase.org/wcd/default.asp.

Interviews and Field Notes

Brother Joe, Chennai, June 11, 2009.
Field Notes, Chennai, July 29, 2009, December 16, 18, and 20, 2010.
Fr. Charles, Chennai, July 8, 2009.
Fr. Lawrence Raj, Chennai, June 15, 2009.
———, Chennai, June 30, 2009.
———, Chennai, December 15, 2010.
Mr. Franks, Chennai, July 16, 2009.
Mr. Mark, Chennai, July 23, 2009.
Mr. Sam, Chennai, March 27, 2009.
Mr. Zander, Chennai, August 5, 2009.
Sr. Merrill, Chennai, June 13, 2009.

Index